Rhetoric and Educational Discourse

Educational policy is often dismissed as simply rhetoric and a collection of half-truths. However, this is to underestimate the power of rhetoric and the ways in which rhetorical strategies are integral to persuasive acts – whether this is in the proposing of a particular policy or in teaching a specific subject.

Through a series of illustrative chapters, this book argues that, rather than something to be dismissed, rhetorical analysis offers a rich and deep arena through which to explore and examine educational issues and practices. It adopts an original stance in relation to contemporary debates and will make a significant contribution to educational debates in elucidating and illustrating the pervasiveness of persuasive strategies in educational practices.

Rhetoric and Educational Discourse is a useful resource for postgraduate and research students in education and applied linguistics. The book will also be of interest to academics and researchers in these fields of study and those interested in discursive approaches to research and scholarship.

Richard Edwards is Professor of Education and **Katherine Nicoll** is Lecturer in Education, both at the University of Stirling. **Nicky Solomon** is Associate Professor of Education at the University of Technology, Sydney. **Robin Usher** is Professor of Education at RMIT University in Melbourne.

Rhetoric and Educational Discourse

Persuasive texts?

Richard Edwards,
Katherine Nicoll,
Nicky Solomon and
Robin Usher

RoutledgeFalmer
Taylor & Francis Group

LONDON AND NEW YORK

First published 2004
by RoutledgeFalmer
11 New Fetter Lane, London EC4P 4EE

Simultaneously published in the USA and Canada
by RoutledgeFalmer
29 West 35th Street, New York, NY 10001

RoutledgeFalmer is an imprint of the Taylor & Francis Group

© 2004 Richard Edwards, Katherine Nicoll, Nicky Solomon and
Robin Usher

Typeset in Goudy by
HWA Text and Data Management, Tunbridge Wells
Printed and bound in Great Britain by
Biddles Ltd, King's Lynn, Norfolk

British Library Cataloguing in Publication Data
A catalogue record for this book is available from the British Library

Library of Congress Cataloging in Publication Data
Edwards, Richard, 1956 July 2–
  Rhetoric and educational discourse : persuasive texts / Richard George
Edwards, Katherine Gordon Nicoll, Nicky Solomon. – 1st ed.
      p. cm.
1. Rhetoric. 2. Language and education. I. Nicoll, Kathy, 1954–
II. Solomon, Nicky, 1951– III. Title.

P301 .E3 2004 808–dc22   2003024357

ISBN 0–415–29670–6 (hbk)
ISBN 0–415–29671–4 (pbk)

Contents

Acknowledgements

All writing is intertextual and this text is no exception. Many have contributed to its production through our (en)counters with them over the years. Some of what is here has been presented elsewhere, some has been drawn from work that one or other of us has produced in collaboration with others. Some no doubt is hidden from us, forgotten traces that we have carried forward without realizing it. Such is the nature of writing. We are indebted to all those who have participated in the processes of assembling us as authors for this text. Richard Edwards would also like to acknowledge the financial support of the Carnegie Trust for the Universities of Scotland, which enabled him to travel to Australia to work with Nicky Solomon and Robin Usher while writing this text together. Personal debts are many and varied. In particular, we would like to thank Clive Chappell, Julia Clarke, John Field, Roger Harrison and Fiona Reeve. We would also like to thank Anna Clarkson, our editor at RoutledgeFalmer, for supporting this project and Margaret Tooey for providing some secretarial support to us. In including some, we are inevitably excluding others, but to include all would be to fill a book on its own. If you find your traces in this text, we thank you all.

Abbreviations

ANT	actor-network theory
ARPANET	Advanced Research Project Agency Network
CBE	competence-based education
EU	European Union
FE	further education
html	hypertext mark-up language
ICT	information and communication technology
ILTHE	Institute for Learning and Teaching in Higher Education
IMRDS	introduction, methodology, results, discussion and summary
MUDs	multiple user dimensions
NAGCELL	National Advisory Group for Continuing Education and Lifelong Learning
NCIHE	National Committee of Inquiry into Higher Education
NPOK	*The New Production of Knowledge*
NSFNET	National Science Foundation Network
OECD	Organization for Economic Co-operation and Development
PC	politically correct
UK	United Kingdom
UNESCO	United Nations Economic, Scientific and Cultural Organization
US(A)	United States (of America)
WBL	work-based learning

Chapter 1

Introduction
Acts of seduction?

An impossible task

Writing about rhetoric is inevitably an impossible task. How is it possible to pin down what rhetoric *is* and do this without resorting to rhetoric? Whatever conception we hold of rhetoric we are bound to find ourselves in an aporia, perplexed. If we take the dominant conventional view that rhetoric is a matter of embellishment and half-truths, then our enterprise is doomed from the start. Clearly, we, the writers of this text, do not take this view. However, even the alternative that we will argue for does not resolve the problem.

In what follows, we present a text which will purport to explain rhetoric 'as it really is', which is itself a rhetorical statement. In writing and presenting this text we are ourselves engaging in persuasion. Our text is a speech act, which will 'talk' about rhetoric and its place in education, but this talking will also be a doing. There would be no point in writing it and presenting it if we had no hope that it would be persuasive. And rhetoric, no matter what view one takes of its nature, is at the very least about persuasion. We could of course argue that our aim is to persuade with robust, logical and clearly presented arguments. But is that not rhetorical too? The elements of good rhetoric – logos, pathos and ethos – are all present here. It seems we cannot therefore construct a 'good' text about rhetoric without resorting to rhetoric.

For some, this would be construed as a fundamental weakness, a failure to find a position outside of rhetoric. For us, however, we see our text as an exemplar of the rhetoricity of language, that there is actually no position outside rhetoric so long as one continues to communicate. In adopting this position, the implication is the need for reflexivity and we have done this throughout the text. Yet in doing so there is also a need to recognize the limits of reflexivity since it is itself a form of rhetoric. It is itself meant to persuade even though it may appear otherwise. Thus we find ourselves in a position of having to acknowledge that it is rhetoric through and through.

Thus, while reflexivity is necessary, there are limits to how far one can take it for us to be able to engage you as readers. This means there is no escape. Rhetoric just keeps popping up whatever writing strategies we might adopt. We simply have to accept therefore that we are embarking on an impossible task. However, the response to that need not be negative. Even if the task is impossible, that does not mean that we should inevitably abandon the effort. It is possible to recognize that texts are rhetorical through and through, that any attempt to write about rhetoric is always going to be rhetorical, and still write. This is what we have attempted in the text that follows. We recognize and accept its rhetoricity. We are reflexive about it, we hope we have constructed an 'open' and honest text and most important perhaps we recognize its limitations, which are themselves the limits of language.

Seductive acts?

In much contemporary debate, 'reality' is often contrasted with rhetoric, where the latter, as we have noted, is often taken to be a collection of half-truths, embellishments or even lies. Listen to the radio, watch the television, read the newspaper, overhear conversations and you will soon find plenty of examples of this:

> That rhetorical adepts are impostors who tell lies and twist the facts, we know from the frequent testimony of the daily newspapers, in which rhetoric is both castigated and manifested. Rhetoric has what is known as a 'bad press', and this is almost certainly because it thrives on something the Press regards as its own particular sustenance; a perception of the limitations of the human mind, an exploitation of predictable responses, a grasp of the ideas that rule races, classes and individuals.
>
> (Nash 1989: 198)

The distrust of rhetoric has a long history, but is no doubt enhanced by the new public discourse of 'spin', which it is argued places greater emphasis on presentation than on substance. In this view, the deficiencies of rhetoric 'are not only epistemological (sundered from truth and fact) and moral (sundered from true knowledge and sincerity) but social: it panders to the worst in people and moves them to base actions' (Fish 1989: 472). All the world, it is alleged, has become an advertisement. Yet this is not the argument we wish to pursue, directly at least. For while rhetoric has a bad name, there has been, in recent years, a massive growth in interest in the notion of discourse in the social sciences and more widely. Our interest is in exploring the rhetorical practices of educational discourses, as we feel that the latter cannot be fully pursued without an understanding of the former.

Any contemporary study of education demonstrates the growing influence of discourse. Concern for issues of language, text and discourse in policy, practice and research are no longer at the periphery but have begun to develop as distinct strands of interest (MacLure 2003). Partly as a result of the spreading influence of poststructuralism and, more generally, what is known as the 'linguistic turn' in the social sciences and the 'social turn' in linguistics, the study of discourse and discursive approaches to research have spread beyond the realm of applied linguistics, psychology and the philosophy of language. In a sense, they have become part of the mainstream of social science research. This is particularly marked among those who locate education within the broader social sciences and not simply as an applied area of professional practice and development. This interest in discourse has manifested itself in the study of educational policies and the management of institutions, as well as in relation to pedagogic practices, either in more traditional classroom environments or more recently in relation to information and communications technologies and computer-mediated communication approaches to teaching and learning. Discursive studies can be found in all branches of education: for example, initial schooling, higher education, training, lifelong learning, workplace learning, and vocational education and training. It is also to be found in the reflexive concern for how research is itself to be represented and the types of discourse through which research is fabricated. The discourse of discourse is pervasive.

Yet interestingly, with some notable exceptions, little of this work to date has been located specifically in relation to the 'noble art' of rhetoric. Rhetoric examines the practices through which discourse and texts attempt to achieve their goals. The *Oxford English Dictionary* (1992) defines rhetoric as 'the art of using language so as to persuade or influence others'. For Potter (1996: 106), 'rhetoric should be seen as a pervasive feature of the way people interact and arrive at understanding'. This is a definition for which we have much sympathy and whose implications we will explore further as we go along. Rhetorical analysis is conventionally thought of as the study of the ways in which we attempt to persuade or influence in our discursive and textual practices. Yet until recently it largely remained a ghost haunting the machinations of contemporary interest in educational discourses. It is in an attempt to redress this situation that we set out on the journey of this text.

The study of rhetoric and rhetorical education have a long and not always auspicious history from ancient Greece onwards. Even then, for many, the art of persuasion – rhetoric – was an underhand activity. Even then, rhetoric was contrasted with the real and found wanting. We find this stance problematic and, in this text, aim to challenge all reductionist notions of rhetoric based on binary thinking. Not least, we argue, because education, like so many other aspects of human endeavour, is inherently a rhetorical practice. Policy, practice and research are not simply neutral statements of facts but are attempts to persuade in some shape or form. Policy makers, for example, attempt to persuade the public that extending educational opportunities does not impact upon standards of achievement. Facts about standards of achievement are deployed but the persuasive force of the policy does not lie in the facts alone. The phenomenon of interest groups attempting to persuade policy makers that one course of action will achieve better results than another is well known. Governments consult, often on policy levers rather than policy goals. Educational managers attempt to persuade staff that one way of running an institution is better than another.

Teachers and lecturers attempt to persuade their students that learning is a worthwhile activity. Motivation may be considered at least in part an outcome of persuasion, for when one is persuaded of the benefits of something, one may be more inclined to learn. Researchers are desperate to persuade themselves, each other and the funders of their research that they have an audience and that their endeavours are worthwhile, or, more potently, useful. And so it goes on ...

Yet to study education as rhetorical practices, while not entirely unheard of, seems somehow unseemly, an act to be undertaken in the dark corners of urban streets, since it seems to challenge the role of reason, rationality, science and evidence in education. It seems to suggest that policy and practice-informed evidence should take priority over evidence-informed policy and practice. Propaganda seems a more appropriate bed-partner for persuasion and, while education is recognized as playing a role in supporting the ideologies of specific states, this is in some ways seen as questionable. While itself rhetorically powerful as an argument, this is not our position. For us, rhetoric problematizes the role of education as a crucial aspect of modernity. This of course is not in itself new. But to undertake rhetorical studies of education is to position it as a rhetorical practice and it is this that we would claim is distinctive about the argument in this text. Whether it is persuasive is another matter. Persuasion may be coercive, reasoned or seductive. Power, reason and desire are therefore embedded within rhetorical acts but these acts always have one vital characteristic and that is that they are embodied in language. In this text we aim to explore the multiple workings of rhetoric in many aspects of education. In the process, we are not only attempting to locate educational practices within rhetoric, but also to demonstrate that the 'linguistic turn' has historical forerunners, which positions as not entirely new, poststructuralist and postmodern approaches that focus on discourse, language and text.

Science and rhetoric

Simplifying to a large extent, in ancient Greece, a distinction was made between rhetoric and philosophy. Rhetoric was about the form of communication, while the content of communication was the concern of philosophy. This developed into a distinction between rhetoric as persuasion and philosophy as truth. According to Plato, it was only through philosophy that truth and justice could be established and it was this which had to constitute the content of speech. Its form, on the other hand, could be constructed, analysed and pedagogized as rhetoric.

Science eventually replaced classical deductive philosophy as the basis for establishing what was true about the natural world, with empirical evidence replacing contemplation and logic. Reason and truth was contrasted with the emotions and ignorance. Attempts began to develop a scientific discourse based in a literal rather than metaphorical use of language. Here then we find in some ways a return to Plato, who associated rhetoric with the appeal to emotions. But now science rather than philosophy became concerned with establishing what was rational, what was true, what was the case. A distinction between the cognitive and emotive aspects of language came to be made. This, 'coupled with the belief that scientific knowledge can be reduced to a system of literal sentences, implies that metaphor has no cognitive import' (Bicchieri 1988: 102). Rhetoric became positioned as part of the arts and humanities, a line of literary enquiry separate from that of the experimental sciences. 'As rhetoric is a classical "art" or *techne*, its historical attitude toward knowledge production is much more at home with literary criticism than with sociology' (Leach 2000: 211, emphasis in original). Insofar as education became eventually positioned as part of the social sciences, the rhetorical aspects of the practices associated with education were overlooked. A rhetorical understanding of education being an art rather than a social science was considered beyond the boundaries of legitimate investigation. One may still have had an education *in* rhetoric, but the analysis of education *as* rhetoric was positioned outside the boundary of legitimate concern, although occasional eruptions of interest can be found (e.g. Taylor 1984a). In other words, the discourse of science played a powerful rhetorical role in positioning education as a science, distinct from rhetoric, and in strongly policing the boundaries between arts and sciences. Over time, the influence of rhetoric itself waned in the arts. This meant, as Nelson *et al.* (1987a: 15–16) comment, that 'the role of rhetoric has been played down in the humanities, but it has been downright ignored in the social sciences. In consequence, the social sciences float in warm seas of unexamined rhetoric.' It is those seas we are entering here.

Modern science attempts to establish the truth of the world, or the best approximating truth to date. It is a discourse of facts, of how things are, or are thought to be, constituted by empirical evidence. It rhetorically appeals to evidence and logic and by so doing positions itself as eschewing the need for rhetoric. In the development of modern science, rhetoric and truth were therefore held to be mutually exclusive, with science concerned with truth devoid of rhetoric. The persuasiveness of science was held to rest in its truth claims, not in its rhetoric, an aspect fundamental to the struggle against social practices based on superstition and religion. Yet, for much of its history and even today, scientific discourse has itself been circumscribed by strict rules of what can be written and how it can be written. Witness, for example, the guidelines for the submission of journal articles published by organizations such as the American Psychological Association (Bazerman 1987). Even in less positivistic research, the power of rhetoric is clear once one starts being aware of and looking for it. For example, Atkinson (1996: 17) argues that the impact of Whyte's classic ethnography, *Street Corner Society*, on modern sociology was made 'very largely by virtue of its textual features ... we cannot afford to lose sight of the persuasive power of style and rhetoric even in the context of such scholarly written products'. And indeed there has been much discussion of rhetoric among ethnographers over the years (Clifford and Marcus 1986). In addition, philosophers of science, such as Kuhn and Feyerabend, have pointed to the discursive conventions that govern science.

More radically, Freedman and Medway (1994a: 8) argue that 'science advances not by the inexorable logic of successive revelations of nature but by the persuasion of influential groups; arguments are only locally valid; there are no truths, only assertions with a backing that is not universal but communal'. In other words, truth, rather than a faithful representation of the real world out there, is a convention constituted by agreement among a socio-rhetorical network. This position undermines the rhetoric of science by arguing that 'truth itself is a contingent affair and assumes a different shape in the light of differing local urgencies and the convictions associated with them' (Fish 1989: 481). What emerges from this is the argument that whenever a case needs to be made that something is true, therein lies a situation ripe for the play of rhetoric.

> It is imperative that we recognize that scholarly, factual work is inescapably rhetorical. It draws on conventions of representation and argumentation in order to convey plausible arguments to readers or hearers. A recognition of rhetoric is not an abnegation of scientific or scholarly responsibility. The either/or separation of rhetoric from science is an unnecessary and indeed misleading legacy of Enlightenment thinking. Rhetoric has been relegated to the fringes of the social sciences for too long. It is vital that we recognize and celebrate its rightful place.
>
> (Atkinson 1996: 145)

The linguistic turn in the social sciences over the last century has resulted in an increased interest in scientific discourse rather than science as such. Yet overall this has been informed by the development of the social science of applied linguistics more than the study of rhetoric, which once again reflects the concern for scientific legitimacy and the power of the signifiers of science and arts in attempting to divide different understandings of the world.

Rhetoric and discourse

Alongside the study of rhetoric in the arts, an area of relative decline in many parts of the world over the last hundred years, we have seen the emergence and growth of applied linguistics as a social science. The study of language has moved to the fore and, with the linguistic turn in the social sciences, language, discourses and texts have made a major appearance in social sciences in general and in the arena of education specifically. For some, like Vickers (1999), who wishes to argue for a revitalized understanding of rhetoric, the primacy of linguistics represents an atrophying of the study of rhetoric. This echoes the argument of Leith and Myerson (1989: xiii) about 'the imperialism of linguistics within the field of language study'. However, perhaps this is too gloomy an assessment. Developments in a range of disciplines – for example, speech act theory in philosophy, critical discourse analysis in applied linguistics, semiotics in cultural studies, genre studies, actor-network theory in the sociology of science and technology, and poststructuralism and postmodernism in a range of subjects – have all, in different ways, drawn upon and pointed to the centrality of language and rhetoric in human practices. Names such as Bahktin, Barthes, Searle, Latour, Fairclough and Swales spring to mind. Thus, Freedman and Medway (1994a: 3) argue that 'if twentieth century humanists and social scientists have tended to define and differentiate human beings by their ability to use language, more recently it is the rhetorical dimensions of that capacity that have captured our attention'. The study of rhetoric has therefore itself become persuasive, with increasing numbers of studies examining the rhetoric of scientific and social scientific discourse – spoken, visual and written texts (for example, Taylor 1984a; Nelson *et al.* 1987b; Klamer *et al.* 1988; Swales 1990; Henderson *et al.* 1993; Collin 2000).

The bringing to the fore of the rhetorical aspects of human interaction and communication have resulted in many developments and arguments, such as that:

- different types of writing develop different, rhetorical forms of rationality;
- the formation of discourse communities entails the development of socio-rhetorical networks (Swales 1990);
- generic discourse forms are resources upon which we draw to persuade (Coe 1994), what Fairclough (1999) refers to as membership resources;
- texts are not objects to be consumed, but are 'experienced as part of an activity, as a production, in which the reader participates through his or her trans-actions with the text' (Atkinson 1996: 19).

Thus, Atkinson (1996: 32) can argue that 'although it creates ire and resent-ment in some quarters where views are entrenched, it is by no means novel or revolutionary to suggest that science is a human activity suffused with rhetoric'.

It has been the work of those identified as post-structuralists that has informed much of our own previous individual and collective works to date. The analysis as well as production of discourses and texts has been our mainstay for a number of years in both research and teaching. Nor are we alone in these endeavours. The works of Foucault, Derrida and Lyotard have been particularly influential in this respect. Foucault's notion of discourse as power-knowledge and the positional orderings of subjectivity have been particularly influential in educational research. Derrida's concept of deconstruction in the play of difference and the metaphoricity of language has been used to challenge more conventional understandings of meaning-making and has opened up new areas of debate. Deconstruction 'systematically asserts and demonstrates the mediated, constructed, partial, socially constituted nature of all realities, whether they be phenomenal, linguistic or psychological' (Fish 1989: 492). However, unlike in forms of discourse analysis linked to ideology critique, where the idea is to 'unmask', to name a truth, deconstruction 'continually uncovers the truth of rhetorical operations, the truth that all operations, including the operation of deconstruction itself, are rhetorical'

(Fish 1989: 493). In addition, Lyotard's notions of language games and perform-ativity have pointed to directions of change within social practices. A performative economy is one in which all practices are based on a strategy of maximizing usefulness. Language games themselves become subject to performativity; their rhetorical effectiveness pointing to their usefulness, their usefulness itself a rhetorical effect. Here rhetoric is both performed and performative.

Yet, despite this clear growth of interest in rhetoric in educational research, most writing and analysis has focused on discourse with relatively little detailed engagement in the wider debates in the social sciences about rhetoric. A range of approaches to the analysis of discourses and texts has developed. These mostly focus on issues of knowledge, power and identity in educational discourse. They tend to be linked to forms of ideology critique to explore how power is exercized through the constitution of knowledge and subjectivity in discursive practices. Some are more inclined towards the use of linguistic 'method' than others. We ourselves have contributed to such discussions over the years. However, only few such analyses have drawn explicitly upon rhetoric as an established area of study. Here

> the goal of rhetoric is never to be 'scientific', or to be able to categorize persuasion for all times and all places. The power of rhetorical analysis is its immediacy, its ability to talk about the particular and the possible, not the universal and the probable.
>
> (Leach 2000: 211)

The focus is on the embodied and embedded exploration of the practices of rhetoric within the wider discursive analysis of education. It is often suggested that discursive analyses, particularly those informed by the work of Foucault, do not provide a basis for a political response to exercises of power. For us, such an (en)counter is fabricated precisely through a rhetorical analysis.

We therefore see that, rather than something to be dismissed, rhetorical analysis offers a rich and deep arena through which to explore and examine educational issues. This text will draw on this tradition to contextualize the contemporary interest in discursive approaches to education and to examine rhetorically a number of key areas of policy, research and pedagogy.

Rhetoric and educational discourse

There is much that is oversimplified and/or overstated in the discussion of rhetoric, when it is discussed at all. Hyperbole is the stuff of much educational discourse, including that of educational research. Thus, for instance, educational policy is often dismissed as *simply* rhetoric, perhaps most powerfully signified in the concern over 'spin-doctoring' by governments in recent years. Apart from rhetoric never being 'simple', given what we have written above, we obviously feel that this is to underestimate the power of rhetoric and the ways in which rhetorical strategies are integral to acts designed to persuade, whether this is in the proposing of a particular policy or in teaching a specific subject. For us, therefore 'rhetoric is the cure, not the disease' (Nelson *et al.* 1987a: 11). We cannot do without rhetoric, and therefore an engagement with rhetorical analysis is essential. To argue that rhetoric gets in the way of the 'real' work of education is to miss the point and also is itself to engage in a powerful rhetorical practice.

Language is central to education, where centring has a powerful rhetorical pull. Whether it is pedagogic practices, the management of organizations, the development and implementation of educational policies, or educational research, they all involve multiple forms of communication, symbolic exchange and interaction. Students are constantly asked to engage in rhetorical practices, to engage in different forms of academic literacy and persuade teachers through their assignments, portfolios, theses, etc. that they are capable or competent enough to be awarded a 'pass'. The arguments over the purposes of education are themselves framed by that most powerful of rhetorical practices, metaphor. Education as social engineering, as initiation, as information processing and as emancipation are but a few of the metaphors in play (Taylor 1984b). Thus, as Elliott (1984: 44) argues, 'the chief importance of metaphors of education, generally, lies in their rhetorical function, which is to stimulate imagination, to arouse feeling, and to prompt action'. Whether discourses of quality assurance and effectiveness have quite this impact is another matter of course, except maybe for the new 'class' of educational managers and entrepreneurs. The point remains, however, that educators are like rhetoricians and gatekeepers of rhetoric.

Our intention in this text therefore is to explore and examine what a rhetorical analysis of educational discourses brings to light. The most obvious point here is that we will be making the case that there is a hidden rhetorical aspect to educational discourses, which needs to be brought out and examined. Psychological and sociological understandings of education will therefore be put under erasure, in order that, for instance, we can explore what it might mean to locate teaching as a rhetorical practice, or the evolution of educational policies, or indeed research and scholarly practices, such as we are engaged in here. In their influential collection, attempting to raise the significance of rhetoric for the human sciences, Nelson *et al.* (1987a: 15) point to a number of questions to be addressed:

> What does the rhetoric of a piece of scholarship imply for its uses? Why do genres of scholarship differ from one field to another? How do narratives matter? What roles do metaphors play in scientific persuasion? How have rhetorical conventions affected particular fields? How does their rhetoric affect their public reception? What do theories of rhetoric imply for the conduct of research? What does rhetoric imply for relations among the humanities, social sciences, natural sciences and professions? How might recent theories of rhetoric revise our conceptions of rationality? What are the connections among rhetoric, epistemology, ethics, logics, myths, poetics, politics, psychology, sociology and other aspects of inquiry? How might increased awareness of rhetoric reform education in the disciplines?

Their focus is on research in the human sciences. However, many of these questions are those we ourselves wish to address in relation to research, practice and policy in education. In the following chapters therefore we shall attempt a systematic exploration of rhetoric in certain aspects of educational discourse.

Before doing this, however, in the next chapter, we will outline more fully some of the principal concepts in rhetoric upon which we will draw in later chapters. In particular, we will explore the persuasive genres and the work of metaphor in discourses. The contributions of speech act philosophy and poststructuralism will be explored more fully in the context of wider and more historical understandings of rhetoric and rhetorical analysis. In Chapter 3 we will enter into our examination of specific educational discourses. We will explore some of the metaphors through which attempts are made to describe and explain teaching and learning practices. In particular, there will be a focus on the spatial nature of many such metaphors, such as student-centredness, legitimate peripheral participation, distributed cognition, and their persuasiveness in encouraging educators to adopt particular approaches. Chapter 4 will extend this focus on teaching and learning by examining discourses of professional development in teaching. It will look at discourses of competence and reflective practice and the ways in which such discourses work to produce specific forms of professional development, in the process shaping the values and identities of those participating in such programmes. It will examine the ways in which practitioners are positioned as an audience in such discourses, the assumptions upon which they are based and inventions to which they are subject. We then boldly go into the realm of information and communications technologies in education. Chapter 5 will examine the speculative strategies through which the use of information and communications technology in education is promoted, in particular the fictions and fantasies of cyberspace. Technologies may be changing the practices of education, but there are also new sites that are being given greater prominence, beyond conventional schools, colleges and universities, signified particularly in discourses of lifelong learning. Chapter 6 will examine therefore the ways in which workplace learning is promoted as a 'new' direction for educational provision and the ways in which this reconfigures educational discourses both about the workplace and within the workplace. The ceremonial uptake of workplace learning will be explored. Educational institutions are themselves workplaces, of course. In Chapter 7 therefore we focus on the use of the rhetoric of managing and management in the reconfiguring of educational institutions. We focus more specifically the ways in which research is being reconstituted through notions of research management in higher education. The rhetoric of management and that of managers is explored for its significance in reshaping organizational life.

The next two chapters focus on different aspects of the rhetoric of education policy. Chapter 8 will examine the education policy context in the United Kingdom to explore the ways in which rhetorical strategies are deployed to produce notions of inevitable change and their implications for institutions and practitioners. Chapter 9 then explores some of the ideas that are being propounded by international bodies, such as the Organization for Economic Co-operation and Development and European Union to reform education around the globe and how the notion of globalization is being deployed as a metaphor through which to promote these changes as both desirable and necessary. In these chapters we attempt to address the rhetorical implications of the discourse of spin.

In this text we are engaged in practices of research and scholarship, and whether this text is seen as a work of scholarship and/or research and by whom is itself significant. Chapter 10 therefore examines the rhetorical strategies deployed in the writing of different traditions of research. In particular, it will examine the different ways in which truth claims are fabricated. Much of our argument points to how changes in education are producing new and different audiences, which impact on the identities and practices of educators and the importance of rhetorical understanding in engaging with these processes. By the end of this text, we hope to have demonstrated that rhetoric should not be dismissed, but needs to be encountered and countered in relation to policy, management, research and pedagogy, if the study of educational discourses is to do more than simply undertake analysis of what is occurring.

Each of the chapters provides examples and case studies. Inevitably, given our geographical locations and areas of expertise, these are drawn largely from the UK and Australia and from the post-compulsory arena of education and training. However, they are merely illustrative of the broader argument of the significance of rhetoric to the study and practice of education. We believe our argument would have been equally convincing had we drawn illustrations and cases from other countries and/or phases of education. We leave it to others so to do.

Reflexivity and rhetoric

We have indicated earlier that we are conscious of the irony that we are ourselves engaged in a rhetorical practice in writing this text on rhetoric. We are engaged in a reflexive project, already entwined within that about which we write. There is an integral link between reflexivity and rhetoric as 'reflexive discourses make the rules and conventions of representation their topic by viewing objects as a site of rhetorical work, and thus problematizing taken-for-granted attitudes and intentionalities' (Sandywell 1996: 8). In the process of writing this text, we aim to persuade. We will almost certainly appeal to evidence, values and emotion. We will be playful and might well disorientate, and we make no apologies for this.

Yet we are also very serious about the research and scholarship in which we are engaged here, now. We feel the failure to examine the rhetorical practices of education limits the understanding of the processes in play and the possibilities for education and the ways we engage in and with it. We follow Atkinson (1996: 36, emphasis in original) who argues that 'scholarship and rhetoric imply choices, decisions and responsibility. They both imply aesthetic and ethical judgements. A self-conscious awareness of the *forms* of our inquiry implies a *responsibility* for those forms'. We accept that responsibility. In writing this text, we therefore wish to demonstrate the importance and power of rhetoric as well as discuss its significance for education. In the process, of course, we are engaged in selection and arrangement of our argument, what is referred to in rhetoric as *taxis*. Whilst in some respects, as we have already noted, we recognize our task is well-nigh impossible, we nonetheless hope to open new possibilities for educational practice and research. And we should point out that the 'we' we represent in this text is not a unified voice. It represents a temporary coalescing of our individual and collective travels, an oasis of dialogue, where we have agreed to pass over any broad areas of disagreement in silence, in order that we can make our cases more persuasively. 'Rhetorical analysis is an interpretative art ... On the one hand, it is flexible and interpretative; on the other hand, it is inconsistent and subject to the strengths and weaknesses of the analyst' (Leach 2000: 218). In writing together rather than separately, we hope to have added to our strengths and lessened our weaknesses. At which stage

> there comes a point in any rhetorical proceeding when the silent partners in the dialogue – the listeners, the readers – are no longer being told; they start to tell themselves, and in doing so help to shape the rhetoric that persuades them.
>
> (Nash 1989: 197)

Chapter 2

Rhetorical practices

In Chapter 1, we outlined some of the contestations surrounding the history and understanding of rhetoric. We continue to examine this in Chapter 2. However, rather than use this as the basis for a broad argument for the importance of rhetoric to the study of education at this point, we wish first to introduce some of the key concepts of rhetoric more specifically in order to inform later chapters in this text. We feel that much of the talk about rhetoric is based upon misunderstandings that result in it being devalued. Implicit to many dismissals of educational discourse as 'rhetoric' (and the quotation marks convey the sense of the sneer in tone often used in the evocation of rhetoric) are forms of ideology critique. These construe certain representations in texts as mystifications of the material world by those who exercise power. Here the notion of rhetoric is collapsed into ideology. Thus, 'in everyday talk, we contrast "rhetoric" with "action", and suggest that something "rhetorical" is tantamount to a collection of lies and half-truths' (Leach 2000: 207). By contrast, we want to suggest that the study of educational discourse precisely as rhetoric can illuminate our understanding in different ways that point to the very real and powerful practices in play. We see that 'part of the job of the rhetorical analyst is to determine how constructions of "the real" are made persuasive' (Simons 1990: 11), one aspect of which is the use of metaphor. Here the question is not so much about whether reality matches rhetoric or not, but which fabrications of the real are more persuasive and why.

Rhetorical analysis involves the study of the ways in which we attempt to persuade or influence in our discursive, textual and gestural practices. As such, it is an embodied practice, more than a mere mark on a page or sounds to be heard. As we have indicated, such analysis, and indeed the teaching of rhetoric, has a long history going back to Ancient Greece. In Europe, rhetoric was part of the core curriculum through to the Enlightenment. However, as we have also noted earlier, the growth of modern science from that period, with its emphasis on induction from empirical observation and experiment, resulted in less emphasis being given to the art of rhetoric, although contemporary academic literacies and composition studies do draw upon it. This situation has shifted somewhat. Whether or not one classifies it as part of the postmodern condition of knowledge (Lyotard 1984), or the 'linguistic turn' in the social sciences, there has been increased inter-disciplinary research and scholarship and a questioning of the firm boundary between rhetoric and truth. Increasingly now the claim to truth is itself seen as a powerful rhetorical practice, warranted through all sorts of discursive devices. A range of approaches to the analysis of discourses and texts have developed, although only some of them have drawn explicitly upon rhetoric as an established area of study (Gill 2000).

Back to basics

The *basic* is a powerful metaphor that masquerades as a natural category. What do we consider to be basic or canonical? What do we consider to be basic in education? The notions of the basic points to the foundational, to that upon which all else can be built. Basic education and basic skills have been used at certain times and in certain places to position reading, writing and arithmetic as *foundations* of learning. This assumes a culture that is based on inscriptions rather than oracy and/or apprenticeship and therefore helps to fashion learning towards certain approaches and ends rather than others. So we might suggest that the basic is foundational for certain forms of learning. However, even here there are challenges, as basic skills have themselves been redefined and extended to take account of different contexts. So, in addition to literacy and numeracy, it is now common to see information technology, problem-solving and communications skills also identified as being basic to education, part of the discourses of generic skills and core competences. What does this indicate? For one, that the basic and the foundational are not solid categories invariant of all times and all places; they are neither basic nor foundational in the sense we might be led to understand them rhetorically. This indicates that the conditions of possibility for the use of notions such as basic skills already point to their *lack* of basicness. To suggest this might be to argue that we should be developing contingent skills, or offering a contingent education. But is this as persuasive as providing a basic education?

Back to basics is a dangerous rhetorical manoeuvre, as it precisely points to the difficulty of identifying what constitutes the basic and foundational, and with that, that there may be none. It precisely points to the rhetorical work that is being attempted by mobilizing the *basics* as part of a persuasive strategy – in part, its effectiveness is perhaps due to a nostalgic emotion with which it is inflected. With this in mind, we therefore ask ourselves what the basics may be for the study of rhetoric.

As we have already said, rhetoric has been much discussed and studied since Ancient Greece. This is a geographical as well as temporal and cultural locatedness of which we should be wary, given that different languages and cultures have different rhetorical conventions (Kaplan 2000). Perhaps more significantly, these classical studies of rhetoric have been written down and translated into modern English, so we are reliant on these texts for evidence of the existence of debates about the pros and cons of rhetoric. We ourselves are therefore culturally and linguistically located in specific discourse networks. Do these texts constitute 'the basics' upon which we build this text on the rhetoric of education? Here we might appear slippery, as at one level the answer is 'yes'. However, for us, these texts may be basic – we weave a text that positions Ancient Greece as our originary point of reference – but they are not foundational. They are resources upon which we draw and to which we connect for our own purposes, rather than foundations upon which we build. They are routes to our understanding as much as roots of it. It is a networked-based rather than building approach we are adopting in writing this text, as the former allows for a degree of travelling, while the latter would keep us fixed in one place. And this text is a journey in a number of ways, not least the number of electronic journeys it has made between us, as we have written it. In a sense, we are ourselves using travelling rhetorically to signify a desire to disrupt and change, to not stand still. In the process, we indicate that this text is not written at the end of a process of thinking about rhetoric and educational practices, but is itself part of the process through which we will establish what we think. It is also the case that the Sophists, the early teachers of rhetoric, were themselves *travelling* teachers. Our view on rhetoric echoes in part that of Swales (1990: 44–5, emphasis in original) on the related notion of genre:

1   A *distrust* of classification and of facile or premature prescriptivism;
2   A *sense* that genres are important for integrating the past and present;
3   A *recognition* that genres are situated within discourse communities, wherein the beliefs and naming practices of members have relevance;
4   An *emphasis* on communicative purpose and social action;
5   An *interest* in generic structure (and its rationale);
6   An *understanding* of the double generative capacity of genres – to establish rhetorical goals and to further their accomplishment.

As an initial location, we travel to Ancient Greece to highlight Plato's concern at the influence of the Sophists and sophistry, the negative connotations of which have been carried forward into the current era. Yet, as Vickers (1999: 1) suggests, 'rhetoric, the art of persuasive communication, has long been recognized as the systemisation of natural eloquence'. In other words, rhetoric takes what is happening in naturalistic communication, systematizes it and then teaches it as a practice to be mastered. The initial focus was very much on the spoken word. This was certainly the case for the Greeks, as the public life of the polis involved orating in a persuasive way to gatherings of citizens, as well as for more specialized bodies, such as law courts. This points to the importance of understanding the place of the rhetorical in all social practices, not merely those of significance in classical times.

It also involves us recognizing that from its earliest manifestations through to the Renaissance, for many, the art of persuasion was seen as part of what was necessary for the liberty and prosperity of the polis as well as for success in civic life. Teachers of rhetoric were seen as dangerous by tyrannical regimes and authoritarian philosophers, both of whom disliked democracy and feared that the masses would be persuaded to political revolt by the rhetorical skills of demagogues. The rhetorical positioning of the Sophists as engaging in the dangers of rhetoric was therefore a political act. The Sophists, who Plato so staunchly attacked, thereby giving sophistry a bad name, specialized in the teaching of political oratory. The positive valuation of rhetoric and the art of persuasion is not generally reflected in the contemporary understandings of sophistry and rhetoric, given that these rest largely on the works of Plato. We would suggest that for many the art of rhetoric is not recognized for the positive contribution it can make, but is rather positioned as working to undermine democratic politics. We shall examine this more later.

Evidence and emotion

Fundamental to the different valuations of rhetoric over the years has been the extent to which acts of persuasion are viewed as based upon appeals to evidence or to emotion, to reason or to feelings. But we need to be cautious here as the 'or' already positions you and us into making binary choices. Either rhetoric is an appeal to reason or it is an appeal to feelings, one or the other. Rhetorical work is already in play with the introduction of 'or' into the sentence. 'Or' inscribes a binary, which results in primacy being given to one end of the spectrum over the other end.

However, if we are wary of the 'or', what can we put in its place and what is the impact of alternatives? If we are not persuaded by an either–or approach, we could perhaps suggest a continuum. Some rhetorical practices may appeal more to the emotions and some more to evidence. For instance, in educational discourses there is often much invested in the notion of meeting students' needs. Such a discourse has a powerful emotive ring to it, yet the evidence for what it brings to the fore seems to be lacking both theoretically – these things called 'needs' are powerful rhetorical devices – and substantively – evaluations do not tend to focus specifically on a clearly articulated category of 'need'. The calls for evidence-informed practice in education may seem to counter this and to result in a research-informed approach. However, the appeal to evidence is itself a powerful emotive move. It would therefore appear that even the notion of a continuum itself starts to deconstruct once examined. There is power therefore in those forms of rhetoric that are privileged as against those which are not.

Thus, even as we attempt to discuss different aspects of rhetoric, we are drawing upon certain cultural resources to orchestrate our own discussion, thereby both engaging in rhetorical work and caught within the rhetorical resources of our own cultural positionings. And, as yet, we are only working with two aspects of rhetoric. If we introduce a third, an appeal to values, to ethics, then the picture becomes even more complex, kaleidoscopic perhaps. The interweaving of values, emotion and evidence in rhetorical acts is not hard to identify, but it is difficult to disentangle.

But we have moved ahead of where we intended. It is the work of Aristotle,

Plato's student, which provides an early systematic account of rhetoric, continuing to influence those who study it today. For Aristotle (1954: 24), rhetoric was 'the faculty of observing in any given case the available means of persuasion'. He outlined three modes of persuasion – ethos, pathos and logos. Ethos is to do with the personal character and attitude of the speaker. Pathos rests on the capacity of the speaker to put the audience into a fit state of mind. Logos is about providing evidence or proof of what is being stated. Aristotle therefore argues that persuasion depends on a number of aspects, upon the moral character of the speaker, on whether or not they can be trusted, on the capacity to place the audience into a fit emotional state and on the reasonableness of that which is stated. There is thus a formal structure to Aristotle's understanding of rhetoric – ethos/speaker/ethics; pathos/audience/emotions; logos/argument/reason – upon which a rhetorical education can be built. A rhetorician then is a person – male in Ancient Greece – of good standing that can be trusted; who can both put his audience into a suitable state of emotion, as a condition for, and outcome of, providing a reasoned argument. Unlike Plato, who associated rhetoric with the work of the Sophists and the dominance of pathos, the appeal to emotions, Aristotle argued for the legitimacy and intertwining of different forms of rhetorical practice. However, this did not involve a wholesale acceptance of the work of rhetoric. It was only in the hands of certain types of speaker engaged in certain types of rhetorical work that rhetoric was legitimate and served appropriate ends. And 'hands' here is significant, as 'rhetorical training in Ancient Greece and Rome … also covered the use of appropriate bodily gestures to enhance the effect of speech' (Ree 1999: 124). Rhetoric was an embodied practice; something which developed in part into the manual rhetoric of sign language for the deaf and what we can refer to as the language of dance. More generally, it points to the importance of gesture in persuasive practices. For Aristotle, the capacity to provide reasoned argument was to the fore and this continues to be influential in education. For example, student assignments in most subjects and disciplines are assessed in relation to the manifestation of reasoned argument.

For Aristotle then, it was only in the hands of certain types of speaker engaged in certain types of rhetorical work that rhetoric could be legitimate and serve appropriate ends. These ends depended on the audience. Here once again we find a triad. First there is the audience as judge, deciding on what has already happened. Second, there is a political audience deciding upon what must be done. Third, there is the audience as observer, from whom no decision is necessary. These three senses of audience were associated with the practices of the law courts, the political assembly and the public ceremony, in many ways reflecting the context and concerns of certain parts of Ancient Greek society. Each of these is elaborated by Aristotle to provide a detailed typology of rhetorical practices. It is not our intention to examine these in detail here, although elements of his argument inform later developments and will be drawn upon in our analysis of educational discourses as we proceed with this text. Needless to say, aspects of Aristotle's analysis can be explored in relation to the legal, political and ceremonial aspects of educational practices, but we wish to extend them into the organizational and pedagogic aspects of education as well. For Aristotle, an education in rhetoric was to provide those who entered the legal, political and ceremonial domains with the appropriate ways of acting and speaking. Our argument is that the work of rhetoric extends into all aspects of human practices.

What Aristotle's analysis does, through systematization, is to provide a means of distinguishing 'good' from 'bad', legitimate from illegitimate, rhetoric. However, ultimately, it posits an appeal to reason, to evidence and logic, as that which is to be valued most in the work of rhetoric. A person of good standing will try and ensure their audience is moved emotionally to accept the logic of the position being presented. However, to disentangle the play of reason, emotion and values in this way, to locate them in separate aspects of rhetorical practices, while analytically neat, seems to point us away from the complexity at play. For us, pathos, ethos and logos are intertwined in all aspects of social practices, as both speakers/writers and audiences are embedded in, and draw upon, certain rhetorical resources in their interactions and communications.

Rhetorical performances

There are a number of categories central to a rhetorical analysis – exigence, audience and persuasive genres. Exigence is 'an imperfection marked by urgency' (Bitzer, in Leach 2000: 212). It is the problem that demands a response. In rhetorical analysis, identification of the exigence contextualizes and locates the discursive or textual practice. In policy analysis, for instance, the exigence would be that to which policy is being addressed: for example, lack of economic competitiveness, social exclusion, lack of participation, inequality of participation, etc. One of the things that contextualization does is to establish the timeliness and appropriateness of the particular intervention, or to use a term from classical rhetoric, its 'kairos'.

> Exigence is a form of social knowledge – a mutual construing of objects, events, interests and purposes that not only links them but makes them what they are: an objectified social need ... exigence provides the rhetor with a sense of rhetorical purpose.
>
> (Miller 1994a: 30)

Rhetorical analysis also examines the ways in which the audience is positioned or mobilized through the rhetorical act. To whom is the text or discourse addressed and how are they positioned? This is important, as 'one of the means of persuasion is making arguments with which the audience may already agree, in order to create a sense of identity between the implied author and the implied audience' (Leach 2000: 210). Rhetoric is therefore both responsive to existing networks and at the same time attempts to mobilize such networks: rhetoric and audience are co-emergent.

A rhetorical community ... is ... a discursive projection, a rhetorical construct. It is the community as invoked, represented, presupposed, or developed in rhetorical discourse ... rhetorical communities 'exist' in human memories and in their specific instantiations in words: they are not invented anew but persist as structuring aspects of all forms of socio-rhetorical action.

(Miller 1994b: 73)

Thus, for instance, the audience for policy texts on lifelong learning may be large and diverse, yet the very bringing together of such an audience through a discourse of lifelong learning creates and cements affinities that might not be possible through other types of discourse that focus more specifically on, for instance, human resource management, community education, vocational education, higher education or adult education.

Rhetorical analysis works with three main types of persuasive genre: forensic, deliberative and epideictic, respectively associated with the law, politics and ceremonies. The deliberative genre is associated with policy and is future orientated and speculative. In relation to this genre, Zimmerman (1994) points out that who may take part in the deliberation, who is to be persuaded and who coerced varies according to historical and political circumstances. A liberal democratic regime may involve far more people in deliberation than more tyrannical forms of governing. It may therefore be that deliberative rhetoric is of greater significance than contemporary discussions of spin may suggest. Second, there is the forensic genre, which focuses on past events and attempts to provide an account that is taken to be true. Finally, there is the epideictic genre of rhetoric associated with ceremonial occasions that focuses on the contemporary and whether people, organizations or events merit praise or blame. Epideictic rhetoric can be found in the notion of 'naming and shaming', publicly denouncing organizations and individuals who fail to meet the quality standards and inspection criteria to which they are subject. Needless to say, many rhetorical practices will draw upon more than one of these genres. Vickers (1999) points out how, during the period from Ancient Greece to the Renaissance, there was a relative decline in the deliberative and forensic genres of rhetoric. The epideictic, through the praising of the epideictic rhetor, came to the fore, no doubt reflecting changing historical and social conditions in the valuation of particular forms of rhetoric.

Leach (2000) argues that once one has identified the type of persuasive genre being analysed, there are five areas to examine: invention, disposition, style, memory and delivery. Invention explores how certain rhetoric comes to be, examining the moral authority of the author to make claims, the logic or reasonableness of what they are propounding and the appeal to the emotions in their rhetoric. Each of these can be examined in the practitioner, policy and scholarly fabrications of education. Disposition involves examining the ways in which the rhetoric is organized and its effects on audiences. Style draws most closely on literary criticism to examine the rituals and imagery through which rhetoric attempts to persuade. Examining the metaphors and metonymy at play in rhetorical acts points to the ways in which meaning can be conveyed through analogies and figures of speech. These are particularly powerful when there is an appeal to pathos. Memory examines those cultural memories shared by audience and authors, while delivery examines the patterns of dissemination through the different forms and media available.

Over the centuries there have been many attempts to systematize rhetoric through turning an analysis of rhetorical forms into a curriculum. That is not our intention here. We value such scholarly endeavours but eschew them ourselves in the spirit of Leith and Meyerson (1989: xii, emphasis in original):

> We do not ... see Rhetoric as a system of rigid categories but as a *process* in the production, transmission and interpretation of utterances, spoken or written, scripted or unprepared. It is not the 'letter' of Rhetoric that we want to reactivate so much as what we see as central to its 'spirit'.

Attempts to persuade and influence are pervasive. Lyotard (1984) suggests that this is part of the language wars of the postmodern condition. Potter (1996: 107, emphasis in original) argues that these metaphorical 'wars' have a longer history, one that he divides into forms of offensive and defensive rhetoric: 'a description will work as *offensive rhetoric* in so far as it undermines alternative descriptions ... a description may provide *defensive rhetoric* depending on its capacity to resist discounting or undermining'. It is important to bear in mind that this is not a distinction between the more and the less powerful, since both dimensions will be found in any discourse or text. While we think Potter is right to point to rhetorical wars as more than a contemporary phenomenon, we also consider that Lyotard is highlighting a radicalization of these processes through the proliferation of texts, discourses and signs that we now experience. There is an incitement to rhetorical practices, which itself is reflected in the growth of discourse analysis as a way of investigating their significance. The different elements above may be combined in a variety of ways to produce different types of analyses that focus on a particular range of practices and issues. They are not part of a method to be applied, but nodes in an interpretative art. As Potter (1996: 181) suggests somewhat obviously, 'all discourse can be studied for its rhetorical and constructive work'.

Walking the talk

But is rhetoric just about persuasion? We would argue that the 'just' in this utterance is problematic and that there is more to rhetoric than persuasion. At the very least, we need to recognize that if rhetoric is about persuasion, we are getting an audience to *do* something. More 'basically', in persuading, we are communicating through a particular kind of language use where words have performative force as well as (or often instead of) propositional meaning. Here, language becomes performative. It is not just saying something, communicating a propositional content, but is doing by saying and, of course, one of the things it can do by saying is to persuade. When language is performative in this way, it is referred to as a *speech act*. We would argue that a rhetorical utterance is therefore a speech act as it not only conveys a propositional content but also has force *and* is uttered with the intention of bringing about consequent effects. And in doing so, it fabricates the material world. We therefore need to take a brief excursion into the philosophy of language.

Earlier we raised the distinction between 'good' and 'bad' rhetoric. We saw that whilst it was possible to see why this distinction was made and why it continues to have resonance even today, it is nonetheless a problematic distinction. What are the criteria of rightness by which good rhetoric can be distinguished from bad? How can these be expressed without the use of rhetorical tropes? If, however, we think of rhetoric as a particular kind of speech act, we can resolve this difficulty. A speech act is neither right nor wrong, similarly an utterance is neither good nor bad. Speech acts can only be judged by whether they are felicitous: or infelicitous that is, whether they work because they are appropriate for the context in which they are uttered. Thus for example, an 'I do' performs a marriage only when the ceremony is carried out in a place and by a person designated for this purpose: that is, an appropriate social situation. In the same way, we can say that a rhetorical utterance can be best judged by whether it works, whether it has the intended effect, and whether it is appropriate for its context. This then brings us back to our dimensions of rhetoric – logos, pathos, ethos and not forgetting kairos. Getting these right is what makes rhetoric felicitous. The rhetorical utterance works, it does the job it is intended to do. It is the lack of felicitousness that means that some of the more experimental writing of educational research, such as poems, may rightly be considered inappropriate and unpersuasive; it is inappropriate for its situation.

The distinction between good and bad rhetoric is a longstanding one, not easily abandoned. Even Plato recognized that, however truthful the proposition, it was much more likely to be accepted if it was uttered with style. Good rhetoric was therefore stylish speech that spoke the truth. Bad rhetoric was style without substance, the attempt to persuade without the force of truth. What this shows of course is that Plato, despite his opposition to the Sophists, was not prepared to condemn rhetoric altogether. Unfortunately, and particularly with the rise of modern science, good rhetoric was largely forgotten. The notion that all rhetoric was bad rhetoric became dominant and, if it was thought of as having any virtues, it was mainly in its bringing to the fore of style and expression.

We would argue that the distinction between good and bad rhetoric has been historically unfortunate. It is a distinction that forms an essential part of an ideological position, but is a dead end apart from that. It does hide, albeit in plain view, the rhetoricity of communicative practices. This failure to recognize the place of rhetoric hinges to a very large extent on how truth is to be understood. If truth is understood as something out there waiting to be discovered and external to communicative practices, then rhetoric will come to be defined in opposition to truth. Hence the only place for rhetoric will inevitably be one solely of style and embellishment. However, if truth is understood as being fabricated by negotiation within communicative practices, then another and altogether more positive view of rhetoric becomes possible. Truth becomes something that emerges from transactions between speakers/writers and their audience(s) within the constraints and possibilities of particular socio-rhetorical networks. Thus in revivifying rhetoric there is no need to abandon truth. Truth happens and it happens when there are transactions which involve meaningful content, where the transactions have emotional force, where they are conducted by those who are perceived as trustworthy, credible and authoritative, and where the transaction is appropriate for the situation. Given these conditions, speech acts have a felicitous status.

In its current form, speech act theory, even though its roots in Western thought go back to the Sophists, is inseparably linked with the work of Austin (1962). Austin's original formulation of speech act theory framed a distinction between the constative, an utterance used for stating things or conveying information, and the performative, an utterance used for doing things, for performing actions. For example, 'I bet you five dollars' is not a constative since it conveys no information; the action, that is, betting, is *performed* by the saying of it. Further-more, the utterance can be deemed neither true nor false. Austin later abandoned the distinction between constatives and performatives. He came to realize that constatives also perform actions and that performatives also convey information.

Speech act theory is about how language is to be conceived. On the one side is the view that it is a system of structures and meanings. On the other, it is a set of acts and practices. This contestation replays in contemporary form the classical debates about the distinctions between philosophy and rhetoric. The issue is the grounding of language. Is it grounded in a transcendental structure or fabricated in human practices? As we have seen, the Sophists lost the debate and the notion that language is fabricated in practices became ideologically deviant with the transcendental privileged over the human. Speech act theory shifts the focus from text, whether spoken or written, conceived formally as a stable object with intrinsic characteristics, to what we *do* with texts. Every text is a speech act in the sense that it is an utterance in an ongoing speech situation shaped by interpretation, context and medium. By stressing the performative aspects of language, Austin appears to have a positive view of rhetoric.

Searle (1969) took the view that Austin had not said what he truly meant and in so doing had unwittingly lined up with rhetoric against philosophy. For Searle, this was an unacceptable position. He attempted to correct Austin by arguing that there is only a single speech act, that of promising. By this argument Searle thought he could bring speech acts back into the linguistic mainstream by bringing to the fore their transcendental structure. If speech acts are all reducible to promising, then here is a conceptual centre that stands above everyday human practices of interpersonal communication. Searle believed that by cutting out the embellishment, or to put it another way, Austin's rhetoricity, he had discovered the centre of Austin's work, in the process recuperating Austin for philosophy.

However, Derrida argues against Searle that, given his concern was language as performance, Austin was doing rhetoric rather than philosophy, or more precisely that Austin was doing both. Rhetoric and philosophy cannot be separated since they are both located in language. For Derrida, the problem with Austin is different. It arises because Austin did not know what to do with figurative or metaphorical language. Austin therefore split it off as outside his concerns. However, Derrida (1988) argues that by doing this, Austin thereby undermines the explanatory power of speech act theory. He shows that serious or non-figurative speech acts are necessarily grounded in the very possibility of figurative language, or as Searle terms it, linguistic parasitism. This is because of what Derrida refers to as iterability:

> a standard act depends as much upon the possibility of being repeated, and thus potentially of being mimed, feigned, cited, played, simulated, or in general 'parasited', since all these possibilities depend upon the possibility said to be opposed to it.
>
> (Derrida 1988: 91–2)

This implies that there is no substantial difference between, for example, promising on stage and promising in 'real life'. Both are performances that the speaker/actor has witnessed and internalized as the ways other speakers/actors have of saying/doing a thing (promising), but which are realized as *acts* only in the performing or iterating of them. To put this simply, we are always acting, in both senses of the word, regardless of whether we have memorized our lines from a specific script for a specific play or, more generally, from 'life', from previous speech encounters. Our acting always relies on that script, the iterable or 'always already', a socially regulated pattern for our behaviour that is nonetheless located in situated and dynamically contingent contexts. Furthermore, speech acts embodied in figurative or metaphorical language are just as much speech acts with performative force as are those embodied in 'serious' or non-figurative language, even if they make work in different ways for different purposes and audiences.

Many would not be happy with this position. What about the figural language of hyperbole, which involves the 'conveying of a proposition that so distorts the obvious truth the hearer recognizes the non-literal intention on the speaker's part' (Fraser 1979: 175)? It is not our intention to pursue this debate further here. What we do want to emphasize is the closeness of rhetoric and the figurative, in particular, metaphor. As it is about understanding and persuasion, metaphor will be deployed in rhetoric. Thus metaphor and rhetoric are inextricably linked.

Metaphor and the figurative in educational discourse

Vickers (1999: 442) argues that rhetoric has atrophied in part because 'modern theory reduces the tropes to two only, metaphor and metonymy'. This is something we are in danger of contributing to in emphasizing metaphor in our own discussion.

However, in view of the importance given to metaphorical analysis in contemporary educational discourses, we find ourselves caught on the horns of a dilemma. We need to reflect the importance of metaphor, but we do not wish to suggest that it is all that can be said about rhetoric in educational discourse. We both add to the discourse of metaphor even as we seek to go beyond it. We have commented already about the ongoing discussion of metaphor and metaphorical analysis (e.g. Ortony 1979a; Alvesson 1993; Cameron and Low 1999). These focus on issues such as: different types of metaphor, for example, live, dead, root; the means by which they work, for example the notion of topic and vehicle; and appropriate methods for researching metaphor. In her review of the literature of organizational studies, Inns (2002) identifies six ways in which metaphor is used in research:

1   Examination of the root metaphor of a subject;
2   Metaphor as a qualitative research tool;
3   Metaphor as a generative tool for creative thinking;
4   Metaphor as a hegemonic tool to influence perception and interpretation;
5   Metaphor as an explicatory, teaching tool;
6   Metaphor as a tool for deconstruction and the questioning of embedded assumptions.

In the process, of course, a range of metaphors is deployed through which to write about metaphor. Thus, for instance, how one feels about the vehicular aspects of metaphor may depend somewhat upon if one associates vehicles with traffic jams or the open road. Fundamental to much of the debate is the concern as to whether we see (where vision itself acts as a metaphor for knowledge) metaphor 'as an essential characteristic of the creativity of language; [or] as deviant and parasitic upon normal usage' (Ortony 1979b: 2).

These debates draw upon and are part of philosophy, psychology and linguistics as well as the wider arena of rhetoric. It is not our intention to pursue these debates in detail, as our interest is in metaphor within educational discourse rather than the study of metaphor per se. However, we cannot avoid the fact that we shall be adopting specific notions of metaphor implicitly in what we write. We follow Coe (1994: 183) in seeing metaphors as 'not merely decorative or emotionally suasive, but heuristic and conceptually suasive as they direct (and deflect) our attention'. Where relevant, therefore, we will relate our discussion to some of the wider debates to which we have referred. What motivates us is that which in an earlier era concerned Taylor (1984b: 8):

> ... in educational, as in other forms of discourse, it is a matter of no little importance that the implications of the metaphors we employ or accept are made explicit, and the ways in which they structure our thought, and even our action, are better understood.

The interest in exploring the metaphors of educational discourse has become more commonplace in recent years (for example, see Stronach and MacLure 1997; Parker 1997; Sfard 1998 and Cameron 2003). From diverse disciplines, such as poststructuralist philosophy, organizational studies and applied linguistics, there has been an increased focus on metaphor and its significance for social practices. However, although often derived from other intellectual traditions, interest in metaphors of education and the use of metaphor in education is more longstanding (see, for example, Petrie 1979; Sticht 1979 and Taylor 1984a). In their influential book, *Metaphors We Live By*, Lakoff and Johnson (1980: 3) argue that 'our ordinary conceptual system, in terms of which we both think and act, is fundamentally metaphorical in nature'. For them (1980: 6, emphasis in original) 'human thought *processes* are largely metaphorical'. It would therefore appear to be crucial to our understanding of educational practices that we begin to engage with the play of metaphor. Similarly Sfard (1998: 4) argues that 'metaphors are the most primitive, most elusive, and yet amazingly informative objects of analysis. Their special power stems from the fact they often cross the borders between the spontaneous and the scientific, between the intuitive and the formal'. Yet often, even where the notion of metaphor is drawn upon, it is ill-defined or understood, used to embrace a range of otherwise discrete rhetorical practices.

As we have noted, '*the essence of metaphor is understanding and experiencing one kind of thing in terms of another*' (Lakoff and Johnson 1980: 5, emphasis in original). Yet there are different ways of achieving this. We will focus on four here: metaphor, metonymy, simile and synedoche. The first three will have more relevance to the analysis within this text and are probably more familiar. However, as part of our argument is that rhetoric provides us with valuable resources that should not be overlooked in examining educational discourse, we feel it important to at least allude to concepts upon which we do not necessarily draw directly. We can relate metaphor and simile, and metonymy and synedoche, as they signify different types of process. The former two can be conceived as involving replacement, where one concept or idea is conceived in terms of another. For example, in the work of the North American critical theorist Henry Giroux (1992), pedagogy is conceived as 'border crossing'. To discuss critical pedagogy as a form of border crossing and to extend that metaphor into different aspects of teaching and learning is to free up our thinking and help us to conceive things differently. It is that freeing up that is fundamental to all four of these aspects of rhetoric. The difference between metaphor and simile is that the latter is always flagged by an 'as if' or 'like'. So for instance, 'teaching first-year higher education students can be like pulling teeth'. This will of course be read differently according to your view of dentistry and your relationship with pain.

By contrast, metonymy and synedoche involve substitution, where one idea or concept stands in for another with which it is related. In particular, metonymy substitutes 'a particular instance, property, characteristic or association for the general principle or function' (Nash 1989: 122). So for instance, 'the cane' might symbolize school discipline, 'chalk and talk' a particular approach to teaching.

Gibbs (1999: 36) provides a useful summary distinction between metaphor and metonymy:

> ... in metaphor, there are two conceptual domains, and one is understood in terms of another, usually very different, knowledge domain. Metonymy involves only one conceptual domain, in that the mapping or connection between two things is within the same domain.

Synedoche also substitutes, but displaces a whole with a part, 'the substitution of one term for another within a predetermined hierarchy' (Fraser 1979: 175). So teachers in a school playground may do a 'head count' where head refers to students. Each of these concepts therefore specifies a particular way in which a phenomenon can be discussed in other than literal terms through the use of figures of speech. Metaphor in this sense is only one possibility for making analogies.

Yet it is metaphor that has been mostly used in examining educational discourses, often to illuminate the familiar in an unfamiliar way. To think of educational discourses in ways which may appear more literary and poetic may seem absurd, but, as we have indicated, it is precisely through an exploration of their textuality and the rhetorical strategies deployed that fresh (en)counters can be developed. The reasons for this become clear when we think of the distinction between the literal and the metaphorical and the implications of reading discourses of learning and teaching as literal when they might be productively read as metaphorical. As Potter (1996: 180) suggests, 'literal descriptions may be just telling it how it is, while metaphorical ones are doing something sneaky'. However, the distinction is important as

> ... someone may discount a description as 'only a metaphor'; or build it up as 'quite literally' the case; and this can be an important topic for study. Indeed the literal–metaphorical distinction is hard to keep separate from the factual–fictional distinction.
>
> (Potter 1996:181)

What this suggests is that in the fabrication of discourses there are rhetorical strategies deployed to position certain aspects as metaphorical and others as literal in attempting to engender certain effects and meanings as opposed to others. Partly this is related to the fabrication of facts. This is not to equate the literal with the factual or the metaphorical with the fictional in some common-sense manner, as is the case in more positivistic understandings of language and science. In the latter,

> ... literal language is the only vehicle for expressing meaning and making truth claims, and metaphor is a deviant use of words other than in their proper places ... figurative discourse is used only for rhetorical purposes or stylish embellishment; metaphor is denied any autonomous cognitive content.
>
> (Bicchieri 1988: 102)

This is the view that sees metaphor merely as ornamental language rather than fundamental to an understanding of and for acting in the world. Thus, *'taken as literal*, a metaphorical statement appears to be perversely asserting something to be what it is plainly known not to be' (Black 1979: 21, emphasis in original). For us, however, it forces us to consider the rhetorical strategies at play where certain things are constructed as facts and others as fictions.

> The literal/metaphorical distinction is particularly important ... it is em-ployed, for example, in drawing a distinction between serious and non-serious writing, academic and colloquial language, research and poetry, where, in each case, the former, truer, more referential medium is legitimised partly by the extent to which it manages to exorcise metaphor from its modes of expression.
>
> (Parker 1997: 84)

Here the most powerful metaphors might be those that hide their own work by making metaphor appear to be an illegitimate part of a text. In this situation, metaphorical readings become disruptive of the literalness of texts. 'Metaphor opens potentialities of understanding rather than fixing understanding detriment-ally and uniquely. A metaphor is permanently an opening for re-reading, re-interpretation ...' (Parker 1997: 84). However, that is not to say that they should be viewed only in a positive light. In the early 1980s, Taylor (1984b: 11) was suggesting that 'metaphors can be seductively reductionist, a tendency much in evidence with the rise of ideas about "accountability", "quality control", "common cores" and the like'. As 'metaphor is itself a metaphor for the meaning–displacing characteristics of deconstruction' (Parker 1997: 84), we are mostly interested in the use of metaphor as a strategy of analysis, as part of a deconstructive rewriting of educational practices.

Needless to say, these categorizations and interpretations are not watertight. There is always a real possibility that one might drown in attempting to achieve hermetic sealing. Further, it is not always entirely clear where a particular example of language use sits in its deployment within these differing rhetorical devices. However, given that 'clarity' is itself a rhetorical achievement and therefore subject to rhetorical analysis, this will not be entirely surprising. For some, embedded in certain scientific and/or realist discourses, these rhetorical practices may be deemed legitimate in the realms of art: for example, fiction and poetry. But when trying to describe and explain the world accurately and truthfully, it might be suggested that language is not being used properly when metaphor inappropriately articulates the literal.

However, not all view science in this way (for example, Kuhn 1979; Latour and Wolgar 1979). Also, one does not have to look far in scientific texts to find important examples of metaphors in play, such as in the concepts of black holes and worm holes, or in the view that an atom is like a miniature solar system. We also learn from and through metaphor. Lakoff and Johnson (1980) provide many examples of the play of metaphor in everyday experience. In this and later texts they argue that it is from an embodied experience of the world that these meta-phors emerge. In the latter, they (Lakoff and Johnson 1999: 128) argue that

> ... we all acquire ... metaphorical modes of thought automatically and unconsciously and have no choice as to whether to use them ... The fundamental role of metaphor is to project inference patterns from the source domain to the target domain. Much of our reasoning is therefore metaphorical ... Metaphorical thought is what makes abstract scientific theorizing possible ... Metaphorical concepts are inconsistent with the classical correspondence theory of truth.

Theirs is a much bigger and more ambitious project than that being carried forward here, one that we appreciate, but do not altogether agree with in certain respects. What Lakoff and Johnson have certainly done is demonstrate convincingly the centrality of metaphor to everyday experience. What we hope to have done in these opening chapters is to have persuaded you of the importance of rhetoric for the study of education. Moving on, we now turn to a range of analyses drawing upon the resources we have harnessed.

Chapter 3

Metaphors of and in learning and teaching

Metaphor is part of a linguistic code that helps to create relevance and to constrain social identities. Educational discourse is conducted in accordance with codes associated with certain role performances – for example those of educational psychologists, sociologists, philosophers and historians; school, college and university administrators; teachers and headmasters (sic); inspectors, curriculum consultants and others involved in educational activities. These codes embrace a variety of metaphorical usages, some of which are common, many of which are particular to a group of 'insiders', who share a set of agreed references.

(Taylor 1984b: 17)

To use certain linguistic codes and metaphors is therefore partly about mobilizing 'insider' groups. Let us now pursue rhetoric within the specific context of education in our attempt to be an insider group within education. In this chapter, we will explore broadly some of the metaphors through which attempts have been made to describe and explain learning and teaching practices and their persuasiveness in encouraging educators to adopt particular approaches. The issue is complicated by the fact that, on one reading, notions of teaching and learning are themselves metaphors. Teaching and learning cannot as such be directly observed. Of course we can describe what a teacher does within the rubric of teaching, for example asking questions, giving out work sheets, professing, marking. These are all practices amongst others that constitute 'teaching'. Similarly, we can describe what someone does when they are learning. They read, take notes, practice a skill set. The practices are empirically describable, but their significance as 'teaching' and 'learning' can only be inferred. In other words, they both stand for and stand in for something; they are inherently metaphorical. In this chapter, therefore, we wish to explore some of the range of metaphors through which these inferences are made, their assumptions and effects. In particular, we want to explore the metaphors of teaching and teacher identity – for example, gardener, fire starter – and the spatializing metaphors of learning – for example, student-centredness and distributed cognition – with a view to examining how these practices are ordered through the persuasive metaphors that are in play. But first to metaphors of learning.

Learning

> Theories of learning are dependent on metaphors, either because they are
> centrally concerned with mental acts and conscious processes or with the
> operations of mental mechanisms below the level of consciousness, all of which
> are only describable by metaphorical means.
>
> (Elliott 1984: 38)

> As blueprints of thinking, metaphors of learning will guide and facilitate
> teachers' understanding of what it means to learn, but these same tools of
> thinking may also limit the thoughts, attitudes and actions of prospective
> educators.
>
> (Martinez *et al.* 2001: 966)

There are many different educational discourses of learning. For instance, there
are the discourses of those participants in learning we variously refer to as pupils,
students, freshmen (sic), learners, adult returners and, perhaps more unfamiliarly,
knowing locations (Law 2000). These are discourses of learning where the focus
is learners themselves. There are also discourses of learning by those who are
variously referred to as teachers, lecturers, trainers, facilitators and professors, to
name a few and only in English. Perhaps more widely available, in the sense that
they find their way into published texts, are the discourses about learning. These
can take many forms but are, most notably, managerial, policy and academic. In
the latter, the study of learning has largely, but not solely, taken place in the
different branches of psychology – behavioural, cognitive, humanist, socio-cultural
– a fraught location, with different branches aspiring to be part of the natural or/
and social sciences, duly naturalized or socially constructed.

Pratt and Nesbit (2000) chart some of the movements that have emerged and
compete with each other to articulate and explain learning. In the process, they
indirectly point to the rhetorical power of differing notions of learning. For
instance, what are the rhetorical effects if learning is positioned as the achievement
of competence? Who would want an incompetent plumber, surgeon or even
teacher? Competence models have been critiqued for ignoring the cognitive
processes of learning, which themselves draw upon metaphors from computing
and information technology to extend understanding. 'Learning was constructed
in terms of storage and retrieval of information, short-term and long-term memory,
speed of processing, types of intelligence; and the effects of age on information
processing' (Pratt and Nesbit 2000: 120). Boyd (1979) provides a number of
examples of the ways in which the terminology of computer science, information
theory and the like have become metaphors within cognitive psychology: the brain
is a computer; certain cognitive process are pre-programmed; certain information
is encoded in memory store; development is produced by the maturation of pre-
programmed subroutines; learning is an adaptive response of a self-organizing
machine; and consciousness is a feedback phenomenon. Construed literally, these

are very powerful in shaping our understanding of learning. Initially it was an analogue computer that underpinned the metaphor for the mind/brain, but cognitive psychology has moved on to use more sophisticated notions drawn from computing. These are what Cameron (1999: 10) refers to as 'a connectionist model of human processing, in which information is represented by the activation of networks of pathways between nodes'. The simple information processing model of learning therefore was in turn challenged by constructivist and social constructivist models where the metaphors are of building bridges and the like. Depth and breadth also play an important part in discourses of learning, with 'deep' and 'surface' learning indicating different strategies adopted by students. In their view of learning as 'a love affair', and with a view to disrupting ideas that learning is all in the mind, McWilliam and Jones (1996) draw upon a range of metaphors from personal relationships, most notably the view of teaching as seduction. Elsewhere McWilliam (1996) refers to this interpersonal understanding as a 'touchy subject'.

McWilliam is using the language of love/passion to disrupt certain rational/ mentalist notions of learning. She provides the metaphors through which to write learning differently, wherein notions of learning style might take on a certain risqué quality not imagined by many of its advocates and supporters. The metaphors of learning that emerge from empirical studies seem to have less hyperbole associated with them. In their cross-cultural study of primary teachers and university students, Cortazzi and Jin (1999) provide a number of generic metaphors of learning, teaching and language that they identified. Thus learning was identified as 'movement', 'click', 'light', 'taking' and a 'jigsaw'. Of these five, metaphors of movement were by far the most popular, even if they also took many forms, for example children 'taking off' and 'zooming away like a rocket' or 'making headway' in 'spurts' and 'surges' like 'moving through water'. The notion of learning as a movement or journey is perhaps not surprising given the educational goal of transforming a person. Harrison *et al.* (2002) argue that the notion of learning as a journey is a root metaphor around which a range of other metaphors coalesce to produce an individualized understanding of learning and the roles of teachers and learners. The metaphor of journey

> ... provides a discursive context in which related ideas such as 'ladders of learning', 'routes for success', or 'pathways to opportunity' are easily assimi-lated, and in which policy developments such as credit accumulation and transfer, targets and learning outcomes are readily understood. Each refers to the progressive and cumulative nature of the journey, in which arrival at certain pre-determined staging posts is recognized through qualifications or portfolio entries.
>
> (Harrison *et al.* 2002)

This might be overstating the situation, overextending the analysis derived from a broad metaphor. It might well be in the specific metaphors of movement that we get some idea of the differing ways in which that journey is conceived – up- or downhill for example – and the relationship between, and practices engaged in by, learners and teachers. Some forms of moving may signify a relationship with authority more than an autonomous journey, something of particular importance in cross-cultural spaces. Whatever, it would certainly appear that learning is a moving experience ...

In many ways, metaphors of learning are integrally linked to those of teaching, conceptions of the curriculum and the purposes of education. Indeed we would argue that the rhetorical fabrication of learning and teaching as somehow divorced from the context of curriculum and pedagogy in much contemporary discourse is itself having powerful effects in framing these situated social practices as decontextualized skills to be learnt. This is something to which we may be contributing in the structuring of this chapter in the way we have. We will return to this issue in the next chapter. For now, though, let us focus on the curriculum and the purposes of education to explore the extent to which they might be linked, as part of a metaphorical system, to the metaphors of learning we have identified. Lawton (1984) argues that there might be differences of teaching style and practice based on the metaphors of the curriculum with which teachers work. He gives five examples: the curriculum as a building operation, as food, as a plant, as a product and as a commodity. He also points to the importance given to notions of balance, coherence and breadth, which play a powerful role in curriculum discourses. However, linked to his concern (1984: 79) that 'many metaphors confuse rather than clarify', he also indicates that these metaphors only work if one has prior agreement about the different components of the curriculum and their relative value. We might add 'progression' to the list of curriculum metaphors that are seemingly clear, but may lead to confusion. Talking of his own research on careers, Hudson (1984) admits that he initially focused on progress up ladders or races across hurdles. These are both familiar metaphors of movement, as are those that he used to reconceptualize educational and career progression once he realized that the movements were more complex and diverse.

> Instead of ladders or hurdles, we could have imagined a movement across thresholds from field to field, or from room to room, in which the requirements placed on the individual might be as dissimilar as those imposed on us by kitchen and dining room, bathroom and bedroom.
>
> (Hudson 1984: 69)

In other words, careers are not simply progressive or linear and indeed may at times involve revolving doors. Similarly plants die, buildings fall down and diet depends in part on the resources available to one. And the curriculum as a commodity puts knowledge and skills into a marketplace, making learning a consuming matter.

Knowledge – of whatever kind – is seen as a commodity to be packaged, and transmitted or sold to others. The commodity metaphor supports and is reinforced by a network of other metaphors which picture knowledge as something that can be assembled and acquired in a purely linear, additive manner.

(Parker 1997: 15)

The situation is complex. Thus, as Davis and Sumara (2004) suggest, this points to a notion of the curriculum based less on Euclidian geometric metaphors of linearity, norms and right angles and more towards conceptions based on fractual geometry and chaos. 'People are not fumbling along a more-or-less straight road towards a totalizing and self-contained knowledge of the universe. Rather, they are all taking part in structuring knowledge ... and this requires a completely different image' (Davis and Sumara 2000: 821). However, how persuasive the notion of a chaotic or non-normal school might be is open to question. In some ways, concepts from complexity theory may more literally describe a learning experience, but be less powerful rhetorically as they are counter-intuitive to a certain notion of education.

Sfard (1998) identifies two types of metaphor in discussions of learning that encapsulate, at a certain level of generality, notions of learning as moving and consuming. She refers to participation metaphors, such as the notion of community of practice (Lave and Wenger 1991; Wenger 1998), which she positions as gradually displacing acquisition metaphors of learning. The former orientate us towards a view of learning as activity and process, while the latter position 'the human mind as a container to be filled' (Sfard 1998: 5). Similarly participation metaphors point to the social and relational dimensions of learning, while acquisition metaphors, with their emphasis on having rather than being, point to a more individualized, self-interested view of learning, ultimately expressed in the notion of intellectual property rights (see Figure 3.1). While this is a useful framing, the level of generality may be unhelpful in examining specific learning contexts. Also it is based on a false binary of being and having, where the form

	Acquisition metaphor	Participation metaphor
Goal of learning	Individual enrichment	Community building
Learning	Acquisition of something	Becoming a participant
Student	Recipient (consumer)	Peripheral participant
Teacher	Provider, facilitator	Expert participant
Knowledge	Property, possession, commodity	Aspect of practice/ discourse/activity
Knowing	Having, possessing	Belonging, participating, communicating

Figure 3.1 Metaphorical mappings of learning
(Source: adapted from Sfard 1998)

that one takes inevitably is dependent on the other. For instance, one may participate in certain forms of education in part because of the prior cultural capital one possesses – although caution is necessary here as to turn all social goods into forms of capital is itself a powerful metaphorical statement.

From their study of experienced and prospective teachers' metaphors of learning, Martinez et al. (2001) develop a different typology to that of Sfard. They locate certain metaphors within specific theories of learning – behaviourism, constructivism and situated. They found that prospective teachers were far more likely to view learning through constructivist metaphors than were experienced teachers. The latter were far more likely to use behaviourist metaphors. Despite its popularity in academic discourses of learning, metaphors associated with situated understandings of cognition were not to the fore in either group. This is an interesting study, although we would question whether metaphors can be made to fit so tidily in a typology of this sort. However, it is suggestive of the links between metaphors, wider theories of learning and the practices of teaching.

What is clear, if anything can be clear, is that many conceptions of learning and the curriculum draw from horticulture and architecture in their framings. We see this also in various notions of the purposes of education. Nurturing plants and scaffolding learning both give a certain sense to that in which educators are engaged. Elliott (1984) identifies four metaphors of educational purpose: initiation, growth, guidance and liberation. All involve movement on the part of the learner, if of different sorts, with different destinations and different relationships between the learner, teacher and the curriculum. And so it goes on with each model of learning constituting and constituted by a range of metaphors through which a certain view of learning, learners, teaching and teachers is expressed.

But briefly, what of those who identify rhetoric and metaphor as integral to learning? What do they do? A good example is provided in Kress et al. (2002). In their study of the rhetoric of the science classroom, they took the view that:

> Our understanding of the process of learning as a dynamic process of sign-making is informed by social semiotics … We view the ensemble of the situated communicative actions of the teacher as semiotic material which contributes importantly to the resources involved in students' production of texts in the science classroom, though we can see in the data we have that students constantly draw on all kinds of other resources from all kinds of other contexts of their interest … The students' signs are always transformations of the resources that were made available to them, made in the light of their interest at the point of making the sign. Learning is thus always transformative, innovative and creative.
>
> (Kress et al. 2002: 129)

Cameron (2002 and 2003) looked more specifically at the use of metaphor in the learning of science among primary schoolchildren in the north of England. She identified three ways in which metaphors could be involved in the learning of concepts. First, building understanding of theory-constitutive metaphors is necessary in the learning of scientific knowledge and discourse. Second, learners' informal theories of science could themselves be already metaphorically structured. Third, metaphors could be used as 'stepping stones' between informal and more formal understanding of science. In other words, metaphors shape formal and informal theories of science and can be explicitly used to move from one to the other. Reflexively, therefore, metaphors provide an important meaning-making resource in learning, in this case of science. Interestingly, in the conclusion of her study Cameron also points to the need to understand better the role of visual metaphors in learning.

More widely, Swales (1990) argues for the continuing importance of developing a rhetorical consciousness among students. Such an approach has a number of advantages:

1   The problem of heterogeneous content interests in the class (medics and economists) is partly if temporarily sidestepped.
2   Insight into rhetorical structure is useful for both the reading and the writing of research.
3   General features are examined before specific details.
4   Discussion of rhetorical structure usefully develops in participants' increasing control of the metalanguage (negotiation of knowledge claims, self-citation, metadiscourse, etc.) which, in turn, provides a perspective for critiquing their own writing and that of others.
5   Rhetorical structure may have 'novelty' value, and may thus identify the class as being different from others that participants have experienced.
6   The rhetorical element is likely to present the instructor as having something to contribute over and above methodology.

(Swales 1990: 215)

In their study, Fuller and Lee (1997: 411) have pointed towards the 'rhetorical collusions between writers and readers, students and teachers in their enactment of the curriculum'. They explore the ways in which quoting, interpolation and probalization are used in students' assignments to demonstrate learning through the rhetorical devices of speaking, echoing and distancing. Their own research is based on an undergraduate women's studies course and we would expect the rhetorical collusions to differ across contexts. However, their study points to the rhetorical performances in students' writing and the feedback received from teachers. It is these sorts of works that have resulted from and in the growth of interest in the arena of academic literacies in recent years (for example, Lea and Stierer 2000; Lillis 2001). Here, as we saw in the turning of the study of rhetoric into rhetorical education, the study of metaphor and genre are turned into a pedagogical set of practices.

However, it is one of the paradoxes for those who explore learning and teaching as a communicative practice that, like us in writing this text, they too are as situated in their meaning-making as those about whom they write. Thus, in making sense of the science classroom, Kress *et al.* (2002) reflexively draw upon the membership resources (Fairclough 1999) available to them. Thus, they introduce metaphors of transformation into their view of learning, a constructivist stance, which positions them broadly with those who draw upon metaphors of participation and movement in their framing of learning rather than those of acquisition. We are back to Sfard's binary, with signs being transformed rather than acquired. Thus, 'we believe that "acquisition" is an inappropriate metaphor to describe the processes of learning: it implies a stable system which is statically acquired by an individual' (Kress *et al.* 2002: 28). Even as we engage reflexively with notions of metaphor, therefore, we are, as Sfard (1998: 12) says, 'doomed to living in a reality constructed from a variety of metaphors'. Doom may be a little on the bleak side, as we feel the notion of metaphor opens up spaces in many different ways, some more productive than others, recognizing that one's notion of productivity depends upon where you are positioned. It is the spatial forms educational metaphors take to which we now turn.

Spatializing metaphors

The spatial dimensions of social practices have been given increased attention in recent years and, with that, the importance of spatial metaphors in the fabricating of such practices (Edwards and Usher 2000; Edwards and Usher 2004). Lakoff and Johnson (1980) argue that orientational metaphors are fundamental to and arise from experience. These are spatial orientations and they focus in particular on use of 'up' and 'down' and the positive valuations of the former in relation to the latter in various types of discourse. On the basis of this, they argue that

> ... most of our fundamental concepts are organized in terms of one or more spatialization metaphors ... In some cases spatialization is so essential a part of a concept that it is difficult for us to imagine any alternative metaphor that might structure the concept.
>
> (Lakoff and Johnson 1980: 17–18)

Our argument here is that within discourses of learning, spatialization metaphors are at play and indeed there are spatial metaphorical contestations in play, which attempt to be persuasive in relation to what constitutes 'good', 'effective' educational practices – themselves to be treated cautiously. Thus, the metaphors of movement and journeys already introduce a certain spatial relationship, depending upon the emphasis placed upon the point of departure and arrival, and the moving experience itself.

Let us take a moment here to pause and brainstorm some of the different discourses of learning that exist. In no particular order and certainly not being exhaustive, we have teacher-centred, student-centred, subject-centred, ladders of learning, distance learning, open learning, flexible learning, situated learning, distributed learning, distributed cognition, deep and surface learning, legitimate peripheral participation, communities of practice, actor-networks, work-based learning, border crossing and pedagogies of (dis)location. Hughes (2002) has explored the notion of women 'returners' as nomads and exiles. In each of these there is a spatial orientation, drawing upon and supporting a particular spatial-ization of learning and learners, as well as often locating learning in particular places. Paechter (2004, forthcoming) provides a helpful typology of the spatial metaphors she identified through her own research:

- Area space – concerned with the drawing of boundaries: for example, field of study.
- Movement through space – concerned with how learners move in, through and around the curriculum: for example, learning as a journey.
- Structural space – concerned with how learning is constructed: for instance, on foundations.
- Hierarchical space – concerned with assessment and attainment: for example, top of the class.
- Distance space – concerned with teacher/student interactions: for example, distance learning.

While such categorizations are helpful, it is also important to be aware of their limitations. As with the typologies above, many of the metaphors can be situated in more than one category and often are deployed as part of a metaphorical complex. However, Paechter rightly points out the significance of such metaphors in the different discourses of teaching, learning and the curriculum and the conflicting ideologies they represent. This points to the ways in which many of the struggles in education are played out discursively through contrasting spatial metaphors.

Some of the metaphors of learning and teaching are more explicitly spatial in their orientation than others. The interest in the spatial reflects moves more generally in the social sciences wherein 'it is at least empirically arguable that our daily life, our psychic experience, our cultural languages are today dominated by categories of space rather than categories of time ...' (Jameson 1991: 16). Our own view is that Jameson's argument is based upon a too simple dichotomy, as categories of space are temporal and vice versa. For instance, a spatial ordering of learning is also a temporal ordering, a notion embedded in the texts of timetables, which distribute people and artefacts to both times *and* places, ostensibly to learn and to teach. Each such ordering has effects for what is learnt, by whom, where, what identity work is being attempted and how power is exercised in these particular social formations (Edwards 2003). As Paechter (2004, forthcoming) points out, this is not trivial and to achieve their discursive goals these spatializing metaphors have to be rhetorically powerful.

The question we now wish to pose is in what ways do these different discourses about learning appeal to reason, emotion and values? What metaphorical work is being done in adopting particular spatial metaphors as figures of speech? Let us take some examples. For instance, in certain contexts student-centred learning has been prominent among progressive educators as an approach for many years. The ideas, derived from and supported by the humanist psychology of Carl Rogers (1983), position the student at the centre of the learning process. In responding to their full range of needs – intellectual, practical and, most importantly, emotional – it is argued that teachers will enable students to learn more effectively. Learning is 'facilitated' rather than poured into the empty heads of students, as is argued to be the case with teacher-centred approaches. This points to the embodied as well as the spatial work of metaphor. The argument is, of course, in itself, an attempt to persuade by fabricating a polarized choice of either student- or teacher-centred approaches and projecting a simplified caricature of the latter, one in which interestingly the subjects to be learnt and taught, the curriculum, becomes largely invisible. At one level, this positioning of the learner as central in the learning process seems like common sense, as does the notion that learning is about the whole person and not simply about the mind and the acquisition of abstract bodies of knowledge – the latter resonating with a kind of intellectual cannibalism found in approaches to the curriculum that seek to cut the subject into modular 'bite size' chunks for consumption by students. In contrast, student-centredness seems to be about student autonomy and responsibility, which are obviously worthwhile. Obviously?

Student-centred learning is powerful as a rhetorical notion, generating warm feelings among many educators in providing a discourse through which to manage and legitimize their practices. It is persuasive as a discourse of learning, even if it cannot be taken literally. One reason for this is that the spatializing of the student at the centre of the learning process cannot be matched in pedagogic practices founded on the mass processing of students through educational institutions. Nor should we ignore the performative aspects of such discourses. To promote a student-centred approach, every aspect of students are put under the spotlight and they are thereby more subject to surveillance. Normalizing processes of learning relate not merely to the mind, but extend to the person's values and feelings, evidenced in the growth of use of portfolios, reflective diaries and learning logs. There is no escape. The student is both worked on (or over) and encouraged to work on themselves, to become a liberally educated subjectivity. There is a sense of Foucault's (1979) panopticon in the discourses of student-centredness, wherein the learner is constantly subject to the real and imagined gaze of the educator, a gaze that is internalized to produce self-disciplining subjects caring for themselves (Edwards 2001). Centring the student puts them under the spotlight, yet this is rhetorically erased through the positioning of such discourses as progressive.

Let us take another example. The notion of communities of practice and its associated concepts of legitimate peripheral participation and situated learning have found much favour in certain quarters in recent years. Based on ethnographic studies of learning in diverse settings, Lave and Wenger (1991) provide illuminating descriptions of the practices though which people move from the periphery, from apprenticeship to mastery, in specific areas. They learn to participate by participating; they become part of the community of practice, which is in itself a community of discourse. Learning in these contexts is located in the specific day-to-day practices of groups; it is situated. Wenger (1998) later went on to develop a pedagogy from this description and explanation of learning, which has almost become a technology, mobilized to support the development of communities of practice in many settings.

An interesting aspect of this particular discourse of learning is the spatial tension within it. On the one hand, it could be said to decentre learning, as the latter is constructed as taking place not simply in educational institutions but in any number of settings. Once again, there is a common sense to this, even if it is not always fully articulated. There is also a decentring of the teacher, as learning is the work of the community, not simply the individual expert. However, as well as this decentring there is also a centring at play, as each community has a boundary, however fuzzy, which one crosses – legitimate peripheral participation – and then moves within as one gains mastery of the particular practice. This centring does not focus on the individual student, as we discussed above, but is inherent in the practices of the community. Thus, rather than the student being the centre, the focus, in this discourse of learning, is on centring as such as the metaphor for learning.

The persuasiveness of this as a discourse of learning is interesting, as there is evidence for it based on empirical studies. However, to adopt it is not simply a matter of rational choice, as there is an emotional and values-based appeal as well. Lave and Wenger (1991) refer to 'communities' and the positive value of the notion of community is apparent. It evokes feelings of belonging and certain shared collective values. There is a rhetorical warmth in the notion of community, even though many communities are far from inclusive or warm. This is why it is important to consider the significance and effect of terms rather than taking them literally. Lave and Wenger may or may not provide an accurate description of learning. At one level, there is no resolution to this. However, in their conceptualization of learning, they bring together certain discursive resources to make their case, to establish the credibility of their study. The spatial ordering of a community of practice to which one belongs or could belong evokes powerful feelings of identification. This is so, even when to be part of a community of practice means to exclude others (Edwards *et al.* 2001a), when communities can be oppressive to those who do not accept their explicit and implicit rules, and are riven by tensions and conflicts. And what happens to those who belong or aspire to belong to numerous communities of practice? The community may be centred, but the individual learner is in pieces, torn and stretched between the various communities and situations to which they belong: for example, workplace, family, pub, political party, pre-natal group. The learner is on the rack here ...

On a more measured note, we offer Nespor's (1994) critique of the notion of communities of practice, itself based on an empirical study of undergraduate education in the USA, which suggests that it is more appropriate to think of learners being mobilized within different actor-networks made up of animate and inanimate objects. Understanding learning as a networking practice is explicitly spatial. It is noticeable, however, that this critique has not dented the warmth with which discourses of student-centredness and communities of practice continue to be received in educational circles.

Sfard (1998: 12) concludes with the view that

> the sooner we accept the thought that our work is bound to produce a patchwork of metaphors rather than a unified, homogenous theory of learning, the better for us and for those whose lives are likely to be affected by our work.

While we do not agree entirely with the detail of her argument, we do agree with this sentiment. In other words, we are not totally persuaded, but nonetheless are happy to give space to her text in this one.

Spaces and places: places to learn?

We have been exploring discourses about learning. What of the discourses of the experiences of learning? Recently, one of us was involved in an empirical study of flexibility in further education colleges in the UK (Edwards et al. 2001b; Clarke et al. 2002b). We introduce this here to both continue the argument for the centrality of spatializing metaphors in learning, but also to provide evidence for this, to embellish the logos of our argument. Flexibility has become a key metaphor for change in contemporary times (R. Edwards 1997). In educational discourses flexibility seems at one level to deny space and time, to obliterate it, so that learning is made available when and where it is required. Space and time become irrelevant with flexible learning, in particular as it is supported through information and communications technologies. Yet the study, which set out to explore the meanings of flexibility for students and staff, found something different, something which pointed to the importance of the spatial, but where this was translated into a sense of place and an experience of belonging. In this section, therefore, we are not discussing academic discourses of learning, but the spatial representations in the colleges' prospectuses and in the discourses of learners and those working in the colleges. Here there is a tension between the rhetoric of flexibility and that of place, of certain forms of movement and belonging.

The project worked with two colleges that were distinguished by designating one 'Techcity' and the other 'Shiptown'. The former is in a large metropolitan area in the south of England, the latter is in a large town in East Anglia. In the course of the study, which took place between July 1999 and January 2000, 50 interviews were conducted with managers, support staff, lecturers and students. Each interview lasted about an hour and was taped and transcribed. Documents from the colleges were also analysed. Here we draw on the prospectuses of the colleges to explore the images they project in order to attract students. What views of learning do they embody in these images, bearing in mind that images are persuasive too?

The two prospectuses for the year in which the study took place are very similar. The front cover of the Shiptown prospectus is laid out with 16 black-and-white photographs arranged in a box shape around the name of the college. The layout positions the reader on the outside of 16 windows looking in at individual and group portraits of young men and women. There is some ethnic diversity in these portraits, but they also suggest that the college attracts the 16–19 age group that has been traditionally served by these colleges. Students are engaged in various activities. The emphasis on student presence and activity is explicit in the slogan, 'Develop yourself'. The latter is repeated three times on the front cover and twice on the back of this prospectus. Vocational activities are signified by students wearing hard hats or a chef's cap and overalls, a young man holding a spanner and a young woman wielding a can of hairspray. Artistic expression is represented by a sculpture or collage and an aerial shot of an art studio. Among these images are a photograph of rows of empty study booths in a library and two exterior views of buildings in which sharp lines of concrete and glass are partially obscured by trees in full leaf. On the back cover a local map shows the college in relation to the shopping centre, railway station, harbour, parks and the town football club. Inside, the same photographs appear larger and in colour. There is also a picture-postcard-style image of yachts in the harbour.

Although there are fewer photographs on the front of the Techcity prospectus, these are in full colour and they are also laid out geometrically as a series of windows into the college. Again there are representations of ethnic diversity and an even gender mix. However, the students in these photographs span a wider age range. Only one photograph suggests vocational training, and the library and computer stations – unlike the empty places represented in the images of Shiptown College – are full of people. The photograph of a building included among these frames comprises a night-time shot of lighted windows and a concrete façade with floodlights illuminating the college name and logo. Again the location map features railway stations, and the local football stadium is represented in one of the photographs inside. Other picture-postcard images include a famous skyline, street market scenes and other cultural sites.

These images have been carefully composed to fabricate vibrant, modern places in interesting and attractive locations, teeming with active, accomplished and smiling people. In other words, the spaces are presented as particular types of place to which one might want to belong. The people framed in these windows are enclosed in a place that stands firmly in a marked location that the reader is invited to occupy. There is a sense of people moving between places within the college environment. In addition, the work clothes and accessories set up a strong relationship between college and workplaces. All these places are located within clearly delineated institutional boundaries. Where the world of work has been brought inside the college, the characters dressed to represent particular trades are all young and able-bodied. They also suggest traditionally gendered occupational divisions. Thus, the prospectuses would appear to position these colleges as places within which to develop oneself within conventional categories and classifications. Semiotically we are invited to occupy these colleges as particular places. They are appealing to us, in both senses of this word and possibly more. They therefore cut across discourses of flexible learning insofar as they seek to represent specific places rather than a denial of space and time. They represent situated trajectories through which to script learning.

The appeal and the investment of spaces as places in which to learn is also to be found in the student interviews. However, this was not unambiguous, as there was also the sense that, as well as providing windows of opportunity, colleges could become places that overwhelm. For instance, Simone, a student at Shiptown College, had left school when she was 14 and had had her first child at the age of 17. While bringing up her son, she had a number of 'little mundane jobs' like 'bar work, stacking shelves, you know, cleaning …'. She had 'put education on the back burner' until

> … four years ago I had my second child and I thought to myself, right, what do I want to do? Do I want to keep doing these, like, little jobs that are getting nowhere? Or shall I, sort of, you know take the plunge and go back into education again?

Thus education is represented as an object that can be both 'put on the back burner', but also as a container which might threaten to engulf you if you 'take the plunge'. Going back into education was contrasted with 'getting nowhere', a standing still rather than a movement. Simone had enrolled for a Fresh Start for Women course at one of the college's community-based centres, which was 'a lovely sort of easing me back into it'. She described this place as 'a very close-knit little college and I felt very cocooned there'. The comfort and safety of the 'cocoon' belongs to, but may also be in tension with, the same metaphorical idea of the container into which you can plunge, but in which you are also in danger of being overwhelmed. At the time of the interview, Simone had just begun a full-time course at one of the main sites of the college. She described her initial anxiety at the thought of coming to this 'bigger college': 'I thought oh my gosh, maybe I won't be able to cope, maybe I'm not academic enough and you know, it's all going to be overwhelming for me.' In Hughes' (2002: 420) terms, given her status as a woman returner, Simone's story may signify more of the experience of the exile than of the nomad, 'located and dislocated within the culture of origin and the host culture'.

A material factor in the construction of further education colleges at the time was a funding methodology that, as well as rewarding specific outcomes, rewarded the 'retention' of students on courses for specified periods of time. Thus lecturers came to evaluate aspects of teaching and learning in terms of the extent to which they could hold on to or contain students. For example, Ruth, a lecturer at Techcity College, described her course as one in which 'the retention is actually quite good … what holds them there is the fact that they're in a group and they're working with others and that they're sharing their learning'. From the lecturers' perspective, there was a tension between the vocational goals of further education and the pressure to retain students on courses, taking them further, but also keeping them in. There is a sense therefore in which containment was a significant spatial metaphor for both students and lecturers, in which there can be investment in a feeling of belonging by the space of the colleges becoming a place. But containment also has resonances of imprisonment. However, the feeling of being inside seems to evoke belonging and provides a way of protecting the 'inside' of learning from the 'outside' of other pressures.

These representations by learners and staff proved to be largely those of containment and movement in and through contained spaces. Similar spatial metaphors are to be found everywhere in educational discourse. A recent billboard advertisement for a London college proclaims: 'Give yourself the edge … Fill the skills gap'. This is a notion resonating with opportunity and danger, wondering how deep the chasm beyond the edge is. Mostly, education in general, and further education colleges in particular, are represented as bounded places. The prospectuses also show the colleges as containers full of desirable objects, activities and social relationships – windows of opportunity – rather than presenting time and place as constraints from which flexible arrangements will liberate students and staff. Thus, while there may be attempts to position colleges as more flexible, the project briefly represented here suggested a range of spatial-temporal containments and movements more than a denial of the importance of space and time. The same senior managers who tended to embrace discourses of flexibility, of supporting learning in any time and at any place, also endorsed the production of images in the college prospectus that say 'come inside – this is a place in which to be nurtured, stimulated, developed'. We therefore see how in the discourses of learners and staff and the texts of education, spaces of containment are also constituted as desirable places in which to be. Place, closure and constraint would therefore seem to have a positive value for many involved in learning and teaching and this is signified through the spatial metaphors at play. Certainly different spaces and different senses of place inform the discourses and images of education among those participating therein. This suggests a tension between the notion of flexibility as a liberation from constraint and the desire to be inside a place, to be contained, to belong, however dangerous that might be.

Spatial metaphors are not simply about learning, therefore, but are embedded in the institutional practices and discourses of those within education. The experience of learning and the attempts to make education desirable are fabricated by metaphors that not only have a spatial dimension, but also express a certain relationship to particular places. Having brought to the fore the work of metaphor in discourses of education, curriculum and learning, what then of teaching?

Teaching and teacher identity

Cortazzi and Jin (1999) identify seven reasons why teachers use metaphor, some of which are to do with their identity as teachers and others to do with the practice of teaching. They are to:

- identify for themselves what they experience
- add dramatic effect to the narratives of learning
- express meaning more concisely
- invite interaction
- organize concepts
- transform images into models
- organize their interpretation of learning.

While we will not address all of these here, they indicate the range of meta-phorical work at play in teaching. What then are the metaphors and similes for teachers and teaching? What do they indicate about those involved? Teaching is very much a rhetorical practice, the attempt to persuade others to learn. In this sense, teachers and lecturers have been referred to, following the work of Fairclough, as 'discourse technologists' (Farrell 2000). To say this might appear dangerous, implying that teaching is propaganda and a form of brainwashing. However, the genres of teaching are different to those of propaganda. Even if they both involve rhetorical performances, they are marked by different exigencies; they are timely (*kairos*) and appropriate (*phronesis*) for different contexts (Freadman 1994b). But this is not our main focus here.

As we have already seen above, typologies – a particular rhetorical organization of information – are a common feature of all educational discourse. In the world of adult education, one well-known typology (Darkenwald and Merriam 1982) classifies adult educators by using the metaphor of tribes. This typology presents five tribes of adult education, each with its own distinct aims, concerns, pedagogic styles and teaching–learning metaphors. Each tribe has its own plot, characters and (usually) heroes. The tribes are summarized in Figure 3.2. On the face of it, this typology appears to be simply a classification device for systematically describing a pre-existing world. In other words, it appears to simply represent that world. However, a rhetorical reading is also possible. This highlights the representational features of the typology, the ways in which it constructs a particular perspective. First, the typology is itself a narrative about working with adults as 'adult education'. Second, it is about adult education as 'tribal', a view also put forward in an influential analysis of academics by Becher (1989). Third, it suggests that workers locate themselves as adult educators and that, within that field, they locate themselves and are located in particular tribal stories which define worlds, influence practice and shape processes of identification. Our concern here is to explore the metaphors through which this is achieved.

Metaphors are lived and, through membership of a tribe, teachers may accept and tell a narrative with which they feel comfortable, which feels like a good

Tribe	Aim	Focus	Content	Relationship with learners	Teaching/learning metaphors
Traditionalist	Discipline of the mind. Pass on worthwhile knowledge, skills and attitudes	Individual	Classics – perennially valuable knowledge	Teacher superior to learner	Empty vessels, conduit, doctor–patient
Self-actualizer	Full personal happiness	Individual	Feelings, personal experience	Teacher inferior to learner	Social director
Progressive	Growth of all individuals (especially disadvantaged) to benefit society	Individual in a social context/life	Immediate problems and needs of the learners	Teacher and learner equals	Coach
Guerilla	Creation of a new and better social order	Individual in a struggle to transform societal structures and priorities	Sources of oppression	Teacher and learner equals	Guide, leader, joint venturer
Organizational maintainer	Better organizational effectiveness	Organization's needs	Determined by organizational needs assessment and broken down into objectives and performance indicators.	Teacher superior to learner	Manufacturer, shaper, builder

Figure 3.2 The tribes of adult education

story that makes sense of the world for them. Thus, a worker with adults identifies with a particular story and equally is identified by it. To become a member of a particular tribe is to be provided with clear and secure definitions (ways of knowing) and bounded ways of practising (ways of doing). It is to be provided with a set of signifiers by means of which allegiance becomes a matter of emotional investment, of pathos, rather than merely rational calculation, of logos, or mere convenience. To be a member of a tribe involves commitment, a belief in the value and worth of what one is doing. It is this combination of ways of knowing, doing and feeling that produces a bounded and unambiguous identity (ways of being). A tribal identity therefore provides a sense of place and placement.

Adult education has always been characterized by more than one discourse. This is particularly the case as it itself becomes re-storied by discourses of lifelong learning in many places. Some discourses have declined in their impact since each has to be told and re-told to maintain their significatory power. In the literature, the identities of workers are described and forged in a multiplicity of ways in addition to the five tribes outlined above. Miller (1993: 76) for example recounts her fears of being discovered as an 'impostor' in the academic world of university adult education, a view Brookfield (1993: 69) feels is also relevant for many students in adult education. Miller (1994: 82) says of her initiation into work in adult education that she initially identified herself as a 'sociologist' because of her background discipline. Mezirow et al. (1990) construct the adult educator involved in social action as an 'empathetic provocateur'. In his discussion of metaphors as shorthand encapsulations of reality, Brookfield (1993: 75) uses the metaphors of 'midwives', 'gatekeepers' and 'enablers' as ways of framing practices. Specific identities are adopted according to the perceived roles of teachers – pedagogic identity – and what they teach – subject identity. These metaphors are fashioned as part of the rhetorical practices through which the character of the teacher is mobilized.

Here, while there may be different metaphors, the difference is fabricated largely as playing out between individuals rather than within individuals. This suggests a grounded and bounded concept of identity. Similarly, in their research on identity among Canadian adult educators, Fenwick and Parsons (1996: 242) suggest that the use of metaphors 'provided an identifiable and coherent picture that synthe-sized fragments of practice and belief into something concrete and communicable'. Participants in their research produced metaphors such as 'fire-starter', 'safari guide', 'hiking leader', 'adventure outfitter' and 'museum curator' to describe their practices. While these vary from the tribal stories of adult education described above, once again the individual metaphors suggest a bounded, if complex, single identity. However, this would appear to be in part an outcome of the methodology and focus of this particular piece of research, which asked educators to choose a single metaphor for themselves to describe their practices of teaching and learning. While displaying a certain metaphorical richness, this research would appear to both assume and produce an individualized and bounded sense of identity. In a sense, then, we would suggest that the ways in which metaphors of teacher identity are represented in many cases already assume a tribal ordering, although this may be represented in notions, for example, such as communities of practice that we discussed above.

We can disrupt this by representing an alternative metaphorical framing which suggests that rather than a single bounded, tribal identity, adult educators, and teachers more generally, are increasingly having to adopt multiple identities and be part of many discourses as a way of negotiating the complexity of their working lives. Rather than tribal identities, therefore, we suggest an alternative metaphor of neo-tribalism. This is concerned with the forms of sociality, of shared sentiment, collective bonds and customs through which groups constitute themselves (Maffesoli 1996; Hetherington 1998). In addition, we would suggest there are shared metaphorical resources in play in the constitution of specific discourse networks. Here selves position themselves in a range of tribe-like allegiances with others. Identification rather than identity is brought to the fore (Hall 2000). In contrast to the classic tribalism of ethnographic studies, with their tightly controlled membership shaping all aspects of the individual's existence, these neo-tribes '"exist" solely by individual decisions to sport the symbolic traits of tribal allegiance' (Bauman 1991: 249). It is self-identification that establishes the neo-tribe. Rather than occupying a position within a single discourse or tribe, a bounded identity with a single metaphor, 'neo-tribalism is characterized by fluidity, occasional gatherings and dispersal' (Maffesoli 1996: 76).

Accordingly, we can say that teachers belong to many and various neo-tribes within which they play diverse roles as expressions of their sociality. The metaphorical identification by teachers becomes multiple, ambivalent and shifting, signifying the complexity of the worlds within and between which they operate. Singular, bounded tribal metaphors of identity lose their power to give meaning in relation to this complexity. Thus, for instance, Morgan (1996: 40–1) says of the personal trainer she interviewed, that she identified herself as 'superhuman and invincible; as an authority and expert; as friend; as coach and motivator; as preacher; as whip wielder and disciplinarian'. Here stories, discourses and metaphors are 'mediators and filters through which we not only live our lives with others in our environment but understand and symbolize that life and our-selves' (Adam 1994: 157). This is echoed in the work by Fenwick and Parsons (1996) noted earlier. They draw out a number of overlapping themes from their own research and argue that the metaphors in use portray, in their case, the adult educator as: one who shows the way; catalyst; one who knows how; caregiver; dispenser of provisions; and good host. 'People use patterns already developed to define their new "self" and to understand the concrete relations between self, objects, and systems of the material world' (Fenwick and Parsons 1996: 242). This illustrates the intertextuality and cultural locatedness of self-identity, image and metaphor. It also signifies a space of work that contrasts strongly with that which existed in the context of discipline-based interest groups such as sociology, psychology and history, or tribal identities. It suggests that teachers in this terrain need to be able to fashion themselves not as a uniform community, but as networks of difference. Of course how far this is the case for all teachers or is specific to the groups studied remains a question, particularly given the importance of place and belonging we mentioned in relation to the study outlined above.

In undertaking a bibliographical mapping of the pedagogic identities implicit in writing on higher education teaching, Zukas and Malcolm (2002) propose a different set of what they refer to as 'masks'. These masks are: the educator as critical practitioner; the educator as psycho-diagnostician and facilitator of learning; the educator as reflective practitioner; the educator as situated learner within a community of practice; and the educator as assurer of organizational quality and efficiency. Each of these can be mapped onto a set of continua that they identify in the literature as dimensions of pedagogic identity. These are:

- learning in community – individualized learning
- disciplinary community – pedagogic community
- moral/social accountability – organizational accountability
- educator as person in the world – anonymous/invisible educator
- learner-centred evaluated – objective measures of learning
- focus on process – focus on product
- content contested – content given
- social orientation – psychological orientation.

While these differ from those we have already discussed, there is sufficient overlap to suggest that some of what we have outlined above from within the world of adult education may be relevant to teachers and teaching more widely. Certainly Zukas and Malcolm (2002) are not working with a tribal understanding of teacher identity, as each of the masks can be adopted by individual teachers according to circumstances. This is in line with our argument regarding neo-tribalism. However, the use of the metaphor of the mask is itself interesting, as it suggests we need to ask what lies behind the mask and maybe even impels us to be suspicious of the authenticity of teachers. We might also ask what masks Zukas and Malcolm are hiding behind. For instance, the continua are represented as horizontal with no explicit privileging of either the left- or right-hand terms. However, implicitly we suspect a slope, with the left-hand terms being privileged over the right-hand. They have a certain pathos that is appealing.

Other metaphors and typologies are to be found in the literature on teaching. For instance, Cortazzi and Jin (1999) identified 236 metaphors of teaching in responses elicited from 140 British postgraduate primary teacher-training students. These they condensed into 10 broad metaphorical themes, listed in order of frequency. Teaching is

1   a journey
2   food/drink/cooking
3   plant growth/cultivation
4   a skill

5 an occupation (other than teaching)
6 entertainment
7 searching for treasure
8 family relationships
9 war
10 construction of a building.

In this list it is important to bear in mind the frequency of usage of different metaphors. Journey metaphors occurred almost twice as many times (44) as the next most popular metaphorical theme to do with food. Given that movement metaphors were the most frequent in the same study's view on learning, perhaps it is unsurprising that journey metaphors are also to the fore in the view of teaching. However, given institutional concerns with retention, there may be a question about how moving an experience it is and whose movement is to the fore. Having said this, it may be reflexively unsurprising that movement metaphors are to the fore in discourses of teaching and learning, for, as we have said of metaphor itself, it involves the translating of discourses of one domain into another; metaphor itself is movement. Metaphors:

> ... may provide the most memorable ways of learning and thus be our most efficient and effective tools. But further, they are epistemologically necessary in that they seem to provide a basic way of passing from the well-known to the unknown ... the crucial use of metaphor is in moving from one conceptual scheme with its associated way of knowing to another conceptual scheme with *its* associated way of knowing.
>
> (Petrie 1979: 460, emphasis in original)

Metaphors of teaching and teacher identity abound. Midwife, artist, technician, authority, caregiver, party host, referee. In their study of generative and surface metaphors used by pre-service and in-service teachers, Vadeboncoeur and Torres (2003) found that the former used notions of gardener, giver of knowledge, change agent and mediator of culture, while the latter fabricated narratives of home-building, rafting, quilting and a Bobius strip. The richness of the latter compared to the former suggests that the pre-service teachers were not developing the metaphorical resources through which to articulate the complexities of their intended careers. However, this seems to be in tension with other research where it is the pre-service teachers who seem to use more generative metaphors (Martinez *et al.* 2001). Metaphors abound even before we enter into the metaphorical terrain of cyberspace and the metaphors of teaching online. Each carries different sets of associations and rhetorical appeal. They inform day-to-day practices. They also mobilize support in different ways among different socio-rhetorical networks. Much is therefore to be found in the metaphors through which educators rhetorically frame their teaching practices and self-identity as teachers, including matters of status and power. Each story maps out the professional landscape in particular ways. Thus, for instance, Clandinin and Connelly (1996: 25) investigate the various stories of classroom teachers:

> Classrooms are, for the most part, safe spaces, generally free from scrutiny, where teachers are free to live stories of practice. These lived stories are essentially secret ones ... When teachers move out of their classrooms into the out-of-classroom place on the landscape, they often live and tell cover stories, stories in which they portray themselves as experts, certain characters whose teacher stories fit within the acceptable range of the story of school being lived in the school.

In addition to the secret and cover stories, the authors identify sacred stories, which are the 'theory-driven' views of practice. Each of these are stories told by teachers themselves, some of which will be more persuasive than others, dependent on context and audience. They are expressed through the metaphors used by those who teach and those who speak of teachers. They also find expression and are mobilized through the forms of professional development in which educators participate, to which we now turn.

Chapter 4

Inventing the 'good teacher'

We have explored some rhetorical dimensions of contemporary discourses of teaching and learning. We now move on to examine professional development, a more specific aspect of educational discourse that affects those who are involved in teaching, as they become increasingly subject to initial and continuing professional development. However, many of those teachers, like ourselves, are involved in organizing and teaching professional development courses themselves. There are many rhetorical aspects we could potentially explore, including the ways in which certain forms of work become positioned as a 'profession' where a higher education credential is a signifier of status and respectability, if not always respect. However, our interests here are more specific.

There has been much debate over the years of the nature of professionalism, professional development and professional practice. We have ourselves contributed to such debates at various times (for example, Nicoll and Harrison 2003). Broadly, these debates have revolved around three notions of professional practice: the technical expert, the competent practitioner and the reflective practitioner. The latter two have been particularly influential as a reaction against the perceived inadequacies of the former, when discussing practice in the human services. And the reflective practitioner notion has become almost hegemonic in many professional development courses in education. However, we do not wish to explore the merits or demerits of any of these ideas per se. Rather we seek to examine the rhetorical work they can be said to do in positioning professional labour in particular ways, in representing certain views of the 'good teacher'. We will focus particularly on the notion of the reflective practitioner, as we want to argue that it assumes and inscribes the very view of the world and practice that is being challenged in this text. In other words, it tends to take a literal, realist view of teaching, thereby displacing the rhetorical and performative from consideration of what constitutes 'good practice'. We will argue that reflection is a rhetorical practice, but one which is mostly positioned as a form of realism, specifically a psychological realism. More on this later.

The first part of the chapter will outline some of the rhetorical work that professional development discourses do. We should point out that the three notions are not necessarily mutually exclusive. Many discourses either explicitly or implicitly draw upon different ideas. This might be argued to be a strategy to build the audience and authority for the particular argument, insofar as ambiguity can enable a range of interests to be mobilized as a supportive audience, as different interests are translated into a common cause. Thus, for instance, it is difficult to be against the notion of professional development, or it might be that a standard of competence to be achieved is in demonstrating reflective practice, often evidenced through (critical) commentary of an aspect of one's professional work. What audience is mobilized and how is dependent upon the extent to which different individuals and groups are persuaded that a particular discourse is about and for them, that they are being invited to participate in the practices of a certain socio-rhetorical network. The second part of the chapter takes a different tack. Here we explore more explicitly some of the ways in which practitioners are invited to become an audience, although many are subject to sanctions if they fail to do so satisfactorily. Here we are returning to the question of the rhetorical work of pedagogy, but in the particular context of professional development.

Technical expertise, competence and reflective practice

The exigencies for professional development are articulated everywhere, it seems. Change and adaptation to change are at the centre of the imperatives to learn throughout life, one aspect of which is in relation to our workplaces. In education, the exigences include:

- the desire to enhance student learning experiences
- the need to reconceptualize learning and teaching in the context of increasing and widening participation
- curriculum change
- the changing nature of work within contexts of globalizing practices and the increasing use of information and communication technologies (ICTs)
- the importance of institutional flexibility in the search for increased efficiency and effectiveness.

You name it, it has got to change, and central to this change is professional development. Promoting better teaching practices through professional development is part of the drive for quality and excellence. Educators are therefore positioned as increasingly required to be flexible and reflexive (R. Edwards 1997), or innovative and creative (Zuber-Skerritt 1992), dynamic in their responses to and engagements with changed circumstances, able to locate, map and translate the different discourses in their arena of practice (Edwards 1998). Change is said to be everywhere and we are urged to be prepared to deal with the uncertainties it engenders. The irony of this is that, rhetorically, change and uncertainty are positioned as certain; the only certainty is uncertainty! The facts of change are positioned to persuade us, the audience, of the need for change. But we can go further than this in our analysis. Change is represented as the reality to which we must adapt. In rhetorical terms, this is a form of 'ontological gerrymandering': 'just as in electoral gerrymandering, where the vote is biased by drawing boundaries in the most efficacious way, the defence is shored up by drawing the rhetorical boundary around the most advantageous issues' (Potter 1996: 185). If, by contrast, change were portrayed as socially constructed, then we might call for preventative measures rather than professional development. By naturalizing change – that is, representing it as a natural and thus inevitable characteristic of the world – it assumes not only a suasive force but in effect attempts to hide its own work as a speech act.

In this context, different views of the professional and professional development are put forward. Professionalism and professional development are mobilized in different ways with different consequences for who participates in this development, the form the development takes and the forms of information and knowledge to which the audience is given access. Let us first address the discourse of competence. If we go to a dentist, butcher, hairdresser or motor mechanic, we certainly expect or at least hope that they will be able to undertake the tasks we ask of them and do so in a skilful way. In general, we prefer to have teeth filled rather than pulled, a well-gutted chicken rather than one with entrails left in place, the hairstyle of our choice rather than a mess, our car fixed rather than left to break down. But why should we view this as competence rather than, for instance, expertise or capability or even skill? Now, we are aware that we are oversimplifying, as neither competence nor expertise can be given definitive meanings and therefore each is capable of doing more than we suggest here. However, in some ways this is a necessary part of our (and perhaps any) argument.

In one tradition, expertise is linked to a model of technical rationality. This assumes two things. First, that a body of theoretical knowledge is learnt and applied in practice situations; and second, that what is learnt in one place *can* then be applied elsewhere. In other words, you learn about surgery in a teaching hospital and you can then go elsewhere and conduct effective surgery; you learn something and then apply it in a context different to that where it was learnt. However, this position has run into increasing difficulty over the years, as it assumes a front-end model of learning; that is, all you need to know will be provided through initial education and training. The exigence of change has undermined this and resulted, as we have seen, in calls for continuing professional development, not only for teachers, but for all workers. However, it has only undermined it in certain ways. The discourse of continuing professional development builds an audience among both the professions and the networks they serve. This does not necessarily displace the notion of the technical expert, for two reasons. First, continuing professional development opportunities can still emphasize the learning of theoretical knowledge as the basis of practice, and second, they can still be provided on the basis of learning away from the workplace, which is then applied within it.

This discourse, in particular, has been upheld by the university as an institution. Expertise here depends upon a body of theoretical/discipinary/subject knowledge that can be produced and taught within the walls of this particular institution. Knowledge is codified and generalized into separate disciplines and conferred with the highest status of all forms of knowledge. Pedagogy is the transmission of this knowledge and the development of critical cognitive capacities. This draws attention to the power of discourses of technical expertise in positioning particular groups as professional or academic, in supporting the privileging of particular forms of knowledge, and affording differential status and roles to different groups. Note here that we introduce a new character into our narrative, which is significant for the persuasiveness of our argument. Discursive power is in part a function of rhetoric, we would argue. Particular rhetorical accomplishments are more or less accepted as persuasive over periods of time. The gerrymandering of change as a naturalized process may be an example of this. Expertise is normalized, in a similar fashion as a denotational reference, even though we would argue that it is conno-tative and performative. 'That is, what counts as the demonstration that someone is indeed worthy of employment ... is constructed through particular linguistic forms which have become conventional ways of articulating what is required or desired' (Holmes 1998: 6). It is thus rhetorical achievements such as expertise that help define boundaries for the possibilities for the action of individuals and groups, deciding what should count as specifically professional. Here profession-alism is not about describing an existing state, but is constantly performed through rhetorical practices, in this case, of continuous professional development and the positioning of certain practices as good practice, eliding any boundaries between professional status, professional working and good practice.

What in some ways is central to technical expertise is that practitioners are positioned as holding expert bodies of knowledge, which are specific to them and their professional group. This provides both the grounds for status but also for demarcations of boundaries by professional associations and trade unions. They have their professional tool kit that they carry around with them. Witness, in particular, in certain situations, the depth of the struggle between doctors and nurses over who should have responsibility for what in treating patients, and the increasing professionalizing of nursing and spread of practice into domains previously requiring the expertise of doctors (Francis and Humphreys 2002). However, this notion of expertise has costs. As discourses highlighting the power of the professions have emerged over the years, arguments that the costs are too high have become more persuasive. Experts, it is argued, cannot be trusted any longer to regulate their own quality and standards. A common criticism is that an expert may know about something, but cannot necessarily do it well. Thus teacher educators may tell students how to teach, but may not necessarily be able to teach well themselves. Student teachers may know the theories of learning, but may not be able to engage a classroom of children. And so on. Such criticism effectively undermines any certainty that expertise is what professional develop-ment should be about. Rhetorically, they both undermine the status and claims to professionalism, while attempting to reinscribe alternative understandings of it. The acquiescence of professionals as a status group is displaced by a discourse in which professionals have to demonstrate their continuing competence. In other words, they have to perform in order to deserve their continuing status. The increasing calls for experts to be publicly accountable means that the ethos of the expert has in many contexts been undermined by the logos and pathos of professional misconduct and incompetence. However, in criticizing certain forms of professional practice, there is the danger that the public is mobilized to critique professionalism per se, as might be witnessed in the rise in compensation claims against professionals. Managing the boundaries of critique and expectations among different parts of an audience is an important rhetorical practice, over which there can be no final mandate, something which becomes a problem for the professions themselves, policy makers and the media.

We have seen how whole ways of working and a range of pedagogical approaches flow from a certain rhetoric of technical expertise and also help to support it. The same is the case for notions of competence and reflective practice. In a sense then, there is a rhetorical struggle between different notions of professional practice and professional development, with very real material affects. This is because, if we act in the social world upon the basis that something is the case or is desirable, we immediately change the nature of the social world. This is the reflexive dilemma for all social actors. It is also the case that different audiences are mobilized in different discourses of professionalism. The questioning of professional expertise has mobilized groups beyond the professions themselves, through which the latter are held to be accountable and subject to scrutiny. In the process, the client has been reinscribed as the consumer, thereby contributing to the changing relationships with professional workers.

In the media and elsewhere experts and expertise have become subject to greater distrust. As we have indicated, this has particularly affected the public sector professions – educators, social workers, doctors, etc. – but has also become part and parcel of the condition for other professions as well – for example, and spectacularly in recent years, accountants. From the Olympian heights, experts have been pulled into what Schon (1983) powerfully referred to as the 'swamplands' of professional practice; a metaphor with a certain pathos for those of us who on a daily basis are wading around and often sinking. In this swampland, professionals are required to demonstrate that they are competent, that they can do what they claim they can do, and maybe sometimes what is claimed by others that they can do. Standards of competence are developed upon the basis of evidence of what already competent practitioners do. Assessments and curricula are built upon the basis of those standards, the logos for which stands in sharp contrast with the more reified, 'arty farty', 'trendy' theory or, even worse, 'jargon' of experts. Professionalism as competence appears more empirically and experientially secure than technical expertise, as appropriate levels of behaviour can be determined through functional analysis. The positivism underpinning this approach acts as a positive warrant that it will produce the necessary outcomes. Competence measures are argued to be real and transparent, fair and valid. Demonstrations that you can do something in the context of practice or in simulations of practice become a key signifier of professionalism. Ethos is built upon doing and not upon knowing, although this powerful binary between ontology and epistemology is itself suspect.

The idea of competent professionals seems entirely reasonable and appealing. It has a strong persuasiveness about it. It does rhetorical work and, as a result, the nature of professional development is subject to upheaval. Greater emphasis is placed on learning in the workplace, upon skills and tacit knowledge and the doing of tasks upon which you reflect, rather than the application of knowledge from elsewhere into the work setting. And there we have performed another manoeuvre, as reflection has slipped into the discourse. The notion of the professional as a reflective practitioner has had its own trajectory but has also been significant in the arguments surrounding the notion of competence. One of the key criticisms of competence has been that it focuses too heavily and in an unreflective way on what one can do. Behaviour alone is all that counts, when, in a situation in which information and knowledge play a greater role in professional work, the capacity to access, interpret and communicate knowledge cannot be overlooked. A cognitive aspect is therefore necessary for competent performance and this is signified through the notion of reflection, around which an increasingly large and noisy socio-rhetorical network has gathered. But note, it is cognitive where the emphasis is on psychological states and processes. Where is the communicative, the rhetorical in all this – itself a rhetorical question it might appear, as all questions are? The answer is that it remains hidden in the folds of much of the discourse of competent and reflective practice.

The idea of the reflective practitioner has a certain pathos to it, the logos for which may rest more in the experience of the audience than in the evidence to support it. Here the professional is positioned in the complex and messy world of practice, where decisions and judgements have to be made on an instant basis. This may require more intuitive than deliberative action (Eraut 2000). Hot action rather than deliberation in the cool spaces after the event often characterize professional practice. However, even when there is not the opportunity to reflect on one's actions in the event, we can nonetheless reflect on them afterwards, and often do, whether in our own thoughts or in dialogue with colleagues, partners, friends, etc. Practice is therefore 'thoughtful', an attractive notion for all concerned. It is also discursive, since reflective practice, as well as being a discourse, also requires discourse. Can one reflect without language? For professionals, it is particularly attractive. It is indicative both that they are serious practitioners and that they are capable of making autonomous judgements in the uncertain situations of practice. As Parker (1997) argues, this positions the professional as adopting an open-minded and questioning approach to practice. Here

> ... reflective teaching's concept of open-mindedness is created out of the hierarchically opposed duality of the concepts *certainty* and *doubt* ... The old certainties of tradition, custom, technical efficiency and nomological universality are rejected as rational grounds for practice and replaced with a process

of dynamic interrogation ... The capacity to articulate doubt becomes the mark of the attitude of seriousness; of an ability to recognize the true depth and gravity of the situation ... This idea of open-mindedness – the exhortation *constantly* to question, criticize and change – issues in a culture of *radical doubt*.

(Parker 1997: 122, emphasis in original)

We feel sure this will resonate with many readers, although ironically the culture of radical doubt might itself be said to undermine the status of professions, even as it is used to give expression to the bogginess they – and we – are negotiating. However, despite its initial persuasiveness, we agree with Parker's further argument that the rhetoric of reflective practice is largely promoted in an unreflexive manner. Reflection is taken literally. Thus, for example, 'reflection is a natural part of human life but for professionals and students, structured reflection can provide a framework within which they can examine their strengths and weaknesses and identify strategies for improvement' (Huddlestone and Unwin 1997: 137). Indeed, it seems to have become a technique to be applied to situations, or even a competence to be practised, rather than conceived as an embedded and embodied part of practice. What do we mean by this?

Reflection is one of the most powerful metaphors in Western society and particularly Western modernity. It implies that you can see one thing in another – the mountains in the lake, your face in the mirror, the external world in your mind. It is this latter that is of concern here, for the notion that one's mind does or can mirror the world, reflect it, points to a particular view of the processes in play. The notion of reflective practice involves looking at what is, in order to see what might be: 'a reflection in a mirror is an exact replica of what is in front of it. Reflection in professional practice, however, gives back not what it is, but what might be, an improvement on the original' (Biggs 1999: 6). In other words, it is a very shiny mirror. Reflection implies an empiricist and realist view of the world. While persuasive for many audiences, partly because it is in tune with many common-sense views of the world – that is, that there is a pre-existing audience to appeal to – we see this as a rhetorical achievement that fails to reflexively articulate its own fabrication. In other words, the notion of reflection does not do justice to the reflexive intertextual and interdiscursive practices that make it possible. Language is taken to be a transparent carrier of meaning, representing reality in an unmediated way. Privilege is also given to visual appreciation of the world. To reflect on practice is to talk about it – in one's head, with others, on paper – but not to take into account the discursive resources upon which one draws and the rhetorical nature of the work being performed. It is to work with a metaphor of a mirror, when, given our view of rhetoric, we would suggest there are many mirrors, mostly cracked, as in a Hall of Mirrors at a funfare, and there is no way out. All is refracted.

Thus, even as reflective practice has become a significant and, for many, a persuasive view of professional work and has become embedded within the curricula of professional development, we are arguing that it is itself not a reflection of how professionals work, a true representation, a mirror on itself, but more an attempt to position professional practice and professionals in a particular way. In the process, a particular professional audience is mobilized through the circles and cycles, single and double loops that rhetorically fabricate the learning of such groups. Here professional practice takes the form of a Whirling Dervish, whipping up a storm. The rhetoric of reflective practice may be powerful, not in the sense of whether it is literally true, but in the ways in which it is persuasive and the work it attempts to do. In other words, reflective practice is not simply a concept, but is a speech act within a contemporary discourse of professionalism and, as such, it does not so much describe as *perform*. To try and make what we mean a little clearer let us turn to some particular examples.

The good teacher?

The exigence for professional development for higher education lecturers is much the same as for other educators. However, there is a crucial difference, as academics are subject specialists, who have not necessarily been taught how to teach. There is a similar exigence for vocational teachers who may have vocational expertise, but come to teaching with no prior training. For both groups, improving the quality of teaching has been positioned as necessary for improving student attainment, despite doubts about the logos of the implied link and the impact of professional development on teaching practices. We will not go into that here, however. Our question is more direct. How do standards of competence operate to normalize and shape what it means to be a good teacher and what it means to act professionally in higher education? Here, we examine the standards identified by the Institute for Learning and Teaching in Higher Education (ILTHE) through which, at the time of writing in 2003, the good practice of those working in higher education in the United Kingdom are being constituted. This analysis is illustrative and not exhaustive, but does indicate some of the rhetorical work at play in normalizing a particular view of good practice and inviting academics to become the audience for particular forms of professional development.

We have earlier discussed professional development as rhetoric. As such, the task is to build an audience in a particular way. Persuasion by appealing to evidence, emotion and values is part of the process of mobilizing an audience. In the process, certain forms of active and productive work within contexts of learning and teaching are fabricated that impact upon the discourses and identities of those involved. Here professional development becomes a form of identity work, attempting to translate the practices, values and attitudes of the worker with those of a profession and, in some situations, the very goals and missions of the organization. This 'enables individuals to actively participate in disciplinary regimes through investing their own identity, subjectivities and desires with those ascribed to them by certain knowledgeable discourses' (Usher and Edwards 1998: 215). But how are they persuaded to do this?

Pedagogical communications can be explored for their work in rhetorically fabricating particular descriptions of the most appropriate or effective work and comportment of the teacher, while simultaneously undermining alternative and resistant discourses. Here 'analysts treat reality construction as something that has to be achieved using some devices or techniques ... realism and factuality are worked up using a set of rhetorical devices and techniques which may be specific to particular settings' (Potter 1996: 102). Our analysis therefore examines the persuasive strategies through which teachers are invited, coerced and maybe seduced into investing their own values, beliefs and identities in particular framings of the good teacher. Our intention here is not to unmask a deliberate and sinister attempt to subvert the true purposes of teaching. We are not sure what such purposes would be. Nor do we consider it inevitable that teachers adopt uncritically the positionings identified for them by others. Rather our aim is to develop a reflexive awareness about the rhetorical work of formulae or prescriptions for how professional practice should be developed. We are rhetorically mobilized to become particular sorts of rhetorician, dependent upon the discourse within which we locate our work and how our work is located by others. Who authoritatively writes/speaks on such matters, upon what basis, and who is mobilized as the audience and how remain constant questions to which attention needs to be given.

In the analysis that follows, we consider the rhetorical devices and techniques that make particular statements possible, persuasive and performative. Our analysis considers the statements of core knowledge and values identified by the ILTHE as those required by a teacher in higher education. These are the demonstrated outcomes of professional development programmes that are accredited by this body. Through our analysis we identify some of the effects of the standards in making discourses of competent and reflective practice possible, and in forging such objects as learning, portfolios of work, design and delivery as naturalistic categories rather than metaphors within a particular discourse of good practice. The suggestion is that as academics (re-)fashion their practices within this rhetorical framework, drawing upon the categories for self-description provided, they are, to a greater or lesser extent, internalizing a normalizing gaze (Foucault 1979), shaping their identities accordingly, thereby coming to understand themselves and act in these terms.

The ILTHE (2003: 22–3, emphasis in original) guidelines for the accreditation of programmes states:

Core knowledge and values

Courses seeking accreditation should be designed with an awareness of the core knowledge and professional values that are expected of Members and Associates of the Institute for Learning and Teaching. It is expected that, as part of the accreditation process, the institution will be asked to explain how the course develops participants' understanding of the ILTHE five areas of learning and teaching activity, core knowledge and adherence to the professional values. These are as follows:

Learning and teaching activities
Members of the ILTHE will be expected to have addressed **all five areas** within both the taught programme (or by independent study) and the assessed elements of the course:

1   teaching and the support of learning;
2   contribution to the design and planning of learning activities and/or programmes of study;
3   assessment and giving feedback to learners;
4   developing effective learning environments and learner support systems;
5   reflective practice and personal development ...

Core knowledge
Members of the ILTHE will be expected to have knowledge and understanding of:

- the subject material that they will be teaching;
- appropriate methods for teaching and learning in the subject area and at the level of the academic programme;
- models of how students learn, both generically and in their subject;
- the use of learning technologies appropriate to the context in which they teach;
- methods for monitoring and evaluating their own teaching;
- the implications of quality assurance for practice ...

Professional values
Members ... of the Institute will be expected to adhere to the following professional values:

- a commitment to scholarship in teaching, both generally and within their own discipline;
- respect for individual learners and for their development and empowerment;
- a commitment to the development of learning communities, including students, teachers and all those engaged in learning support;
- a commitment to encouraging participation in higher education and to equality of educational opportunity;
- a commitment to continued reflection and evaluation and consequent improvement of their own practice.

Generic statements of this kind appear to allow for multiple interpretations. However, our argument is that, as they are translated through the texts of particular courses, within interactions between students and tutors and through assessment practices, they become less open than they appear. In other words, as we indicated in the previous chapter, there are any numbers of rhetorical collusions which are negotiated in the translation from broad principles to specific pedagogic practices, within which forms of closure are pursued in the boundary maintenance of good practice. Potter (1996: 111–12) argues that descriptions work by managing the domain that is to be considered: 'sometimes, the success of a description in action will depend on its selective management of the realm of objects and events that are to be considered'. In this case, specific competence descriptions act to delineate the domains of knowledge and individual activities, responsibilities, relationships and dependencies that are emphasized and given priority within specific programmes. In the process, others are marginalized.

Thus, the learner becomes a pre-existing object within competence statements. In the process, good teachers are fabricated as subjects who understand how students learn and know how to support them in their learning. Good teachers are required to investigate this and base their selection of methods, design and planning, monitoring and evaluation accordingly. This looks alright until you consider the work going on here and what alternatives there might be. 'Within the framework of education as an academic discipline, current literature usually interrogates educational practices through the binary formulation of learning and/*as distinct from* teaching' (McWilliam 1996: 2, emphasis in original). Such a separation has been constituted by and reinforced through the primacy of psychological theories of the individual and, in so doing, teaching as a relational, social and pedagogic practice, and the curriculum as a content, has been partially erased as a focus of professional development. A particular pedagogic identity is positioned as *the* pedagogic identity, mobilizing an audience to practice in particular ways. A stress on learning and the learner was not made in nineteenth century texts on education, where the emphasis was on teaching. By producing the learner as an object within competence statements, alternative foci for the knowledge and practices of the teacher are elided. The teacher is required to learn about how students learn and, for assessment, to provide evidence of their understanding of this in their selection of methods and design of learning and so forth. And it all seems so sensible and even progressive, which is part of its appeal and power perhaps. Similarly, the professional developer or designer of learning opportunities is required to provide opportunities for such learning and assessment. The researcher focuses on producing new knowledge of the learning of the learner. This is not to suggest that there is no room for alternatives or for individual agency, but we suggest that it makes possible a discursive environment within which support for narratives focused on the learner becomes more possible, plausible and more likely, marginalizing issues of pedagogy and power. In the process, the power in the pedagogic relationship is reconfigured on the basis that this is simply a manifestation of what it means to be a good teacher. To challenge that relationship in some ways becomes the sign of a bad teacher, almost regardless of whether or not that is the case.

The ILTHE standards are meant to produce reflective practice and personal development as objects for discussion and elaboration. Rhetorically, a discourse of reflective practice and development of the teacher as learner permits a similar discourse of practice and development of the student as learner. Given that reflection is what teachers need to do to learn and develop themselves, it seems only reasonable that the student should also. They are invited to engage in a technology of the self concerned with the conduct of conduct (Foucault 1988). Thus, for instance:

> One way of helping students to reflect would be to ask them to analyse themselves as learners. They could, for example, do the exercise in which you were asked to consider whether you were a 'good' learner. They could use Honey and Mumfords' *Learning Styles Inventory* (1982) to discover whether, by nature, they adopt one of the following learning styles:
>
> - Activist (rolls up sleeves and rushes into action)
> - Reflector (contemplates the problem and considers how to approach)
> - Theorist (consults 'experts', researches the issues before acting)
> - Pragmatist (selects the most appropriate form of action given the circumstances)
>
> Whichever method is chosen, however, the student has to learn to reflect in a way which suits his or her own style and needs and the teacher has to create a supportive atmosphere in which this can take place.
>
> (Huddlestone and Unwin 1997: 138)

Reflection becomes that which suits the 'natural style' of learning, and the 'needs' of the student. The role of the teacher is to support this reflection and their needs. But 'narrative organization can be used to increase the plausibility of a particular description by embedding it in a sequence where what is described becomes expected or even necessary' (Potter 1996: 119). Rhetorically, we can see that by beginning the narrative at a certain point, a whole range of characteristics become plausible as the focus for further discussion and investigation. The naturalizing of learning styles is only one of these possibilities and the metaphors associated with these styles tell certain stories of learning and learners themselves, including that learning has a certain 'style' associated with it.

Of course this is not a surprise – indeed, we already know this. Programme design has to start from somewhere and we always depend upon prior assumptions about the nature of the task. What makes *these* assumptions different is the way in which generic statements of teaching are represented as real and neutral descriptions of the work of a good teacher, disembedded from context and culture. Similarly, Chappell *et al.* (2000: 203) have pointed to this generalizing tendency in relation to competence-based education (CBE): 'despite the obvious differences between positivist, humanist and critical orientations to CBE, they all assume, albeit from different perspectives, that competency descriptions have the capacity to describe real work'. By beginning a narrative at a particular point, with particular objects already constituted within it, critical discussion becomes difficult. An audience is mobilized to become a socio-rhetorical network of a particular sort, in which the assumptions made set boundaries to what can be considered legitimate discourse, often coded as that which is of interest and relevance. The point at which a description starts is thus rhetorically important. For instance, '... studies of interaction in official hearings and courtrooms emphasize the importance of controlling where an answer starts and stops and what counts as a complete answer' (Potter 1996: 172). Narrative organization depends upon the order of events and who takes part and 'details of this kind can be organized to provide narrative structure to an account; the order of events, who the characters are and so on' (Potter 1996: 118). This is also the case in discourses in and around the professional development of academics and educators more generally. Witness, for example, the rhetorical contortions as educational administration is translated into educational management and then into educational leadership. The good teacher is a character in the many senses of that word ...

Of course a lot more rhetorical work goes on than we are highlighting here. It is worth pointing out that at the same time as teaching is marginalized through the focus on the learner, it is itself divided into separate activities of 'design' and 'delivery'. McWilliam (1996) argues that such separations and elisions tend to reinforce contemporary views of pedagogy as knowledge dissemination and consumption, and take attention away from alternative notions of pedagogy such as, for example, relational practices of cultural exchange. This further elision of teaching has occurred extensively within the UK where views of teaching as 'delivery' also suffuse, for example, the further education (FE) context. 'The language of FE tends to be rooted in the technical – thus tutors "deliver" courses to students' (Scaife et al. 2001: 9). There is a consequent masking of pedagogy as a powerful relational and socio-cultural process of exchange that does not separate the learner from teacher. In the process as well, the professionalizing of teaching results in a translating of good practice into a set of techniques to be performed, the success of which can no doubt be measured against the increased attainment of students.

The ILTHE statements do other forms of rhetorical work. As we have suggested, they imply that descriptions of professional action and identity hold good across a wide variety of geographical, institutional and subject contexts. In this sense, there is an attempt to mobilize academics as a single profession of educators, when their own socio-rhetorical allegiances may be more diverse and complex. They imply a certain stability and universality in the practices in which academics engage. Yet, for instance, studies of academic literacies in Australia and the UK provide more complex and contextualized accounts of teaching and learning in higher education (Candlin et al. 1998; Baynham 2000; Lea and Street 2000). They also point to the diversity of subject cultures and academic practices, and demonstrate that subjects, such as psychology or physics, have quite different expectations of academic performance from the 'emergent disciplines' of the professions, for instance, nursing or teaching. This growing diversity in the higher education curriculum is complemented by the increasingly wide range of educational, cultural and linguistic backgrounds of students, as access to all forms of education and training is extended. In a field of activity characterized by a diversity of settings and discourse networks, therefore, it appears ironic that it is now that there is the attempt to mobilize a single audience of educators through professional development. Generic statements of competence outcomes, principles and values effectively marginalize these more dynamic, contingent and located accounts of academic practice by promoting a generalized and abstracted view of the good teacher.

One could of course argue that details of location and context of practice are taken into account within a competence framework through the reflection of practitioners on situated practice. Generic statements provide a space for this kind of argument. They thus can be taken to act merely as heuristics. However, acceptance of this argument leads to a failure to consider the further positioning of the professional and teacher of professionals, which results in professionalism being resituated as a form of technical expertise, precisely what such approaches are meant to challenge. These are the aporias that those supporting the professionalizing of academics face and that are brought to the fore in the type of deconstructive reading in which we are engaged here. Thus, practitioners can be argued to learn generalized understandings of practice – that is, codified knowledge – which *can* then appropriately be applied by the reflective professional into a form that can be used in their context. This at once puts the onus of responsibility on the academic practitioner to interpret the relationship between existing knowledge and situated action. It produces rhetorical space for a kind of discourse of reflective practice with which we have become very familiar. Thus 'professionals can use reflection as a bridge to help span what is often regarded as a chasm between the reality of their practice as teachers and the theoretical models and concepts put forward by academics who research education' (Huddlestone and Unwin 1997: 137). The academic is positioned as an intermediary interpreter between knowledge and situated action. Evaluative self-assessment of this activity can then become an integral part of being professional and meeting competence standards. This is, again, a narrative start where the sequence of what is described has a certain logos to it, assuming you accept the starting position.

That a space has been made for discourses of reflective practice within that of competence is apparent in the prevalence of the portfolio and reflective text as primary assessment tools within professional development programmes. We know the general form for such tools. A portfolio of performance evidence is compiled by the student, in sections addressing a competence outcome discretely. A short piece of text is written by the student for each outcome, relating the evidence to a claim that it is sufficient to demonstrate performance at the appropriate level. This claim is not just a statement of competence, but is often also a reflective text. It presents an argument of how and why the represented performance is competent, and to what extent it could be improved. The portfolio is in many ways one of the most clearly rhetorical practices in student assessment, as the person has to orchestrate their material to make a convincing claim that they, as individual professionals, are competent. Logos, pathos and ethos are to be found in such practices. This is an act of confession (Foucault 1981) whereby the academic becomes constituted as a reflective practitioner. The normalizing gaze is internalized and turned upon the self, as reflection becomes self-measurement and self-evaluation against the standards and the appropriateness of performance, justified in relation to a combination of codified and practical knowledge. It is, however, limited to a consideration of the relationship between the outcomes, evidence and the theoretical and practical knowledge held as resources. This embeds a particular form of rhetorical achievement, which forms the identity of the professional in a particular way.

Let us pursue the notion of the reflective text as a rhetorical achievement further. What kinds of rhetorical performance are enacted through such practices? For an argument or performance to be taken as correct it has to be warranted. Warranting is a rhetorical move that is used within all kinds of communication and takes various forms according to the use of specific devices appropriate to differing contexts (Gergen 1989). For example, within an academic text such as this one, the consistency of the argument exhibited, the strength of the evidence supplied and that which has already been accepted by colleagues elsewhere needs to be demonstrated if it is to be persuasive. Warranting thus takes place through careful elaboration of the argument and through the use of devices such as referencing and quotation to frame the impression of consistency and consensus about the truth articulated. Often the description is written in the passive voice. This is a device to further erase any impression of subjectivity or bias within the description. Narrative accounts are commonly expected to meet certain standards of coherence and correspondence if they are to 'pass as a plausible account of "the way things really were"' (Potter 1996: 169), but the devices used differ according to context. A portfolio and reflective text of the sort that we are considering commonly draw on both these forms of warranting. Potter discusses such practices as 'externalizing devices'. They all work to persuade a reader that the description provided is not merely a subjective view but an objective account. They 'construct the description as independent of the agent doing the production' (Potter 1996: 150).

The description of competent performance in portfolios is often corroborated by witnesses of that performance. This is often someone in a superior institutional or professional position to that of the student. The description of reflective self-evaluation therefore is warranted through consistency within itself, consensus with others determining codified knowledge elsewhere, consensus with practitioners and the views of individual students. The consequence of this is a professional who is mobilized through hybrid rhetorical performances that draw upon and fabricate consensual communities (academic, practitioner and student) for this work. To persuade an audience that a description is factual, true, or an accurate account of what is, we commonly draw on such devices. Here we see all aspects of rhetoric at work – ethos (the status of the speaker/writer), logos (the nature of the argument made), pathos (its emotional pull) and kairos (appropriateness to context). All these work together to construct the warrant.

What of those who are articulating this particular type of discourse of profes-sional development? What are the 'deliverers' of professional development for academics writing/saying? What rhetorical strategies do they draw upon? The following is an extract taken from the Introduction to a course text offered by one UK university in 1999:

> Teachers in higher education do not usually make choices about teaching, learning and assessment methods on the basis of explicit knowledge of research evidence or educational theory ... The impact of theory and evidence can be very slow ... But it is also the case that such research evidence does not, and cannot, answer all the questions we have as teachers, or provide clear guidance for many of the everyday teaching decisions we need to make ... Simply because we are authors of a theoretical book does not mean that all our teaching is underpinned by theory and evidence or that we could justify everything we do without reference to traditions. In our own development as teachers we have been influenced by only a limited range of all the research and theory we have encountered in books, articles conferences and seminars. While we can talk about quite a wide range of ideas, we find it difficult to hold many concepts or principles in mind at any one time while we are planning our teaching. And while we are actually teaching only one or two very simple and robust ideas enter our consciousness, even if others have become embedded in our practice. We are each of us guided and influenced by different theories and ideas.

It is worth reading this extract more than once to draw out the ways in which it is both authoritative and distant, but also modest and engaging in its attempts to draw in the audience. And it is reassuring about the need for 'only' one or two ideas to inform our teaching and that these can be 'simple' and 'robust', itself an interesting view of research findings. The rhetorical work is carried forward through:

- what is presented as factual with regard to the 'normal' comportment and activity of teachers;
- the positioning of the teacher in relation to other (more authoritative) groups;
- the status of the knowledge upon which teachers are drawing.

The use of the authoritative 'we' is a strategy that works to align the subjectivity of the teacher to a group of teachers within which the authors of the text are also positioned through the shared enterprise of teaching. This attempts to create a certain empathy by providing a sense of an existing community that one is being invited to enter. At the same time, the authors position themselves as authoritative within this group in two ways. First, there is their assertion of 'the' facts of teaching, for example, 'teachers in higher education *do not*', 'it *is* also the case'. Second, the authors construct another authoritative category to which they alone belong. This is the category of theorizers of teaching and learning, for example, as 'authors of a theoretical book'. In certain circles, of course, this may not work: for instance, for those who position theory negatively. However, in relation to an academic audience, it is more likely to increase the authority (ethos) of the authors. They therefore present themselves as role models; individuals who have developed as teachers by encountering research and theory in books, articles, conferences and seminars and who have been influenced by a specific range of ideas. What is going on in this text is complex work that constructs certain activities and understandings of the teacher and teacher development as appropriate in a persuasive way, part of which rests on the ethos of the text's authors and therefore the trust that can be invested in them and their writings.

As well as fabricating categories and hierarchical distinctions between groups, this account also provides categories of and distinctions between forms of knowledge, the cognitive processes and physical practices of the teacher. Specific binaries are in play within which one pole of the binary is favoured – theory/practice, rationality/irrationality, consciousness/subconsciousness. Teachers are considered as not generally being 'in the know' about theories of teaching and learning and, because of the influence of tradition, not necessarily conscious of the rationality of their practices. Teachers who have developed, however, draw consciously on simple, robust theoretical ideas. The identity of the good teacher modelled within this text therefore is that of the rational and reflective practitioner, who is consciously guided by theories and ideas that we have been (en)countering throughout.

Learning is described throughout the course materials generally as the understanding of ideas that takes place through the individual acquisition of concepts, restructuring of cognitive structures, experiences of feedback and reflection and the overcoming of the barriers of negative emotions. Good teaching is to be achieved primarily through the cognitive structuring of learning experiences in ways that facilitate reflection on theory in relation to experience of practice. The logos for these truths of learning and teaching are supported through the contributions of various authoritative researchers to the course texts, and descriptions of and reference to the work of others. In this intertextual way, the materials seek to build and project authority. Key to this, however, is the promotion of knowledge of only certain forms of psychology in the materials, which are presented as representative of the full range of research evidence and educational theory. These are projected as theories that generate best practice. The good teacher therefore is fabricated as progressive, drawing from a given range of robust theory and evidence, who is aware of the influence of tradition, but is also reflective and self-steering in relation to their own professional development. And what is wrong with that?

All courses contain descriptions that do similar rhetorical work, whether these are explicit or implicit. There is nothing wrong in itself with such rhetorical work, but it does raise the issue of what such work includes and excludes, and how explicitly this is addressed. A feature of many of the texts on the professional development of academics is the representation of the learner within a humanist understanding of self and identity. This draws particularly on the writings of people like Rogers (1974) and Schon (1983), where the learner is constructed as a self-directed and autonomous individual. What these individualized and psychologized understandings fail to acknowledge is the role of culture, power and environment in shaping subjectivity. Within a humanist frame, the self is positioned as 'standing apart from any situatedness, outside of history, sociality and human practices' (Usher *et al.* 1997: 99). In these practices, it is the individual who is to be developed, marginalizing the organizational dimensions of professional practice and that work usually entails working with others, what some refer to as collective competence (Boreham *et al.* 2002). Representations of teachers and also learners in terms of a detached rational, reflective consciousness perform important work in ruling in and ruling out certain pedagogical possibilities and in mobilizing an audience as a professional group of a particular type.

By not acknowledging the specific origin of such universalized theories of teaching and learning in a particular branch of psychology, a historical amnesia is promoted, which opens the way to the search for best practice formulae that *can be* encoded in standards and developed as an area of expertise separate from alternative domains of research, disciplinary knowledge or context. This produces a separation of disciplinary and pedagogic knowledge that 'enables pedagogy to be analyzed simply in terms of "teaching and learning" rather than as an aspect of knowledge production, and in effect creates a superfluous community of (decontextualized) pedagogues' (Zukas and Malcolm 2000: 7). As we have argued, in the process pedagogic practice is represented as a technical and atheoretical activity, lacking a reflexive understanding of how knowledge of teaching is rhetorically generated. With such reflexivity, the teacher could fabricate identities that move across and within various discourses, as a means of engagement with practices. These systematic and universalized pedagogic practices are seductive in appearing to offer the possibility for efficiency in delivering learning, but fail to engage with ethical and critical dimensions that are central to processes of teaching and learning. Separating out the 'how' from the 'why' and 'what' of education allows questions about the meanings and purposes of education to be marginalized. For some, it may be persuasive as part of a culture of accountability. For others, the ceremonials surrounding its unfolding remain a baffling mystery.

We could carry on, but we hope we have illustrated our point about the ways in which professional development draw upon a range of rhetorical strategies to promote particular views of what is desirable and appropriate. Whether such discourses – of professional development and our own here – find an audience depends on the success of our rhetoric. In many cases, of course, professionals do not have a choice about attending professional development courses. Whether they become an audience for such events is another matter of course. Many, rightly in our view, remain sceptical. Having explored a range of issues in relation to professional development for educators, we now move on to explore the wider realm of what for some is known as cyberspace, and the rhetorical practices in and around the use of ICT in education, a site of increasing educational interest in recent years.

Chapter 5

Cyberspace, cyberbole
Metaphorizing the virtual

In writing this chapter, we find ourselves (en)countering further aporias. When composing this text, we have largely approached the task as if we are producing a printed book, which we are and which it is. But the writing has taken place through the transmission of electronic files across computers located in different continents and linked to the Internet, with all the resources with which that provides us. In the drafting of the chapter, we adopted the approach that we would write it as if it was an electronic text – which it was – and therefore include links to relevant websites where they existed. And indeed, this text may also appear as an electronic book, in which case those links may be 'live'.

The reason we start this chapter in this way is to point to the felicitousness of particular conventions of writing for particular types of text, in particular the convention of referencing. As this text has and may take different forms – paper and electronic – we have decided here to use two styles of referencing in the same text. In the paper form, where possible, the conventional references will lead you to the Bibliography at the back of this book. In the electronic form, the click of a mouse rather than a flick of the page will take you to the relevant site on the Internet from which we have drawn. Here then we are pointing to the differing communications and rhetorical conventions that are associated with different media, something which has led writers like Kress (2000 and 2003) to argue that conventional notions of literacy are completely inadequate for the complex semiotic practices currently being developed. Here communication in general and language in particular are taken to be multimodal and literacy a far more diverse and complex set of practices.

E-learning, online learning, virtual learning environments, have all become important areas of discussion as the potentialities of information and communication technologies (ICT) in relation to education and training have expanded. Talk of the Internet, virtuality and cyberspace are not to be found in science fiction alone, but are part of everyday discourse, including the discourses of education and training. In this chapter, we will explore two aspects of that discourse. The first is the rhetoric *about* cyberspace. To characterize ICT as cyberspace is to position it in certain ways, as though science fiction has been made real. Indeed, some of the framings of ICT, as we shall see, suggest this. The second is the rhetoric *in* cyberspace. This is the communication practices of those using ICT for teaching and learning (DEETYA 1997). It is the former rather than the latter that will be our primary focus here. Central to our exploration will be the spatial binaries that powerfully inform the fabrications of ICT and the valorization of presence over absence within them: for example, face-to-face/at a distance, real/virtual. We will argue that these are deployed to invoke rhetorical memory and imaginaries that are mobilized through educational discourses

The background murmur of cyberspace

Cyberspace is an imagined network layer sitting on top of the physical infrastructure of cities. Cyberspace is an imagined continuous, worldwide networked city; the global city that never sleeps, always experienced in real time ... We are all dwelling in cyberspace, coursing through the wires, becoming cyborg and becoming human, alone at the keyboard, together online.

[http://www.labyrinth.net.au/~saul/essays/08cyperspace.html]

Cyberspace: the realm of pure information, filling like a lake, siphoning the jangle of messages transfiguring the physical world, decontaminating the natural and physical landscapes, redeeming them, saving them from the chain-dragging bulldozers of the paper industry ... A new universe, a parallel universe created and sustained by the world's computers and communication lines ... through its myriad, unblinking video eyes, distant places and faces, real or unreal, actual or long gone, can be summoned to presence, from vast databases that constitute the culture's deposited wealth ...

[http://www.mystacom/restricted/streams/gnosis/cyber.html]

The above represents a tiny fraction of the outpourings, both in print and online, about cyberspace. Much of it is of the form aptly referred to as 'cyberbole'. In fact, it is so hyperbolic that to talk of the talk of cyberspace as a 'background murmur' has to be the paradigm case of irony. A foreground roar would seem more appropriate somehow. How persuasive such hyperbole is remains an open question of course. Despite this, we want to argue that there is still some purchase in using this characterization.

Over the last decade or so the Internet has grown explosively. For example, at the end of 1994 only 10,000 website servers were connected to the Internet. By 1999 there were seven million. The US Internet Council estimates that in 2000 there were more than 300 million active Internet users, compared to 90,000 in 1993. In the world of business, even though businesses have used computers since the 1940s, the difference now is that the Internet raises the stakes. Computer networks have decreased transaction and co-ordination costs. By networking, businesses can rationalize and standardize their activities. Every major business has a website, using it to sell goods, automate its supply function and generally operate the business. Software systems, especially database management programmes and enterprise communication tools, now form the backbone of businesses (Agin 1999) [http://profs.lp.findlaw.com/e-commerce/ecommerce1.html]. Included in this is the provision of learning for their employees, of course. The situation has become one where businesses using tools made available by the Internet gain such an advantage that they literally cannot afford not to use them if they want to remain in business. In educational settings too, we have witnessed the development of greater connectivity and networking as faster networks lead to newer services and from thence to new uses. Electronic networking has penetrated into all academic disciplines, in the process expanding the space of learning environments. Virtualization, it is said, is creating a global learning space, the 'global matrices of minds' (Hackett 1994) [http://is.gseis.ucla.edu/impact/s94/ students/timothy/timothy_final.html].

Historically, computers were originally seen simply as a medium for storing and analysing scientific data in a secure environment (Feenberg nd) [http://www-rohan.sdsu.edu/faculty/feenberg/talk4.html]. ARPANET (Advanced Research Project Agency Network), the first linking of computers in the form of a decentralized network between universities, the Pentagon and defence contractors, was designed for military-scientific purposes at a time when the Cold War was at its height. The decentralization was to ensure that the whole system would not go down if one computer were knocked out in the event of war. In the mid-1980s, the US National Science Foundation created the NSFNET to provide connectivity to its super-computer centres. This became the high-speed link that enabled the Internet to develop. Graduate students used the system and extended it with Usenet and multiple user dimensions (MUDs). Graphics and audio were added, and eventually hypertext mark-up language (html) protocols were developed. Instead of using ARPANET and NSFNET for long-distance computing alone, scientists also used it for communicating with each other, for sharing results and for gossiping, particularly after the invention of the first e-mail programme in 1972. The most frequent use of the Internet now is precisely for e-mail, a mark of how quickly and completely it has become a communication medium for many (Mayr nd) [http://members.magnet.at/dmayr/history.htm]. 'What began as a Cold War effort to speed up communications has become cyberspace' (Poster 2001: 37).

Everyone, it sometimes seems, has become globally connected – or they believe they are. Is it any longer possible to imagine life without, for example, e-mail? For the majority, of course, it is. However, for many, connectivity has become indispensable. Getting online becomes an everyday part of life, at work, socially, educationally and recreationally. The Internet's openness and accessibility is part of the key to this growth (Poster 1997). Furthermore, many now recognize that the Internet is probably more than instrumental, a convenient tool. The technophiles and cyberutopians, despite their hyperbole, have hit a resonance when they highlight the significance of computers not just as a calculating and information storage device but as a means of communication that has transformative effects on social life. In changing the material basis of communication, they argue from differing perspectives that the Internet has also reconfigured socio-cultural objects (Snyder 2002). The networks (a powerful metaphor here) of the Internet connect people through the space-time compression they make possible. They reproduce and disseminate almost any cultural objects that people are capable of producing (Sterling 1994) [http://www.computerlearning.org/articles/Hype Hope.htm]. But here we must ourselves be cautious of the hyperbole in which many engage, as, for instance, 'everyone' is geographically specific, as debates about the information rich and poor indicate, and it may involve more effort for some than for others in contributing to the murmurings. The Internet has its own closings as well as openings, more on which we shall write later.

This is probably why metaphors of space are so crucial in the discussion of ICT. The Internet becomes constituted as a socially and culturally produced space that constantly stimulates new forms of interaction, and hence identities, 'a vast undiscovered country' (Nunes 1995) [http://www.dc.peachnet.edu/~mnunes/jbnet.html]. Although this is not so often highlighted, in this virtual terrain new power relations come into being at the same time. The spatiality of the Internet is captured well in the prevalent metaphor of cyberspace. Cyberspace itself has been referred to as a frontier, the information superhighway, an electronic marketplace, a new Jerusalem, amongst many other things, thereby fabricating further metaphorical complexes. At the other end of the spectrum from these popular modes of characterization, there are those of a more intellectual (or perhaps pseudo-intellectual) character. The quotes at the start of this section are an example of this. The rhetoric of such characterizations attempt to charm and enchant.

In this chapter, we concentrate mainly on the geographical or topographical metaphors associated with the discussion of cyberspace, returning once again to the spatial metaphors, their assumptions and effects, that we discussed in Chapter 3. There is a lot of emphasis on the space of cyberspace, and also on the paradox that this is a space which is also a non-space or spaceless space. Rheingold (1993) refers to cyberspace as a conceptual space where words, relationships and data are manifested through computer-mediated communication. For Bukatman (1996: 18) 'cyberspace ... [is] a completely malleable realm of transitory data structures in which historical time is measured in nanoseconds and spatiality exists somehow both globally and invisibly'. Here there is an elision of time and space, an eradication of history and distance, something we see expressed in notions of flexible learning, wherein space and time appear to become deniable in the cause of learning (Edwards and Clarke 2003). In another place, two of us have suggested that cyberspace can be understood as a (dis)location, something which is both positioned and not positioned, producing a range of positionings (Edwards and Usher 2000): not least, of course, the space we materially occupy at our terminals, which is often displaced in the rhetoric of virtuality in cyberspace.

As well as these geographical/topological metaphors, the discourse of cyberspace is replete with metaphors of movement and mobility (Featherstone 1995). An example is the metaphor of 'flows', originating in the work of Deleuze and Guattari (1987) with their notion of rhizomatic branching networks, used as a way of critiquing notions of fixed boundaries and identities. Flows have now become a conventional way of articulating the space-time compression and the deterritorialization of people, images, information, commodities, money and ideas (Appadurai 1990). Cicognani (1998) defines cyberspace as an 'electronic fluxus'. Wark (1997), varying the metaphor somewhat and borrowing an image from geometry, refers to flows as 'vectors' (lines of fixed length and direction but with no fixed position) and argues that we all now live in a space of vectoral flows rather than fixed places. These vectors, particularly those along which information passes, have become faster and more flexible, in the process connecting anything to anywhere and creating a new space of possibilities. He points to the experiencing of particular places and the impact on cultural differences: 'vertical differences of locality, ethnicity are doubled by horizontal differences determined not by being rooted in a particular place but by being plugged into a particular circuit' (Wark 1997: 57). Wark then conceptualizes cyberspace as the deterritorialized terrain of vectors. The Internet with its information and image flows becomes articulated as a vector that traverses space and time, abstracting these from the specificities of location and history, simultaneously rendering them into non-space and non-time. With this, comes the experience of (dis)location, the existential condition of being at once 'here' and not 'there', yet also being 'here' and 'there' simultaneously, as the sense of journeying we found associated with learning in Chapter 3 becomes disorienting.

This disorientation arises because metaphors of movement are combined not only with topographical (or space) metaphors but also with ones which evoke speed and travel. The 'information superhighway' is a good case in point. As Nunes (1995) [http://www.dc.peachnet.edu/~mnunes/jbnet.html] points out, at the end of World War Two, a major highway building programme transformed the US topographically, socially and culturally and, in a similar way, the information superhighway 'offers an image of dramatic change in American lives through a change in the virtual landscape'. Although the image does not accurately describe the network architecture of cyberspace, it nonetheless functions as 'a conceptual model for the world created by this technology [of the Internet] – and a very powerful one too' (Nunes 1995) [http://www.dc.peachnet.edu/~mnunes/jbnet. html]. Nunes goes on to argue that the metaphor of the information superhighway creates 'a virtual topography in which speed, motion and direction become possible … the Internet becomes a simulated territory we traverse via computer/modem roadster in which the computer screen replaces the windscreen'. Here we see the strength of the analogies taken from movies and books about the 'road' which are then translated into a vision of cyberspace. It is one often repeated. For example, 'we envision ourselves and our computers as travelling through space to another destination. Sometimes we travel to obtain information along the fiber-optic roadways of the Internet; at other times we take joyrides without particular destinations in mind' (Rohrer 1997) [http://philosophy.uoregon.edu/metaphor/ iclacnf4.htm]. By drawing on certain cultural memories, there is the attempt to persuade us to position ourselves in relation to the Internet in certain ways.

Conceptions of space become reconfigured with its materiality and the relationship between space and place radically restructured. With cyberspace extending social interaction, there are changes in the quality of the interaction (Drodge and Kitchen 2000) [http://www.mappingcyberspace.com]. Online, there is a seeming absence of time and place. Regardless of physical place, one can be in contact with much of the world via the global computer network. Online, one can live next door to everyone else at any time, virtually. As Nunes (1995) [http://www.dc.peachnet.edu/~mnunes/jbnet.html] points out, 'distance disappears into immediacy and presence becomes a state of simultaneity and transparency'. Geographical place has been replaced by existence in the same virtual space. The immediacy of the Internet means that time is no longer a constraint on communication. Place and time are no longer seen as the boundaries they have always been. Or at least, if they are boundaries, they are seen as having become much more permeable. Kaplan (1996) argues that the new relationship between place and space enabled by these technologies creates new and different networks, communities and identities as more and more people are connected electronically through websites than by conventional geographic proximity. Poster (1990) has argued that whereas hitherto identities have been shaped by production practices (I am what I produce), they are now shaped by communication practices (I am what I communicate and with whom I communicate). In the former, identities arc elicited as autonomous and instrumentally rational, in the latter as unstable, multiple and diffuse. Another kind of (dis)location then within and around which possibilities for new communicative practices emerge.

We shall say more about these metaphors later. For the moment, we would argue that cyberspace, whatever the nature of the metaphor deployed, cannot be understood simply as a neutral signifier of a reality. When we discourse about cyberspace, we are obviously referring to some reality but the reference is not neutral, nor is it separable from the discourse in which it is embedded. Consequently, it is impossible for us to fix the signifier onto a stable and single referent or to stipulate a universal meaning. We cannot even begin to conceive of the possible reality referred to without thinking metaphorically, in terms of frontiers, highways, Jerusalem, etc. Our understanding therefore is saturated by the metaphors deployed to characterize cyberspace to the extent that the metaphors have become indispensable to its understanding. We cannot communicate about ICT outside of the different rhetorical practices through which it is fabricated. Another way of putting this is to say cyberspace *is* its metaphors. So cyberspace becomes something that is not simply *like* a frontier or *like* a highway but assumes the *reality* of a frontier or a highway. As Baudrillard (1988: 16) argues, 'that which was previously ... lived as a metaphor in the terrestrial habitat is ... projected entirely without metaphor, into an absolute space of simulation'. In other words, that which was previously recognized as metaphor now becomes taken as reality, albeit a simulated or virtual reality. Cyberspace as superhighway is not just a metaphor for *changes* in communication brought about by information technology, as it actually *becomes* a highway. The fact that it is a *virtual* highway is no longer significant, as it makes it no less real. Here, as we have suggested earlier, the literal/metaphorical binary as an either/or starts to implode and rhetoric as embellishment is fabricated as powerful in spite of or maybe because of the cyberbole we (en)counter.

This is a situation that brings us back to the notion of the impossible task. If cyberspace is fabricated through the metaphors by which it is communicated, and if we argue that these metaphors very often are pure hyperbole, then what would an alternative discourse of cyberspace look like? How are we to talk about cyberspace without using these metaphors, given that they have so thoroughly saturated our understandings? And even if we could manage to break out, would our alternative discourse still not deploy metaphors, albeit different ones but still constituting the virtual as the real? If the truth of cyberspace was just its cyberbole, we could fall back on the conventional way of proceeding. This would be to strip away the hyperbole and get to the underlying kernel of truth, given that hyperbole has conventionally been understood as over-ornamentation or embellishment. If we were to extend this, deploying a critical consciousness, we could say that the task was to uncover whose interests are being served by the cyberbole. We would not want to reject such approaches. However, stripping away the hyperbole to get at the truth is no easy task and is itself an interesting rhetorical characterization of the task to be undertaken. As we have indicated earlier, it may be an impossible one, since the implication here is that there is a truth to be found once the stripping away has been done. Equally, what does it mean to dismiss this discourse as *mere* ornamentation? Is this itself not an example of rhetorical dismissal, an inversion of the rhetoric being criticized?

These positions are all problematic. Accordingly, we would prefer to argue that, for example, when it comes to cyberspace there is not *a* truth but *many* truths, probably each of which are wrapped in some kind of interest, and all of which capture some felicitous aspect of the reality of cyberspace. For instance, let us consider technorealism. It attempts to strip away the cyberbole, to deflate what Turkle (nd) [http://www.prospect.org/print/V7/24/turkle-s.html] has called 'the overheated language that surrounds current discussion of computer mediated communication [and which] falls within a long tradition of American techno-logical optimism'. Shapiro (1997) [http://www.technorealism.org/overview.html], one of the founders of the technorealist movement, agrees about the need to counter the boosterism of the techno-utopians but finds that he too cannot escape metaphor when he characterizes the aim of the movement as expanding 'the fertile middle ground between techno-utopianism and neo-Luddism'. Furthermore, it is also clear what the interest is viz greater government regulation of the Internet and a reigning in of software giants such as Microsoft.

We are arguing then that in the growing use of ICTs, the world is metaphorized as a networked electronic space, a virtual space of multiple flows. One way of understanding cyberspace then is as a metaphorization of the virtual. This is an attempt through metaphor to capture the almost inconceivable, the dream of total connectivity, an interconnectivity on a global scale. This global interconnec-tivity is connectivity taken to its fullest extent, to the extreme, and as such it is most aptly characterized as *hyper-connectivity*. Here, following Baudrillard (1988), we understand hyper-connectivity as referring not only to the multiplicity of connections in a quantitative sense, but also to a situation where it is impossible to conceive the world and one's place within it as not being *always already connected*. The notion of hyper-connectivity blurs any distinction, or dissolves the binary, between the connected and the not connected; or to extend this further, between the abstract and the virtual, the concrete and the face-to-face.

The explosive growth of the Internet seems incontrovertible and for many is now taken for granted. While we may not explicitly articulate it as such, in everyday discourse we *act* as if we are hyper-connected. It is for this reason that the metaphor of the 'background murmur' has resonance, albeit not in an obvious way. A background murmur is there, present and insistent, but as a backdrop, a presence which may also seem an absence. You cannot see it, yet you sense it is there, an alternative world of multiple communication possibilities. This is to constitute cyberspace as something always already there – there behind our backs. The rhetoric of cyberspace is indeed sneaky then …

An imaginary present

> Ideologues, visionaries, or digerati … never in human history have so many people laid down their views on what the future will be like. And never were these views, prognostics, or ideologies changed, and proven to be wrong at such a fast pace.
>
> (Millarch 1998)
> [http://www.millarch.org/francisco/papers/net_ideologies.htm]

One aspect of the rhetoric of cyberspace is its expression of a significant techno-logical and social imaginary. Cyberspace is 'a cluster of different technologies, some familiar, some being developed and some still fictional, all of which have in common the ability to simulate environments within which humans can interact' (Featherstone and Burrows 1995: 5). Many of these technologies have been promoted and popularized within a range of cultural discourses, from the esoteric to the quotidian. If then we conceive of cyberspace as a way of expressing an imaginary and, if we think of the conventional conception of an imaginary as something speculative (fictional?) and located in the future, we also have to recognize that with cyberspace, the imaginary is also present and real. Cyberspace is then constituted as a future-present, a fictional-real.

This is perhaps best manifested in the literary movement of 'cyberpunk'. The term cyberspace was itself coined by William Gibson, the 'father' of cyberpunk, to characterize a notional yet 'real' space – the virtual real or the reality of the virtual. His *Neuromancer* (Gibson 1984), perhaps the best known and influential example of the genre, is now regarded not merely as speculation, but as presenting a theoretically coherent vision of the near future, a narrative of the not far off now which is also the already upon us.

At the time he wrote *Neuromancer*, Gibson had no idea that NASA [National Aeronautical and Space Administration] was working on real artificial reality, or that artificial intelligence researchers were trying to make thinking machines, or even that some physicists were theorizing that the universe could be a computer and God a hacker. But these themes were all 'adrift' in the zeitgeist of science fiction which was Gibson's guilty literary pleasure.

(Hayward 1993)
[http://www.cc.rochester.edu/College/FS/Publications/
HaywardCyberspace.html]

How cyberpunk visualized the future has also shaped how we understand the present. In cyberpunk, speculative science fiction is combined with the actuality of technological change. Disturbing visions of future cyberspace worlds are presented, visions encompassing technological developments, power struggles, post-human forms and boundary-displacing locations on- or offline. But Gibson maintains that he was not predicting:

What's most important to me is that it's about the present. It's not really about an imagined future. It's a way of trying to come to terms with the awe and terror inspired in me by the world in which we live.

(Gibson 1989: 3)

Cyberpunk is thus said to be in a recursive relationship with theorizations of the contemporary condition (Featherstone and Burrows 1995). It presents metaphors reminding us that communicative technology, both virtual and material, mediates to a hitherto unprecedented extent our relationships, our sense of identity and our wider sense of everyday life. And furthermore, that because of this, to polarize the virtual and the real is no longer possible.

In cyberpunk literature, people and digital technology lose the boundaries that divide them. This is a technological/social imagery encapsulated in the metaphor of the 'cyborg', or cybernetic organism, a term theorized by Haraway (1991). Featherstone and Burrows (1995: 2) define a cyborg as 'a self-regulating human-machine system ... a human-machine hybrid in which the machine parts become replacements, which are integrated or act as supplements to the organism to enhance the body's potential'. Cyborgs are simultaneously human and non-human, a blending of nature and culture – a (con)fusion of human and machine. Whilst the cyborg is the product of science fiction, of capitalism and militarism, it is a metaphor that reveals possibilities for a new relationship of the social to technology. Again also, the cyborg points to the impossibility of opposing the virtual to the real, the imaginative to the material. In one sense, the cyborg is science fiction, but in another it can be argued that we are in one way or another all already cyborgs, particularly with the spread of technologies such as transplants and bio-genetic engineering. As a metaphor, the cyborg points to hybridity and the restructuring of boundaries. It performatively embodies the instability and impermeability of hitherto fixed boundaries between nature and culture, tech-nology and nature, bodies and subjects, active agents and involuntary machines. Beyond this, the cyborg metaphor enacts the death of large-scale systematic theory-building and, more positively perhaps, the valuing of difference and complexity. In addition, it invokes a questioning of the analytical categories deriving from fundamental divisions or binary oppositions, such as those between technology and nature that have so powerfully structured the 'reality' of the world. In rendering these categories ambiguous, the cyborg points to hyper-connectivity, the virtual with its multiple connectivities and inconceivable potential. Bigum and Green (1993: 4–5) have gone so far as to talk of the need for a cyborg curriculum to critically address 'the increasing significance of technology in educational practice, particularly those technologies bearing directly on knowledge production and the relationship between language and subjectivity'.

As well as a future cast as an imagined present, cyberspace is also about the present as a past imagined, and metaphors figure significantly here also. We have noted earlier the deployment of the metaphor of the 'frontier'. This is a rich metaphor, as whilst it is clearly meant to evoke notions of unbounded space and trekking, it also has a range of other connotations: for example, rugged individu-alism, freedom without interference and progress through the overcoming of obstacles. The frontier, however, is not the only metaphor. Others, such as social Darwinism, the birth of flight, and human space exploration are also to be found. What all these metaphors have in common is their grounding in a historical story, one that is particularly, although not exclusively, part of the American cultural consciousness. The frontier is itself a very obvious example, with the memories evoked through film and novel. What *work* such metaphors as the frontier do, specifically what potency their location in a story of origins has, is what interests us.

We would argue that the location in a historical narrative gives the metaphor an authenticity such that the social fabrication of any history is concealed. The consequence of this is that the speculative assumes the status of the descriptive, the social is naturalized. The metaphor is understood as literal truth. There is another aspect of this that needs to be taken into account here. The myth of the frontier has exercised a powerful influence in the shaping of a rhetorical memory. As such, it has entered into American cultural consciousness and even those who are not American, but who have shared in this rhetorical memory, are swayed by it. This then is the present as a past imagined. We understand cyberspace in the present, not just in terms of an imagined future, but also as an imagined past where metaphor and rhetorical memory make the present an actualization of the past.

Being human

The space–time metaphor represents a monumental failure of imagination … we've been thinking about virtual presence as if we have to send our bodies out there. If we could design reality for our minds, what powers would we grant ourselves? The ability to be anywhere instantly would be a step in the right direction. The ability to be everywhere, all at once, without going mad is the real challenge ... The surrogate life in cyberspace, makes flesh feel like a prison, a fall from grace, a sinking descent into a dark confusing reality.

[http://www.mystae.com/restricted/streams/gnosis/cyber.html]

Is it really sensible to suggest that the way to revitalize our community is to sit alone in our rooms, typing at our networked computers and filling our life with virtual friends?

(Turkle nd)
[http://www.prospect.org/print/V7/24/turkle-s.html]

It is undoubtedly the case that the world the rhetoric of cyberspace stories into being is one that many would regard as highly problematic. The rapid spread of the Internet and the seepage of cyberspace into everyday life raises fears of the effects of online connectivity, where the more people become electronically connected and simulacra take over from reality, the more they become disconnected from 'real life'. Here real life refers to structured relations of presence whose absence in cyberspace generates fears of a dangerous erasure of the real. We therefore witness the emergence of a fresh crisis narrative regarding the erosion of the social fabric, one that an earlier generation articulated in relation to television. But, as Macrae (1997: 74) points out, 'virtual existence has become so immediate that what constitutes the real is called into question'. Some have argued that the Internet has destroyed face-to-face community, so how can it be possible to create virtual communities?

Many however take an opposite view. For them, cyberspace names a virtual utopia. They argue that cyberspace enables the development of virtual communities. Rheingold (1993: 26) characterizes these communities as 'informal public places where people can rebuild the aspects of community lost when the malt became malls'. Here cyberspace becomes a means of rediscovering a lost utopia. Kapor (1993: 9), the founder of the software giant Lotus and of the EFF (Electronic Frontier Foundation), harks back to American history: 'life in cyberspace seems to be shaping up exactly like Thomas Jefferson would have wanted: founded on the primacy of individual liberty and a commitment to pluralism, diversity and community'. Cyberspace then will put right all that should have been but never was. Also, it is worth noting here the appeal to the rhetorical memory of Jeffersonian democracy, itself a myth, but a powerful one in the American cultural consciousness.

There are those who, without being cyberutopian, nonetheless argue that virtual spaces generate new public spheres and that new technological modes of experiencing and interaction are just as real and life-enhancing as face-to-face interaction, certainly for those who work and play, who have affinities and shared interests in cyberspace. For those, their virtual existence within these communities is as real, if not more so, than their existence outside. For gamesters who spend much of their lives in cyberspace, the disembodied nature of their participation does not negate a sense of community. Cicognani (1998: 17) claims that 'virtual communities offer a communicative engagement which extends beyond mere exchange of information'. Similarly, Poster (2001) argues that the Internet has gone beyond being a mere tool and is itself a form of community. Burbules (2000) also suggests that it needs to be understood as a virtual global community, a primary medium for the transmission of communication, information, culture, goods and services around the world. He says it is actually more of a meta-community, an overarching congregation of communities and a set of conditions that make communities possible, a space in which communities can be enabled or made to happen. The argument here then is that it is therefore a mistake to dismiss digital technology per se as dehumanizing or life negating and to only valorize face-to-face activities and interaction as authentic and 'human'. In this view, to be cyborg is to be human and vica versa.

Others, however, query whether electronic connectivity can ever replace face-to-face interaction in the meaningful communication required by any community. This is part of a wider debate where it is argued that even if it were possible to characterize interactions in cyberspace as communities, given that they are fleeting and anonymous, these cannot be 'real' communities. As Poster (2001) points out, the Internet is seen as eroding sociality and destabilizing community by undermining the face-to-face. Thus it is precisely because electronic connectivity lacks this dimension of the face-to-face that its potential in any social space will always be limited. For example, in education the assumption is that effective learning must always have this dimension and e-learning is somehow considered to be a less adequate form of communication and interaction, despite the semiotically sophisticated (en)counters it may involve. The question posed is whether the Internet can be universally accessible and therefore whether it can ever be a true public sphere as the enthusiastic proponents of virtual communities would argue. Tabbi (1997) argues that it is precisely the disembodiment, disembeddedness and decontextualization (no bodies, no history, no place), or dislocation, of electronic interaction that limit the participative potential of cyberspace. In this view, can cyberspace then ever be a cultural or educational site?

This argument about the limitations of cyberspace is not just about technological considerations but also surfaces deep-rooted cultural understandings, including understandings about the nature of culture itself. We do, however, note in passing that there is an irony, as the highlighting of the value of the face-to-face has grown with the growth in significance of the virtual. But to return to cultural understandings, there has always been a fear of technology on the grounds of its supposed inhuman or unhuman characteristics. The cyborg is an imaginary present that many would fear, but it is only the most contemporary manifestation of the deep-rooted fear of the monster with human characteristics that can work in rhetorical memory. *Frankenstein* remains ever popular, as does the *Terminator*. The other side of this coin is the valorization of direct face-to-face communication to the point where it becomes naturalized, that is, it is considered, without question, that the face-to-face is an *essential* characteristic of human beings. It is our task here to question everything. In that spirit we point out that the face-to-face, far from being natural, is itself a cultural artefact. The unquestioned view about its naturalness springs from what Derrida calls the metaphysics of presence, the humanist tradition of the West that privileges the present as against the 'absent' and, we would add, the 'virtual'. Humanist-shaped culture therefore configures anything that is not face-to-face as a threat to an essential human condition, as the feared and rejected Other. Consequently, the face-to-face has become the mark of authenticity and arguments in favour of this position remain very powerful and felicitous in educational circles.

What follows from this is that these humanist cultural understandings, although powerful, are not hard-wired but historically contingent. The face-to-face as a privileged mode of interaction is itself embedded in practices constituted within particular discourses and cultures with a very long history. Moreover, to define the authentic in terms of the face-to-face is a very obvious piece of rhetoric. This does not make it wrong, but it does make it open to question. As Burbules (2000: 329) points out, it is 'a cultural myth to imagine the more immediate interactions are always the most honest, open and intimate ones'. What needs to be questioned here therefore is not whether the rhetorical claims of the face-to-face are right or wrong, but what their acceptance represses and/or demonizes and with what consequences.

What we have here is a recurrence of binary thinking and, as Poster (1995) points out, the new kinds of interactivity opened up through cyberspace cannot be adequately specified by the binary of real/virtual. To continue thinking this way only serves 'to obscure the manner of the historical construction of forms of community' (Poster 1995: 89). In other words, there is no one authentic form of community, as what constitutes a community can change both in time and space. Poster (1995: 90) goes on to argue that what makes a community vital to its members is 'their treatment of communications as meaningful and important'. This is exactly what virtual communication signifies to its participants, where the absence of the face-to-face interaction is not regarded as a deficit nor as inauthentic. Porter (1997) argues that being able to exhibit mobile, multiple and 'made-up' identities may not necessarily be a bad thing. Perhaps we need to rethink our notions of culture as a homogeneous social sphere, as 'it is the collective response to this experience of ambiguity, the gradual process of adaptation to the semiotic universe of free-floating electronic alibis' (Porter 1997: xii) that constitutes cyberspace as a unique cultural site. Notions of an 'essential' community and a privileged mode of interaction are not found in nature but are rhetorical fabrications that allow us to understand the world and to interact and communicate within it. With the growth of the virtual we need a shift in the way we understand culture (Arnold 1995) [http://technoculture.mira.net.au/storm/storm10.htm].

Right now, we are in a situation where anything seemingly outside the human is rhetorically constructed as non-human, as outside of culture. What we need therefore is an alternative and more persuasive rhetoric that enables us to understand culture and cultural understandings as ongoing and changing achievements.

This clash of rhetoric over the dangers of the virtual in contrast with the face-to-face misses out on an important aspect. The proponents of the face-to-face tend not to take into account the implications of the *immediacy* of online connection. It is of course the case that one of the main characteristics of the face-to-face is its immediacy and this characteristic is one that its proponents value highly. Yet it is also the case that immediacy is a significant characteristic of cyberspace. The fact that it is virtual does not alter its immediacy. The implication to be drawn from this is the need for a reconfiguration of the face-to-face (Krause 2002) [http://www.emunix.emich.edu/~krause/Diss/].

The face-to-face then is itself a metaphor and its privileging is constituted through a metaphoricity of the *ocular*. The ocular, the realm of the gaze, the visual, is the presence that valorizes the face-to-face. Looking someone in the eyes is seen to have a transparency to it lacking from other forms of interaction. However, the ocular is itself only one form of connectivity and communication. Other forms of connectivity, including those based on the virtual, are also possible. Equally, the notion of community needs to be reframed to take account of the fact that a community can no longer be defined simply in terms of geographical proximity or shared physical space. You do not actually have to be able to see others to feel that you are part of a community with them. Yet again, all it is possible to say is that there is no right or wrong position. What is incontrovertible is that communities do exist online. Are they *really* communities or is the very notion yet more cyberbole? As we have suggested, it is not quite that simple, as such binaries are always problematic and, as a rhetorical achievement, they are rarely persuasive. Perhaps a more felicitous position might be to recognize that

> ... virtual communities pose more questions about how individuals construct connections than they answer concerning the ends of achieving an electronic democracy. Rather than work towards (re)producing a model community, cyberspace could just as easily keep us moving beyond our ends, toward new connections ... that would demand new discourses.
>
> (Nunes 1995)
> [http://www.dc.peachnet.edu/~mnunes/jbnet.html]

Cyberspace then can be rhetorically fabricated as disruptive of historically bequeathed models of self and community. We need a different kind of rhetoric, one that will be more persuasive in relation to the reality of the virtual.

Back in the USA

As I sit at my computer, tapping at the keys ... I say a private prayer of thanks to the Pentagon for making it all possible. This personal computer and the information services I accessed via modem are both by-products of the war machine.

(Wark nd)
[http://www.dmc.mq.edu.au/mwark/warchive/21*C/21c-cyberwar.html]

For Virilio, the epoch of Infowar is an era in which unspecified civilian 'enemies' are invoked by the state in order to justify increased spending on the third age of military weaponry and in particular, in the form of new information and communications technologies such as the Internet ... The Internet is a constituent feature of the 'third age of military weaponry' or what Virilio calls the Information Bomb.

(Armitage 2000)
[http://www.ctheory.net/text_file.asp?pick=133]

Paul Virilio argues that we are in a cyborgian age where any distinctions between human bodies and technology has disappeared and whose shape is determined by information and communication technologies. For him, the military-scientific complex is intimately linked with these technologies. In their turn, these have radically changed the nature of warfare. As he puts it, the army now watches the battle from the barracks, occupying the territory once the war is over. The intimate and interactive connection between the US military, the development of digital technologies and their application in modes of communication is well known. As Wark comments in the quote above, without the Pentagon and its gargantuan resources for military research and development, there would be no personal computers, no e-mail and no cyberspace. Many would claim, including ourselves, that the military origin of current technologies is imprinted in their very form (Chesher 1994) [http://eserver.org/cultronix/chesher]. Video games are a good example. The technology for their development originated in research and development on pilot training simulators. War has come to be constituted and depicted as a form of video game. There is thus a potential for a collapsing of rhetorical boundaries as war and entertainment intertwine. Entertainment imitates life imitates entertainment, as reportage of the 2003 Gulf War and the deployment of 'smart' weapons illustrates.

The links between the military and cyberspace are also intertwined with the links between cyberspace and contemporary capitalism. Despite cyberspace being clearly different from other and previous cultural media, the experiences of users, it is argued, are just as much shaped by contemporary capitalism. Capitalism's impetus is towards the commodification of all spheres of life. In this narrative, its latest 'victim' is knowledge and/or information. The heated debates over online piracy and patenting of *intellectual* property, coupled with the growth of capitalist rhetoric that constitutes cyberspace as in need of 'control', is an example. It is the mark of a concerted push to make the Internet a mechanism for commodity distribution (Harris nd) [http://www.greenleft.org.au/back/2000/418/418p11b.html]. Education is not immune from these processes. Bill Gates' vision of a future where every school pupil has their own laptop might be educationally laudable but it would also grow Microsoft's profits even further. An argument put forward here then is that cyberspace is actually an ideological formation, a means of justifying the survival and growth of the latest form of capitalism where knowledge is both a valued outcome and the most important means of production. Birdsall (1996) [http://www.isoc.org/isoc/whatis/conferences/inet/96/proceedings/e3/e3_2.html] refers to it as the ideology of information technology, linking information technology with free market values and the commodification of knowledge, a convergence enhanced by the success of governments in pushing privatization and anti-state agenda. Those peddling this ideology argue strongly that cyberspace will dramatically increase productivity. Failure to seize the potential offered by information technology will be tantamount to missing a historical opportunity and will lead to a country falling behind in the highly competitive global economy. On this reading, the information superhighway is meant to make the world safe for profits and, in particular, as Poster (1995) points out, strengthen US capitalism in a time of significant competition from elsewhere.

Those who see cyberspace as the instrument of militarism and capitalism are vehement that rather than a historical opportunity, this is just capitalism in new clothes. Cut through the rhetoric of openness, community, democracy and what do you find? Capitalism and militarism in the cause of US imperialism. As Harris (nd) puts it, 'when cyberspace comes back to earth, it looks awfully like it is back in the USA' [http://www.greenleft.org.au/back/2000/418/418p11b.html]. In this view, the function of the ideology of information technology, like all capitalist ideology, is to act as a cover for the embedding of free market values and mechanisms into all areas of life. By doing this and by incorporating forms of resistance, it conceals the continuing redirection of wealth, power and resources to an already privileged minority.

That is one side of the picture. There is another, one which whilst not falling into the hype of the cyberutopians and technophiles shows that cyberspace is maybe not just about military and big business domination.

> Consider the following goal: To create a clone of a powerful and complex computer operating system by asking programmers from around the world to donate their time and effort to the project. The operating system would be available free to anyone who wanted it, regardless of whether they had contributed to it or not.
>
> (Kollock 1999: 8)

Actually, this is not a hypothetical case, let alone a fantasy. It happened. The operating system is Linux, referred to by Kollock as 'the impossible public good'. A public good is one that all can benefit from regardless of their contribution to its production. It is indivisible in the sense that our consumption of it does not reduce the consumption of others, and it is non-excludable as no-one can be excluded from benefiting. In 1991, a computer science student, Linus Torvalds, wrote a code for a new operating system for his computer. He then made it available on the Internet, inviting anyone online to contribute to its further development. By 1994, a powerful and useful operating system had been developed through online contributions. As Kollock (1999) points out, it is now available free to anyone who wants it, including ironically businesses, and is constantly being revised and improved through the voluntary labour of many programmers. When asked about the success of Linux, Torvalds attributed this, first, to the collaboration made possible by the Internet and, second, to the virtual community of programmers found in that virtual space.

We would not want to suggest by this example that cyberspace is a realm of benevolent sharing communities. As we have seen, the rhetoric about cyberspace is diverse and contested, the logos for which does not fall neatly in one direction. It is clear that cyberspace is producing new formations of social and economic power and it is intimately connected with contemporary capitalist formations. The democratic participative actuality of Linux might well be the exception. Certainly, cyberpunk, with its dystopic projections, can be read as an anticipatory politics oppositional to corporate manipulation of the Internet and potential cyberfascism (Featherstone and Burrows 1995). As Gabilondo (1995) points out, there is a need to guard against utopian libertarian technophilia. To this extent the critique of cyberspace that deploys the concepts of critical theory does have some resonance. However, at the same time, it would be oversimplistic to see these new capitalist formations as always fixed and hegemonic. Capitalism has a global reach but it does not wipe away everything it encounters. Critical theory in its fervour to uncover is not reflexive about its own rhetorical framings.

To label something an ideology, therefore, is not simply to articulate a description, nor yet to rest content that one has uncovered an underlying truth by this articulation. Saying that those who deploy ideology are cloaking, either consciously or unconsciously, their material, sectional interests in the mantle of progress and democracy for all, is an articulation that is itself a rhetorical formation. Once again, it is not a case of getting to the truth of the matter – is it really an ideology? How could such a question possibly be answered? Perhaps, then, it would be better to say that cyberspace is also a site of conflict, maybe even the stake in a conflict, but a conflict nonetheless over the control of the virtual, where how cyberspace is understood strategically positions the adversaries and where the weapons in the conflict are rhetorical.

Education (en)counters in cyberspace

The notion of cyberspace and the impact of the Internet and the world wide web have provided fertile ground for reconceptualizing education. Open, distance, flexible, distributed and e-learning have become common parts of educational discourse (Lea and Nicoll 2002). Traditionally, metaphors of bounded space have proved particularly potent in education. For example, Lankshear et al. (1996) have argued that education is a modernist institution and as such is characterized by various 'spaces of enclosure' such as the printed text, the classroom and the curriculum. These work to enclose meaning and experience through a fixed and obligatory curriculum, with the book as the paradigm form of text. Here learning is a matter of extracting a singular canonical meaning and teaching that of being the authority in terms of interpretation and accuracy. The assumption in such discourses is that there is a single definitive meaning there (knowledge) waiting to be found. They maintain that cyberspace works in ways which call these spaces of enclosure into question – the fixity and stability of the word, the linear text, the teacher as authoritative bearer of meaning. The possibility is opened up for educational practices to be more egalitarian, purpose-driven, self-imposed and self-monitored than those found in current mainstream educational practices. The claim is that, by creating a reader-controlled environment, knowledge production through the consumption of fixed and definitive meanings become less bounded and hierarchical. Meanings become more readily negotiable by users. Cunningham *et al.* (1997) argue that the hypertextual capacity of cyberspace allows learners more scope to construct knowledge rather than just passively receive it. Hence, where learners do not simply interpret meaning but actively collaborate in its creation, they are more able to determine their own paths of learning. Cyberspace therefore enhances the potential for metaphors of journeying and construction to be more persuasive in educational discourses. Thus, for instance, Burbules (2002) refers to mapping and architecture as key to turning the web from a space into a place.

Potentially, in the virtual classroom, the focus moves from teacher as the central authority transmitting knowledge through the written text, with responsibility for validating input and encouraging consensus, to the learner pursuing a multiplicity of locally defined educational/educative goals in a variety of ways. This would seem to suggest more opportunities for learner-centred pedagogies in shifting from teaching to learning. The emphasis here is on a pedagogy which is self-directed and purpose-driven, encompassing a multiplicity of changing goals and purposes, rather than a pedagogy oriented to achieving externally-imposed and predefined meta-goals of modernist education. There is a reconfiguration of the teacher–student relationship. It is argued that all can be experts, given the abundance and availability of information in the sites and networks of cyberspace. Given that there is a need to develop skills of accessing and using information, and that learners may be more skilful in this regard, this provides a new role for teachers, albeit one they will have to share with learners. Furthermore, Lankshear *et al.* (1996: 172) argue that there are greater possibilities for the development of understanding, or meta-level awareness, through 'communicative practices [that] presuppose openness, self-monitoring and constant reflexivity on the part of participants'. Cyberspace technologies become 'amplifiers of human attributes and capacities, and hence of human potential; as prosthetic devices which enable learners to operate differently' (Green 1993: 28). The learner as cyborg, perhaps …

The transposing of the metaphor of the cyborg to the educational enterprise is undoubtedly provocative. However, it does remind us that in trying to understand the (en)counter of education with cyberspace we have to consider how pedagogy might be affected but also the identity of learners too. This involves consideration of how learning is understood. So the (en)counter with cyberspace is not simply performative in the sense of increasing transactive efficiency and the productivity of learning. Yet again, it involves a change in cultural understandings about what constitutes learning, knowledge and identity. What kind of subject is encouraged? Can we still go along with the foundational metaphors that have hitherto largely shaped our understandings of consciousness and subjectivity? Bigum and Green (1995: 15) point out that much engagement with new technologies is shaped by the rhetoric of the past: 'what becomes crucial in determining what happens in [educational settings] is not so much driven by what is known, as by rhetorics which draw upon a context that has arisen from past practices of and attitudes towards other technologies'. Yet, as we have seen, different possibilities are also framed. The information promiscuity of the Internet can mean that the identities of learners (and their identities *as* learners) are shaped without policing by an external epistemological authority. In cyberspace, the disciplinary distinction between knowledge and information becomes even more difficult to maintain. What is legitimate or worthwhile knowledge increasingly becomes that defined by the self-directing and self-monitored practices of cyberspace's virtual communities. New educational forms require new discourses and new metaphors, which themselves help to shape the form education takes, in the sense that we suggested in Chapter 2 that discourses are performative. Education and schooling displaced by discourses of lifelong learning and edutainment, perhaps.

Earlier, we referred to the rhetorical fabrication of virtual communities as spaces with a potential for democratic participation. We have noted that it is necessary to question the rhetoric of cyberspace in this regard. Nonetheless many see it as an environment where the skills and attitudes necessary for engaging in democratic decision-making can be cultivated. For example, Lankshear et al. (1996) believe that in enabling access to continuously available online information and participation in a range of activities and experiences, cyberspace's virtual communities make the democratization of education a real possibility. Tabbi (1997) argues that whilst the Internet tends to be perceived mainly in terms of enabling learners to more readily access and exchange information, it can also function as a forum where differences amongst learners can be articulated and where a greater equality of participation and interaction can be established. As with the wider discussion of utopianism and cyberspace, therefore, we find similar trends in the discussion of education and technology. Iacono and Kling (1996: 101) argue that the promotion of ICT in education should be understood as a form of social movement, which draws upon 'a rhetorical form, which we call technological utopianism … [This] is a key framing device for portraying societal renewal through technology and allowing people, many of whom know little about computing, to identify with the goals of the movement.' The rhetorical form is one way of mobilizing an audience for changed practices.

Others, however, question this. They point out that, whilst virtual communities may well have a democratic potential, cyberspace, although participative, is not *inherently* democratic. Disciplinary power could well be reinvested from the transmission of inputs to the examination of outputs and surveillance may be even more prevalent. Similarly, ICT may result in the commodification of knowledge (Lyotard 1984) and/or the development of hybrid forms of edutainment (Kenway *et al.* 1993). Kramerae (1995: 43) argues that there has been a singular lack of support for those studying the gender issues and the gendering of computer studies and programmes both within and outside of the classroom. The point Kramerae and others are making is part of a larger problematic, that it is never just a matter of bringing democracy into the classroom by giving every student a laptop and by recreating the classroom as a digital environment. Whilst a decentred and interactive classroom experience can have democratic outcomes, whether it will still depends on the wider social context and dominant cultural understandings about what constitutes knowledge and learning. Technology will affect these but perhaps more significantly new ways of looking at the world, and therefore new metaphors, are likely to be more efficacious. Any democratic impulse could remain unrealized, therefore, if learners are not stimulated to think critically about the impact on their learning of different technologies and the mediating processes that come with them. In other words, learners need to be inscribers lest they become inscribed, skilled in their own semiotic practices (Kress 2000). They need to engage in and with digital rhetorics (DEETYA 1997).

What is being argued here? In a sense, all the modernist metaphors of centre, margin, hierarchy and linearity are being turned on their heads. By doing this, the way is opened for a questioning of modernist educational systems and frame-works. As we suggested in Chapter 3, the metaphors are those of multilinearity, nodes, links, networks and complexity (Davis and Sumara 2000). Cyberspace itself is rhetorically deployed to undermine the apparent stability and coherence of all aspects of the educational project of modernity. Cyberspace provides a powerful means of challenging these modernist spaces of enclosure, for justifying changes in what constitutes knowledge, the way it is produced (research), organized (curriculum), presented and disseminated (the book), delivered (pedagogy) and justified (democracy). This becomes part of a wider questioning of the modernist subject with its notion of core, fixed identity. Lankshear *et al.* (1996) argue that cyberspace's new forms of textuality, intertextuality and hyper-textuality produce a reconfiguration of the subject (in the sense both of the person and the curriculum). With this, comes a justification of the need to reconceptualize the educational project in terms of multiplicity, of multiple paths, non-linear forms of learning and teacher–learner transactions. This entails a move from the fixed institution-based space of education to the more unbounded terrain of lifelong learning. Cyberspace therefore enhances the potential for the deployment of non-Euclidian metaphors in our understanding of learning.

Whilst network is not exactly a new metaphor, it is nonetheless one that is gaining increased currency. To illustrate we will now explore the deployment of this metaphor in actor-network theory (ANT). This is a theorization that deliberately seeks to move learning and knowledge production away from its psychological roots, that is, something that goes on in the mind. It highlights actions rather than beliefs or intentions. Knowledge cannot exist as a thing to be assessed apart from the learning context. It is not a static structure residing in the individual's head. It is a dynamic activity distributed across the knower, the means of knowing and that which is known. It is spread out across extended time frames and multiple resources. Taking the metaphor of networks, actor-network theory characterizes all social life as patterned networks. Furthermore it seeks to break down the distinction between the animate and inanimate and thus the social is cast as consisting of humans and non-humans as equally significant participants (actors) interacting together (networks). For learning, this means a stress on:

- the process of learning rather than just the outcomes;
- relationality where things have significance and meaning, not because of what they are essentially, but in terms of how they are positioned in relation to each other;
- the materiality and heterogeneity of the diverse material of the world – objects, bodies, information and media:
- infrastructure, rather than just people.

Educational practices can be understood as actor-networks consisting of participants organized in time and space. ANT allows a theorizing of the educational environment comprising a complex teaching and learning network(s) (see, for example, Nespor 1994). The network consists of actors both animate and inanimate (for example, computers, books, equipment, space). For the network to function successfully, all actors must be effectively mobilized and in place. Thus learning is distributed throughout the network and becomes the potential of learners to act in a certain way when located within an appropriate network of relationships. Learners can be understood as being engaged in a project of producing new knowledge through learning. The learner is mobilized as a *knowing location* – 'a learner knows because he [sic] is at the right place in a network of materially heterogeneous elements' (Law and Hetherington 2001: 4). Knowing occurs because you are at the right place in a network of heterogeneous elements that have been brought together. Learners are located in more than one network, so learning is distributed through all the networks in which they are interconnected. But networks have to be mobilized. Learners will have different values and interests, as indeed will other human actors and even non-human actors. Their reconciliation is effected through translation, a process whereby actors attempt to construct common definitions and understandings by co-opting each other in the pursuit of their objectives, as we are attempting in the writing of this text. Translation enables the alignment of interests and values. Thus learning involves the enrolment and mobilization of heterogeneous elements: for example, supervisors, colleagues, peers, laboratories, test-tubes, computers, the configuration of space, journal articles, conferences, funders and many more. All these and the relationships between them forges the network that needs continual management. It is perhaps unsurprising that this approach has found greater felicitousness with those who are involved in e-, distributed and networked learning (Fox 2001).

This discussion of actor-network theory is not meant to provide a detailed analysis and critique. What we have tried to do is show how the deployment of the metaphor of the network, synergistically coupled with that of the actor, fabricates learning and the educational environment in a new and different way. Without in any way suggesting that there is causation, we simply want to point to the affinities of actor-network theory with the way in which cyberspace has been understood. It could be argued that actor-network theory deploys metaphors and frames an understanding of the educational enterprise that is particularly appropriate to the realm of the virtual. In this context, we can also point to relationality, process, materiality and the breakdown of the boundary between the animate and inanimate. Actor-network theory therefore provides an interesting and perhaps productive way for new and different (en)counters between education and cyberspace.

A metaphor for the inconceivable?

> No assertion is simply an assertion, for it carries within it the unsaid awareness that it cannot be asserted ... it is as if (speaking metaphorically!) we are caught in the metaphors of language and there is no way to halt their shifting character.
>
> (Lawson 1985: 26)

It is of course not the case that cyberspace is inconceivable. This text, to say nothing of the plethora of literature on the subject, clearly demonstrates this. By naming it as metaphor we have 'conceived' it. To say this, however, is not to say that it can be unequivocally defined. As we have seen, the notion of cyberspace is a site of controversy and conflict. It is easy enough to embrace naïve technophilia and/or technological fetishism and to frame cyberspace as a transcendent location. In a sense this is understandable given that cyberspace is presented as an exciting opening. But there are limitations and dangers to be found in these unbounded spaces. We should not be seduced by a rhetoric which makes cyberspace transcendental, detached from the practices through which it is formed and the powerful constraints to which it is subject and that it itself imposes.

Yet there is still an elusiveness here and that is perhaps because it is not so much cyberspace that is inconceivable but the virtual which it frames. Again, it could be argued that the virtual is not inconceivable. At one level, it is hardware: for example, telephone lines, co-axial cables, hard drives, modems, satellites, desks, chairs. At another level, it is software such as computer programmes. It is also wetware, the actor-networks which live in virtual spaces. Hard, soft and wet are themselves suggestive metaphors in this regard. And even then, the description is not exhausted.

The argument in this chapter is that cyberspace is a way of naming and evoking the virtual through metaphor. Metaphor is the means by which a complex set of elements and relationships is made comprehensible. Virtuality is changing the world as we have come to know it. We need a language that will enable us to reconstruct the world in its virtuality, and metaphor with its power to continuously redefine is the means to do this. As Cicognani (1998: 19) points out, metaphor is language, and vice versa, and cyberspace is 'a linguistic construction since any "object" found in cyberspace is a result of some sort of languages'. Cyberspace is a metaphorical resource and itself provides further resources for a reconceptualization of space through the deployment of 'flows', 'nodes', 'vectors' and 'networks', even as these very same notions inform the concept of cyberspace. Cyberspace then can be seen both as a metaphor of space and a space of metaphors, a space in which there is a multiplicity of possibilities and potentialities. Little wonder the hyperbole both in and around it and the troubling it raises for educators who tend towards knowledge more than rhetoric.

Metaphor then enables the articulation and comprehension of new things but in the case of virtuality, can it even do this, given the infinite set of possibilities which is the virtual? In this text we have attempted to do this, but have been able to do so only by piling metaphor upon metaphor. As Lawson puts it above, we are 'caught in the metaphors of language'.

Chapter 6

Taking up workplace learning

There is little doubt that education practices are more varied than they used to be. Indeed a cursory glimpse at current educational provision reveals a multiplicity and variety of programmes that counters any of the arguments that talk about new learning practices, and new modes of knowledge production are 'just' rhetoric. While we can see many classrooms that resemble a certain tradition of educational experiences, we can also see many other kinds of learning spaces. These different spaces comprise different sites of learning, different technologies for learning and different programmes of learning. As we have outlined in relation to cyber-space in the previous chapter, all of these contribute to and are symptomatic of different discourses about learning, knowledge and education. These new practices have not just suddenly appeared but rather are part of an unfolding and entwining of various (en)counters.

In this chapter we will examine another example of these differing educational practices and the rhetoric through which it is mobilized. Our particular interest here is to explore the ways in which workplace learning is promoted, not for the first time, as a 'new' direction for educational provision and the ways in which this kind of innovation reconfigures and is reconfigured by educational discourses. The practice on which we will focus here is a work-based learning (WBL) post-graduate programme currently offered in a university in Australia. This represents one example of how universities are repositioning themselves in 'new times'. An important aspect of this repositioning is connected to the current construction of workplaces and work as important sites of learning (see, for example, Garrick 1998; Symes and McIntyre 2000; Boud and Solomon 2001). We have chosen to examine this programme because we believe it is a good example of many of the changes in educational provision. It is not good because of any intrinsic value, but rather it is good because it seems to be so different to traditional academic programmes in terms of its structure, content and process. It is not structured around disciplinary areas or subjects. It allows for a dispersal of curriculum responsibilities. Unlike in conventional course designs, in WBL the curriculum is shaped by a learning process that enables individuals to define and design their programme. Importantly though, WBL is a partnership programme, which means that the learner's workplace is a stakeholder and actor during the development and through its implementation. This distribution of curriculum responsibilities can be understood as a particular uptake of the challenges put forward in the rhetoric of flexible learning, lifelong learning and the knowledge economy. It is a programme that mobilizes different subjects in a complex network, where subject refers to the knowledge that is being fabricated as well as the identities of those participating in the practice. These identities are those of teachers, learners and organizations, all of whom are located across multiple sites and are being defined by new relationships within these sites (Usher and Solomon 1999; Boud and Solomon 2001).

In order to examine this WBL programme, we will draw on a particular kind of rhetorical analysis to which we have only referred in passing to date. The key theoretical resource for this exploration is the genre work of Freadman (2002), in particular her use of 'ceremonial place' and 'uptake' as ways of explaining social action. This work is located within a broader set of North American genre studies to which we referred earlier. These studies had been primarily concerned with language teaching, the writing of the professions and composition studies. But we, along with others (for example, Freedman and Medway 1994b; Coe et al. 2002) have been persuaded that this kind of approach does useful work in explaining and analyzing the rhetorical practices of education more generally.

Later in this chapter we draw attention to a number of texts that have been written to describe and promote the WBL programmes on the case university's website. We will explore these texts as particular kinds of uptakes by academics and their institutions. We suggest that these are tactical within a sequence of textual practices that are produced through and within a ceremonial place. As a rhetorical move, we name this ceremonial place as 'Academic Globalizing Communities'. We will explore what work these texts do within this ceremonial place, how they try to persuade, how they position the writer and the reader, and how they themselves encourage particular kinds of uptakes. Here we might say that uptake and audience co-emerge through the rhetorical practices of these WBL texts; uptakes are part of what mobilizes socio-rhetorical networks. In some ways, then, this chapter will be examining more explicitly the how of rhetoric as much as its substance.

As the name 'place' suggests, we take the view that an examination of the location of the text is integral to our consideration of the work that these texts do. We understand this location to be both a global and local one, in which the two are entwined with each other. This helps us to work with the discursive relationship between the global and local as they contingently connect through an infinite series of textual sequences and local uptakes. This is an example of the greater interconnectedness to which we referred in Chapter 5. Indeed one of the understandings of the analysis in this chapter is that individual texts are local uptakes whose shape and purpose are strategically linked to a chain of discourses that are themselves mobilized and made purposeful in the process of their fabrication. Therefore WBL practices become an anticipated uptake of the changing discourses of education and, at the same time, contribute to a reconfiguration and reconstitution of these discourses.

In its exploration of the uptake of workplace learning in universities today, this chapter is itself an uptake of the discourses that it is exploring and, as such, is contributing to the very reconfiguration of that which it is about. First we explain the theoretical frame that we are using. This is followed by a discussion of Academic Globalizing Communities as a ceremonial place for the mobilizing of a socio-rhetorical network. We then briefly provide a description of the WBL programmes and an analysis of a selection of WBL texts. In this chapter, our focus is on the rhetorical work of a number of texts in a particular ceremonial place. We seek to explore a number of questions:

- What work do these texts do within this ceremonial place?
- How have they come to be?
- How do they persuade?
- How do they position the writers and the readers?
- What are they intending to produce?
- How do they encourage particular kinds of uptakes?

These questions are rhetorical ones, not in the sense that they are questions that do not require answers, but they are rhetorical as they signal an exploration of the texts as rhetorical performances that have an explicit desire to persuade, mobilize and position.

Framing the discourse

This text has already drawn attention to a diverse range of theoretical resources that allow us to usefully explore the rhetorical work of educational discourses. One of the resources we have identified is located within the broad area of rhetoric and genre studies, the more recent studies of which are named as the 'new rhetoric' (Freedman and Medway 1994b; Coe et al. 2002). As a rhetorical move, the 'new' in the name, the 'new rhetoric', is a mark of its distinctiveness from the 'old', signalling new interests and directions in genre work. We will have more to say about the rhetorical power of the 'new' in a later chapter and we would question how new the new is in the new rhetoric. While there is great variety in the questions being explored under the name of the new rhetoric, there are important shared interests. One of these is the exploration of the rhetorical work of genres: that is, how genres persuade and act upon the world and how they 'shape both individuals and communities' (Coe et al. 2002: 3). This marks a general shift away from genre's more traditional concern with textual regulations and conventions of form and content. As Coe et al. (2002: 5) point out, 'analysis of what discourse *does* is the hallmark of New Rhetorical inquiry'. The new genre theorists work with a concern with the sociality of discourse. The focus of this concern is on discourse as something that does work, is social and purposeful, is socially situated, and which is fabricated and productive, while also restraining and sanctioned. Rhetoric is understood as a way of thinking and talking about what discourse does: that is, the work it does. If speech acts, therefore, discourse works. Through a different route we come once again to the performativity of/in language.

What is important here is that the new rhetoric is not only concerned with the way genres shape people's discourse but also on how genres mobilize people's identities (Bazerman 2002). The new genre theorists are interested in the production of both subjects and discourse, not as separate processes, but rather as co-emergent: 'the production of genres are inextricable from the social, institutional apparatuses that "obligate" certain kinds of subjectivities for their ongoing maintenance. Thus addressing genre requires thinking through subject production and its attendant questions of power and desire' (Fuller and Lee 2002: 211). These kinds of complexities have a number of appeals. They allow for a way of exploring the relationship between desires and exigencies and their social consequences and actions. But they also allow for an exploration of discursive recurrence, which can be in terms of a discursive freedom as well as discursive connectedness. It is this working of the relationship between recurrence, connections and freedom that is of particular interest to us here.

In order to explore these performances as a rhetorical move we draw on the work of Freadman (1994a, b, c and 2002). Of particular value is an understanding of genre as a set of strategies for social action. Using genre as a way of understanding social action rather than linguistic realization allows us to use it as a resource for exploring the tactics through which things get done and how it persuades us to do. The appeal of 'persuade to do' is connected to understandings of genre in Freadman's (1994c: 13) earlier work, where 'any particular genre is defined primarily by the stake for which its participants engage in it ... [and] the stake of that genre ... become[s] a purpose that can be manipulated tactically'. The notion of tactic is an important one, as it suggests intention and deliberation. As Freadman (1994c: 17) reminds us, 'rhetoricians never taught for competence, let alone for proficiency or accuracy: they taught an art'.

Importantly and not surprisingly, Freadman draws on speech-act theory and takes up Austin's notion of 'uptake' and Wittgenstein's and Lyotard's notion of the 'language game'. Lyotard (1984: 10) describes a language game as a term where 'each of the various categories of utterance can be defined in terms of rules specifying their properties and the uses to which they can be put'. As Lyotard (1984: 10) points out, the rules are not intrinsically legitimate but rather 'are the object of a contract, explicit or not, between the players'. In Lyotard's game the moves or utterances made must abide by the rules, as any modification of the rule changes the nature of the game. In terms of this analysis, 'the observable social bond is composed of language "moves"' (Lyotard 1984: 11), through which there is the mobilization of socio-rhetorical networks. Freadman (1994a) takes up the notion of game, along with 'players' and 'moves'. She works with the idea that the moves are not arbitrary, but tie in with the rules of the game and, as such, are made with certain anticipated, desired uptakes in mind. This nicely connects with an engagement with the notions of 'strategy' and 'tactic' as integral to action working on the exigencies of particular situations. A focus on strategic action has particular relevance here as it draws attention to the relationships between texts. This intertextuality takes account of texts as a practice with a history as well as the moment of interaction between texts. This interaction and the produced textual uptake occur within a ceremonial place as part of a sequence that works towards a desired outcome (Fuller and Lee 2002). In other words, the rhetoric does not come from nowhere and is not going nowhere either. For Freadman (2002), a particular uptake is one that involves boundary crossing through a process of translation, where the translation refers to the mediation of the boundary, but not its obliteration. If we locate this mediation within the notion of a game, as Lyotard (1984: 10) points out, this process is an adversarial one, 'to speak is to fight, in the sense of playing, and speech acts fall within the domain of general agnostics'.

Freadman uses the term uptake to explain the bi-directional relation of a pair of texts or genres. So, for example, a work colleague invites another to present a seminar paper (text one). An anticipated uptake (text two) to this invitation is likely to be something like 'I'd like to' or 'I'll have to think about it', 'Not this time …' or phrases to that effect. These uptakes are anticipated because within our cultural practice texts one and two are a predictable pair in a particular generic sequence. Moreover, by taking up an anticipated response, text two confirms the generic status of the invitation. This is not to say, however, that other uptakes are not possible. There is always the possibility of the unanticipated which may well disturb the predictability of the discursive sequence. Examples of these kinds of disturbances are frequently cited in discussions about cross-cultural encounters, usually when literal meanings are given to vocabularies and phrases that have a metaphorical intent.

Similar examples can be found in any learning space, where the answers that teachers expect are not forthcoming – learners being 'slow' on the uptake perhaps. Unfamiliarity with conventions may be responsible but this is not always the case. Disruptions happen because other kinds of textual uptakes are always possible. Sequencing is not rule-bound. Boundaries are always being crossed. Some of these boundary crossings happen at the interpersonal level, where memories and/or histories of relationships trouble a conventional unfolding of events, actions and language. But they also happen at a discourse level, because discourses intersect and overlap, opening up different sets of textual and subject position possibilities.

The metaphor of the game is therefore important in order to draw attention to the range, scope and potential freedom that is possible within a genre. Freadman (1994a) therefore uses the metaphor of a game to correspond with the notion of genre. She argues against a focus on the rules of the game (or genre), as this unhelpfully suggests that the outcome of a game is the outcome of a set of rules. For her, this amounts to a recipe theory. To counter this determinism, Freadman argues that the emphasis should be on the idea that the rules are for play. This shifts the significance of the game metaphor from the rules to the playing of the game. It provides not only space for tactical movements, but also extends the boundaries of the game to more than the game itself. The notion of *ceremony* is used to draw attention to the multiple social activities within which a game is located.

> Ceremonies are games that situate other games; they are the rules for the setting of the game, for placing and timing it in relation with other places and times. They are the rules for playing the game, but they are not the rules of the game. Games, then, are rules for the production of certain acts in those 'places'. That there may be 'play' at both these levels is important: knowing the rules is knowing how much play the rules allow and how to play with them.
>
> (Freadman 1994a: 47)

She therefore takes and extends the Aristotelian notion of ceremonial rhetoric to which we referred in Chapter 2. The concept of a 'ceremonial place' is a particularly useful one for exploring educational discourses. The WBL programme we discuss is discursively forged and can be understood to fit within sets of textual sequences, which can be explained as ceremonials. The ceremonial place can therefore be used to describe a particular ensemble of actions that are constituted by various rituals, regulations and players. These actions unfold through a set of discursive sequences that mobilize particular kinds of genres that themselves position and reposition the participating subjects. 'It is place that constitutes genre [as it is] the functions and roles entailed by place [that] determine the interlocutory structure of a genre' (Freadman 1994a: 60). Texts arise within ceremonials and their rhetorical form is framed by their ceremonial place and function. In other words, the ceremonial is framed by and frames a time and space, setting it apart from others and marking its specificity. Genre is therefore mobilized by its ceremonial place. In these terms, each text can be understood as both mobilizing and mobilized by a ceremonial place.

This focus on the text, combined with a significance of place, is important for exploring texts as instantiations of written practices, where their significance is found in the way the writer and the reader are positioned (Clark and Ivanic 1997). This chapter therefore 'takes-up' the challenge posed by Freedman and Medway (1994a: 12):

> Genre studies are a particularly promising instrument for illuminating the social process in its detailed operation, and afford an opportunity we should not refuse of examining what it means to be part of an institutional process. What does participation in a genre do to, and for, an individual or group? What opportunities do the relationships reflected in and structured by a genre afford for human creative action, or, alternatively, for the domination of others?

The ceremonial place: academic globalizing communities

In this section we take up the idea that WBL as a higher education programme initiative has a rhetorical relationship with sets of discourses and conventions that operate within a ceremonial place. The name we are giving to this ceremonial place is 'Academic Globalizing Communities'. This name is itself a rhetorical move that is intended to invoke an image of a different space in which academics across the globe are now players. This space is like a macro-game that comprises many other games, some of which are familiar, while others are not. Some moves by players within these games might well resemble those of a decade ago, while others differ significantly.

The idea that academic communities exist is certainly not a new one. Indeed academics have generally positioned themselves in some way or another with an institutional or disciplinary community. While more recently, some academics have problematized the notion of community and suggested alternatives such as tribes (for example, Becher 1989; Bizzell 1992), the term continues to appeal. Perhaps an invocation of a community and its accompanying promise of belonging and membership, which we discussed in relation to communities of practice, is even more important as the boundaries around academic communities have become blurred and more expansive, and have become more like networks. This is to a point where some academics consider the survival of such communities to be at risk. Here the discourse of the academic community is itself a rhetorical move in the game of higher education.

While it is likely that we still understand ourselves as belonging to local, disciplinary or institutional communities, it is also likely that those working in higher education now understand themselves, as we understand ourselves and our work, in relation to broader and more global kinds of relationships. Hence 'globalizing' is included in the name of the ceremonial place. The use of the term 'globalizing' rather than 'globalized' is deliberate. We use the present continuous form of the verb (or process) in order to draw attention to our understanding of the experience of globalization. Here globalization is not a thing (a noun) or a monolithic force that is bearing down on universities in a prescriptive and deterministic way (Edwards and Usher 2000; Boud and Solomon 2001). Rather globalization can be understood as a discursive practice, that is, a way of thinking, speaking and acting that interacts with changes in socio-economic and cultural structures, configurations and relationships. As such it – and in a sense it is not an 'it', but an effect of actions, although rhetorically invoked as a powerful actor in many representations – is a dynamic process and one which has both anticipated and unanticipated effects (Chappell *et al.* 2000). We will return to the significance of globalizing practices in Chapter 9.

Explaining Academic Globalizing Communities as a ceremonial place requires quite a lengthy discussion. It is not a single or simple thing and indeed would be described and characterized in very different ways depending on who is speaking, and how this person positions themselves and is positioned within this complex place. Nevertheless, taking up the idea that Academic Globalizing Communities is a ceremonial place helps to conjure up some characteristics and processes that suggest rituals, genres and practices that contribute to ways of working and being in education. The complexity of the characteristics of this ceremonial place are a consequence of a number of intersecting practices that are linked to a number of historical and contemporary processes. These processes together produce particular kinds of rules and rituals involving sets of players assembled in various loose local, regional and global associations. These associations, while varied in form and practice, are engaged in the education of populations. They are discursively positioned and maybe even position themselves as seeking to produce particular kinds of productive subjects, academic and workplace subjects whose work is consonant with the diverse knowledge needs of the global economy. This view is based on an understanding of a close relationship between education and work. It is this relationship that is experienced as central to much academic work, and indeed to the complex conditions of this ceremonial place, a place within which WBL programmes are located. Not all are persuaded, of course.

The discourses that are contributing to this alignment of education and work are numerous. As many writers draw attention to, globalization is attributed as one of the key causes and effects of this alignment. Whether understood as an economic, political or cultural process, globalization can be seen as a metaphor that enables the migration and thus uptake of certain ways of thinking or acting in various parts of the globe (Edwards *et al.* 1999). Amongst its effects, particularly in countries connected with the Organization for Economic Co-operation and Development (OECD) policies, is the global uptake of the discourses of business and commerce in educational discourses. We witness the 'corporatization', 'commodification' and 'commercialization' of educational services. These are not just 'mere' rhetoric, but practices that contribute to the making of, on the one hand, new conventions and rituals that allow for global patterns of education, and on the other hand, an unruliness of knowledge production (Stronach and MacLure 1997). Attempts to persuade audiences to take up these new practices are through a number of rhetorical devices. One such device is the constant reminder that we are living in *new* and *uncertain* times, an exigence to which we must all respond, if we are to survive. This has a number of effects. For instance, it is suggested that it would be problematic to continue with our existing practices. We are invited to believe that we need to do things differently now. We may be persuaded so to do, because we are told and then experience the world as a different place, where our educational practices and ways of being need to be replaced urgently.

The practices of educators and their institutions take up the economic value of education as a response to an urgency to adapt to new economic conditions, in order that they can more fully contribute to the adaptations required of modern societies. Universities, therefore, in line with all businesses, have taken up the discourses that commonly characterize new economic times, and these times, as we are told, require new workers with new knowledge, skills and dispositions to meet the challenges of the 'new economic order' (Gee *et al.* 1996). All is new if not always shiny. The mobilization of economic discourses in the educational policy formulation of governments has been labelled by many as the 'new vocationalism' (Ball 1994; Grubb 1996; Symes and McIntyre 2000), which emphasizes the need for all educational institutions to contribute to national economic imperatives. For the most part, these discourses are embedded within human capital theories of economic performance. They compellingly promote the idea that economic performance is intimately connected to the level of qualifications, skill and ability of the workforce and are a common feature of the educational discourses of many OECD governments (Papadopoulos 1996).

The discourses of new vocationalism draw attention to significant changes in work and learning and also to workers and learners. They suggest that knowledge production and learning practices are now distributed across various work and learning sites and that there is a privileging of new kinds of workers who are able to 'do things differently' in their everyday work practices. We are led to believe that all workers have to have different understandings of their roles at work. They have to forge different relationships with colleagues, managers and the organization. They need to conceptualize their knowledge and skills differently, to change their understanding of who they are at work. In short, to change their identity. Certain workplaces have therefore to give more attention to their employees, in particular the fashioning of values, attitudes and dispositions in order that we all have 'nice days' (Legge 1995). Human resource development re-stories the workplace and its own practices, the rhetorical effects of which are based on the forms of uptake in which employees engage. Here trainers and developers, often restyled as facilitators, take on the role of discourse technologists (Farrell 2000). Employees may play the game, but also be aware of the game they are playing (Lash and Urry 1994; du Gay 1996). Changing selves has therefore become an *aim* of new vocationalism (Chappell *et al.* 2003).

An emphasis on 'knowledge production' and the 'knowledge worker' in the economy has resulted in a number of commentators questioning the adequacy and utility of the content, organization, production and transmission of knowledge that traditionally takes place in education and training institutions (Senge 1994). This position proposes that the knowledge of the economy is different from that which has occupied traditional education programmes. The position connects easily with popular public discourse on the role of educational institutions today. This in turn perhaps explains the easy uptake by many academics of the Gibbons *et al.* (1994) thesis that there has been a significant shift in emphasis away from 'culturally concentrated' (academic or Mode One) knowledge to 'socially distri-buted' (Mode Two) knowledge. Many academics easily engage with the idea that knowledge is (or should be) now practical, interdisciplinary, informal, applied and contextual rather than theoretical, disciplinary, formal, foundational and generalizable. It all sounds so sensible and appealing. Many writers now consider workplaces themselves as sites of learning, knowledge and knowledge production (Boud and Solomon 2001). Workers within the new economy are now expected to contribute to knowledge production within the workplace rather than merely applying existing knowledge to workplace activities. This new knowledge is not found in traditional subjects or disciplines. Its deployment has to have immediate value for the enterprise and this is more likely if the knowledge is context specific, even though its value may well be short-lived within the organization. This knowledge is not foundational and cannot be codified into generic written texts such as competency standard descriptions, procedural manuals or textbooks, but is fabricated within the context and environment of the immediate workplace. This new form of knowledge is understood and described by some writers as 'working knowledge' (Symes and McIntyre 2000). It is a term that is descriptive of and also contributes to current understandings of knowledge. Arguably, at the same time, it could be said that it is part of a theorizing of non-codified knowledge. Perhaps the coining of the term 'working knowledge' is one way some academics are retrieving what they believe primarily belongs to them, a rhetorical translation and reappropriation.

Meanwhile the privileging of non-codified yet useful knowledge continues to be supported and complemented by certain kinds of pedagogical practices. These practices place the individual student and their life and work experiences as central to their learning. Described by some as a type of 'instrumental progressivism' (Symes and McIntyre 2000), this student-centred style of education is individualized and flexible, and more often than not designed to enhance opportunities for employment. These opportunities are encouraged by the use of experiential learning and practice-based teaching approaches. These approaches are often manifest in learning processes that are framed by project work, which draw on students' workplaces or experiences and are organized around the resolution of 'real' workplace problems. They can be understood as a pedagogical device to assist in the development of learner-workers: that is, people who are motivated, can work in teams, are organized, take responsibility, etc. (Chappell *et al.* 2003). These kinds of pedagogies encourage and contribute to a reconfiguration of educational discourse that further contributes to the pull away from more conventional forms of disciplinary knowledge.

These new ideas about knowledge and learning have had profound consequences on the identity and practices of many universities and academics. They find themselves in almost an unfamiliar place. For many, the rituals and norms have changed. Their institutions are no longer considered to be the primary producers of knowledge. Academics are now told that they work in 'workplaces' and that means they too are employees. Furthermore, the parallels with the economic world are undeniable in the way universities are described as income-generating businesses, driven by quality, relevance and efficiency as defined by governments, corporations and now of course students. Or so we are told at least.

Participating as an academic in this somewhat unfamiliar ceremonial place presents considerable challenges to the identity of those affected. The new and multiple forms of accountability mean that academics are subjected to various institutional regimes – those of the academy, the government and the other participating institutions. In this highly contested area, academics take up ambivalent subject positions as they actively self-regulate in different networks, distributing themselves in various power relations. They engage in different kinds of self-regulating performances as they play the various games: performing as academics

- with disciplinary knowledge in the academy;
- with worthwhile expert knowledge, that can contribute to the construction of productive subjects (the population); and
- who are able to align their goals with those of the academy, business and/or government.

While this space may be a messy and unruly one, this does not mean it is unregulated or undisciplined. The disciplining regulations are just multiple and complex. Academics are under surveillance in relation to the relevance, quality and efficiency of their work, and, at the same time, their performances are subjected to disciplinary and institutional surveillance and the accompanying debates about the legitimacy of socially distributed knowledge (Luke 1996). They struggle with questions about the place of the 'ivory tower' in these times and their role in servicing the instrumental needs of industry and government. Simultaneously, academics are being positioned as slaves of capitalism by some, while, at the same time, congratulated and rewarded for entrepreneurial success by others (Luke 1995). There is a lot of hyperbole, to which we have just contributed through our own uptakes.

The multiple accountabilities involve multiple sets of discursive sequences and rhetorical practices that contribute to the fabrication of the contemporary academic subject. The rules and regulations are no longer the same as in previous decades. One way of understanding the conditions of this ceremonial place is to consider the composition of the players. These include both familiar and unfamiliar participants. The familiar ones include: academics, academic peers, and of course students. The less familiar participants include new sets of players such as senior bureaucrats and accountants within the university and the governments who use the collected information to manage and calculate the allocation of funds. Additional participants are organizations external to the university. These might be industry representatives, or senior managers of large corporations. These new and old participants are engaged in new ruling relationships, which forge new sets of separate and intersecting accountabilities (Ramsden 1998).

As academics struggle with the troubling intersecting accountabilities and the accompanying challenges to the arguable purity of disciplinarity, they are engaged in different kinds of textual uptakes. The boundaries around educational programmes are subjected to sets of ruling relations (Smith 1999) where their effectiveness is bound up with their relationship to the economics of education. The performances of contemporary productive academics therefore become very closely tied into government programmes. The ceremonies within this place are mobilized by globalizing disciplinary communities influenced by government's regulatory exercises, which are mediated locally through institutional regulations. Together these create the boundaries that discipline the textual uptakes. However, the new boundaries, rules, regulations and participants in this ceremonial place are still connected to discursive sequences of the subjects produced in previous decades. But they are a different take and the tactics are seemingly more complicated. Academics and their institutions are being relocated and their knowledge is being repositioned. It is these relocations and repositionings that allow for different textual uptakes. In other words, different ceremonial places allow for different things to be said and to be taken up by different actors. The persuasiveness of the discourse is therefore related to the ceremonial place within which it is located.

Educational practices, such as WBL programmes, are symptomatic of the ambivalent performances that, in a sense, are almost a necessary component of contemporary practices. We suggest that the WBL texts examined in this chapter are academic performances that are symptomatic of the complexity of the games that academics play in the collaborative knowledge production process within this Academic Globalizing Communities ceremonial place. These are games that are bounded by contested rules and regulations as the various participants play through their textual practices within the new hybrid spaces that are created by the opening up of institutional and disciplinary boundaries. These spaces challenge the comfortable, familiar distinctions between public and private domains, between disciplinary knowledge and working knowledge, and between the workplace and the academy that once ruled academic work and academic subjects. Interestingly, ICT is both contributing to these processes and, as we have seen, involves similar uptakes.

A work-based learning programme

The institutional site of the WBL programme is a recently formed technological university in Australia. Its newness means that it has not been characterized by conventional disciplinary programmes. Its image lies in its reputation for practice-based teaching and education for work purposes. A perusal of a number of pro-motional documents reveals the degree to which the university positions itself as a university that produces employees and is a university that works with the relationship between working and learning. The university documents draw attention to the importance the university places on work experience, and on its relationships and partnerships with industry and large corporations. You will not find terms such as 'foundational knowledge', as these are not how the university wishes to position itself. While it may not describe itself in exactly these terms it can be understood as an educational institution that presents itself as a co-producer of knowledge, co-producing very particular kinds of subjects. It has therefore been more open to the uptakes associated with the new vocationalism and the discourses of socially distributed knowledge.

It positions itself as a university that is productive in forming productive graduates, who either are or will be productive employees within their organizations. In doing so, the university signs up as a productive workplace. As the university increasingly works with business partners in varying collaborative arrangements, it also adopts a position that crosses the education and non-education boundary. Thus, it not only performs as a university but is also learning to mimic the rituals, language and practices of other organizations. We suspect that the shared productivity discourse is a key mechanism for aligning academics, workplaces and business personnel. Would any of us be happy to be positioned as unproductive in our workplaces, even if we were allowed to be? This is particularly so in the way productivity is used to highlight the benefits of being in a relationship. For example, for the university, productivity is in terms of the benefits of the partnerships with business. This relates to the image gains in terms of 'working together' and 'being close to the action', as well as to the funding benefits through attracting new groups of fee-paying students. For business, the productivity gains in aligning with universities, in the first instance, are in terms of using academics' expertise in assisting the forging of the 'right kind' of employees. However, they are also, in the way collaborations with the academy are, perceived as enhancing the professional image of those workplaces. Thus, not all workplaces can become part of the ceremonial place of WBL degrees.

The discussion above draws attention to the fact that WBL programmes at this university have not emerged within a vacuum. Their emergence is one of the uptakes that is made possible within the current conditions and discourses of this ceremonial place. The textual sequences within educational discourses of partnerships, the knowledge economy, flexible learning and lifelong learning have meant that, in a university such as this one, WBL can be seen as a natural (and tactical) pedagogical move. Therefore, while perhaps a somewhat radical move for some universities, at this university the establishment of WBL programmes has been a tactical response to a number of related needs and urgencies. When talk about uncertainty and the accompanying unpredictability of higher education income is well-rehearsed, the university needs to differentiate itself in order to find new markets. This means it needs to accelerate its connections with businesses and organizations. Perhaps also there is a need to be seen as responsive, flexible and innovative, all metaphors that are deployed to engender action. These needs themselves are only experienced as needs because of the various discursive practices that have to date been constructing the university's identity and offerings. Furthermore these discursive practices are manifest not just in the language around the relationship between working and learning and the importance of business relationships, but also in the university's institutional structures and processes. In other words, the university's existing conventions, rules and rituals have allowed WBL programmes to be incorporated within its repertoire of educational offerings.

This is not to say that in order to materialize these new programmes existing accreditation and regulatory systems were adequate. Indeed a number of new university committees and processes had to be established (Onyx 2001). Being slightly out of sequence with existing practices, these new committees signalled to the university community that this is a different programme and it is one that the university is taking seriously. Interestingly though, several years into the WBL programme, these new committees no longer exist. It seems that they had done their work. Now WBL quality and accreditation issues are dealt with in the mainstream committees. The reasons for this mainstreaming are articulated in terms of efficiency of structures. This efficiency line could only be possible if we understand that the institutional discourses had been reconfigured in a way that suggests that WBL is no longer experienced as unconventional. One can understand this as a kind of downgrading of accountability. This suggests not a downgrading of the programme, but rather that it has been mainstreamed, which is arguably an indicator that it requires less institutional surveillance.

The texts examined in this section are texts that describe and promote WBL on the university's Faculty of Business website [http://www.business.uts.edu.au/ wbl/what/index.html]. We therefore re-enter cyberspace in our engagement with WBL. This site has been modified several times and indeed during the writing of this book the website has undergone a major textual reconstruction. The latest version, at the time of writing, modified in May 2003, positions the programme, the university and the readers quite differently to the way these are positioned in the earlier May 2002 version. It is these differences that provide the focus here, in order to highlight the co-emergence of audience and uptake through rhetorical practices. It is interesting to note that the fact of the changes, as well as the large number of changes, exemplify some important points raised in the earlier discussions on the complexities of the Academic Globalizing Communities ceremonial place and how these are played out within an infinite sequencing of textual uptakes. Importantly, the two versions indicate that educational textual practices do not simply follow a predetermined, uncontested linear process of development heading relentlessly towards a, perhaps, feared dark powerful place – depending on your point of view – within commercial discourses. By contrast, it seems that directions and thus rhetorical devices shift backwards and forwards across various contested discursive domains. Moreover, these shifts exemplify the performative nature of genres and language games, where new ones emerge if the genre or game does not do the work that it is desired to do.

As a tactical move for this chapter, we have chosen to use Internet texts to describe and promote WBL rather than the print versions. As already indicated, an analysis and discussion of Internet texts invites a different kind of rhetorical analysis than, say, an examination of the textual sequence of the accreditation process of WBL programmes within the university. Certainly an analysis of the rhetorical work of an accreditation process would also disclose the twists and turns within academic discourses, as the institution and those within it move in and out of familiar and unfamiliar disciplining games. However, the following discussion of the rhetorical work of the web descriptions of WBL is a tactical one, drawing attention only to some of the features of the two versions. We focus on those that help to rhetorically position our argument. We consider the work of these texts within the ceremonial place, how they position the readers and the writer in relation to particular kinds of textual uptakes.

The first version, now no longer retrievable, is a textual uptake of other printed documents that had been written for circulation and discussion amongst academics, when the university was internally framing, describing and promoting the programme. The information described in the website is in fact a translation of this earlier internal communication about WBL. The information is similar but it is also a different uptake. It is different because it uses the electronic resources and because it crosses over into another genre to speak to a different audience. There are different moves within this site as the game is within an alternative discursive space, a space that has other purposes, structures, players and rules.

But these differences are ones that are not so different that they are entirely unpredictable in the Academic Globalizing Communities ceremonial place. They may not be ritualized as such, but they are part of a familiar enough discursive process where a movement in and out of educational and non-educational discourses seems to be taken up with relative ease. This is so much so that it could be argued that the boundary between these two sets of discourses is experienced as no longer clearly sustainable. Indeed the first version is written in a way that indicates that the relationship between work and learning, as well as between the economy and education, can no longer be dismissed as mere rhetoric. Indeed it could be said that we no longer need to be persuaded that these relationships are significant ones. They just are.

But is it that simple? Are educational and non-educational institutions and identities the same? Has the business of academics been normalized into a world where its doing of business is just a business? An exploration of the earlier WBL website does reveal many features that suggest the response to these questions could be given in a single word, 'yes'. As you do not have access to this site, you will just have to trust us when we say that the site does have a generic resonance with many corporate websites. It does look like the way businesses describe themselves on equivalent sites, as it takes up the images and language of business. This can be seen in a number of places in the texts. Each page within the site is accompanied by a pictorial image. While the images on each page differ, each is superimposed with the word 'Work'. It is a device that works as a constant reminder that this site, and therefore the WBL programme, is primarily about work. This is reinforced in phrases and words that resonate with the language of business. For example, phrases such as 'Work Strength in Collaboration', 'highly innovative', 'performance and professional development goals' and 'enhancing workplace performance' are scattered throughout the text. Moreover, the site includes information about activities that have become conventional in the games that the business world plays, such as breakfast seminars.

However, perhaps all is not what it seems. The web descriptions work very hard to persuade the audience to take up WBL, to position the university as a legitimate player in the business game, but, at the same time, position organizations as legitimate players in academic games. Arguably, if this dual positioning was a settled or natural one, this amount of persuasion would probably be unnecessary. As it is, there are frequent reminders in the texts about who the multiple players in the game are and the benefits of these collaborations, where everyone is learning and organizational needs can be met but only by working together. Work is being done to mobilize and translate the different interests into a network. A key paragraph in the section, 'How WBL Works', sums it up: 'Customized learning programmes are developed that relate to each participant's work responsibilities and time frames. Everyone's needs are met through this process: individuals' career and professional development needs, employers' organizational goals, and (the university's) academic standards.' Furthermore, just in case the benefits for each of the players are not obvious, a section is included that spells out specifically the benefits for the participants and the organization.

Another sign of the hard rhetorical work that the texts need to do is their use of the question–answer format. They frequently use questions as headings for some of the menu items. For example, we find:

- 'What is WBL?'
- 'What are the Benefits of WBL?'
- 'Questions about getting involved?'

The use of questions does particular kinds of relationship work. They are a rhetorical tactic that invites the reader into the text. This question–answer pairing, as in any bi-directional relation of a pair of texts, sets up a relationship not just between sub-sections of a text but also between the readers and the writer. They are a rhetorical tactic that attempts to personalize the relationship and close the distance between the reader and the writer. Indeed we have used this device ourselves in this text with similar motivations in mind. In these WBL texts these questions also signal to the reader that they know him or her well enough to come up with questions that he or she might be asking. This sign of engagement is reinforced, as it is in many websites, in a 'Frequently Asked Questions' section. This kind of section also does specific kinds of rhetorical work. It signals that, while this might be a new programme, there has already been a lot of interest and for good reason too. It also provides a site to place information that cannot be easily located in other sections of the text. It is a space for lower order information, such as entry requirements, fees, what is involved, university support, etc. While this information might be important and indeed even essential, it is not the information that is to be put to the fore in this rhetorical positioning of WBL programmes.

The WBL website uses the technical resources that make available different spaces to background and bring to the fore various kinds of information. 'WBL Resources', the fifth and final item in the menu on the site, provides a background space that allows for the display of an additional set of characteristics of this discursive site. This item comprises two readings in the form of two PDF files that can be downloaded. These have been lifted from what could be described as more conventional kinds of educational textual sequences. One is an article in an academic peer-reviewed journal and the second is an article from a human resources monthly magazine.

What rhetorical work do these resources do? The answer is not a simple one. The resources signal another kind of legitimacy to the WBL programme and the institution within which it is located. They signal a more complicated identity of the institutional site and in so doing arguably help persuade a potential partner that, while we can talk like you and be like you, in some important ways we are also different. We perform in various ways to various audiences. By drawing on these various performances we have something to offer. One can only speculate whether or not these PDF files are downloaded and read, but perhaps that is immaterial – they certainly are in their electronic format. They do rhetorical work by just being there, reminding the reader that the university does academic work, such as journal writing, and that this work is legitimate and significant within this kind of educational and non-educational partnership game.

The more recent website texts take up some of the rhetorical features of the first one, including the 'Frequently Asked Questions' section and the 'Resources' described above. However, at the same time, they are significantly different texts. While we can only speculate the reasons for the changes, the difference suggests that the first site did not do the work it needed to do. The desired uptakes did not happen. In other words, possibly the web information did not successfully persuade enough. The number of desired new WBL partnerships and learners did not materialize, so the university has had to tactically reposition itself and therefore make different kinds of textual moves.

An obvious, although not entirely predictable, rhetorical difference in this second version is the insertion of talk about knowledge. In the first version, knowledge, let alone a relationship between knowledge and WBL, was not mentioned. In its attempt to be like a business, it is as if the first version texts were deliberately distanced from language that might be considered to be too academic, such as knowledge. Instead language was used that was believed would work to help the university make connections with businesses. The talk therefore in the earlier version was about 'productivity' and 'performance' and 'partnerships' and 'learning' as keys to achieving organizational and individual goals. However, the second version takes up a different rhetorical position and seems to pull the discourse into a more complicated discursive space. It is a space that can be understood as a more academic one, but also one that links in with the economic discourses that speak of knowledge economies, knowledge work and knowledge workers. Markedly, in this version, the opening page, 'Welcome to Work-Based Learning', begins with an opening paragraph that possibly resembles the beginning of an academic paper:

> There can be no denying the importance of knowledge in today's increasingly complex and competitive global markets.

Working knowledge needs to be relevant to individual and organizational needs.

It needs to be trans-disciplinary, valuable economically and applied.

In recognizing the value of knowledge gained through professional practice, the work-based learning process enables individuals to reflect upon, capture and extend this knowledge.

Aligned with this introduction of knowledge into the discourse is an engagement with understandings about learning. This textual move does not assume a shared or common-sense understanding of what learning is or that working and learning are unproblematically the same thing. In these texts, there is talk about the links between learning, knowledge and critical thinking. Moreover, some of the text suggests that 'we', presumably academics, have moved away from 'old-fashioned' ideas about learning and teaching. Indeed it tells the readers that 'we need to go beyond the metaphor of "pouring content into someone's head"'. This statement rhetorically positions 'we' as no longer caught within anachronistic academic conventions. We, like you, are modern, progressive and therefore we can work with you to create a new we through jointly participating in this innovative educational programme. Not coincidentally the photo images in this version reinforce this new we, with images of people, together and individually, located across various workplace and educational sites.

In fact, the text goes on to say that we are already working with the likes of you. While organizations are at times spoken about generically (for example, WBL awards help organizations and learners to achieve their performance and professional goals), they are also spoken about in a very specific way. A corroborative device is the inclusion in the text of the names of organizations that have already established WBL partnerships with the university. As the text suggests, these organizations have already taken up the challenge and the opportunity. This could help persuade readers to align themselves with organizations such as these.

This website and the accompanying texts do different kinds of work for the university and whether or not all the work is productive is no doubt contested. Perhaps, if its productivity is to be judged by the number of people or organizations that have been persuaded to take up a WBL programme, we could find an easy answer. Although perhaps not. How many uptakes are enough to be considered successful? One ... five ... ten ... or more new students? Do any fewer than the desired number suggest that the rhetoric in these texts has not been persuasive enough?

But there are uptakes and uptakes. Our rhetorical interest is located in a different discursive game to the one concerned with numbers of students enrolled in a programme. Certainly the student number game is a relevant and powerful one within educational provision. Yet our discussion hopefully indicates that the productive sequence of 'need more students, develop new course, put forward new promotional materials and enrol new students' is neither a discrete discursive sequence, nor the only game within which education and educators are located.

Our focus has been on the complexity of the rhetorical positioning of academics and their institutions given a multiplicity of discursive possibilities within a ceremonial place that has been named the Academic Globalizing Communities. As suggested, this place is in some ways currently characterized by an increasing disturbance around the boundaries of educational and non-educational discourses. In particular, we have explored the boundary space of WBL. Our analysis has illustrated that this disturbance is symptomatic of a number of discursive changes that have meant that the game academics had been playing in the past is, for many, now different. It is a game that involves the taking up and taking on of various audiences, practices and language moves, none of which are settled. In the process of writing this text, we have ourselves been involved in only certain uptakes rather than others, and there are more and other things that can be said about the rhetoric of and in workplace learning.

By rhetorically placing the WBL texts within a ceremonial place we can understand ways in which educational genres and discourses are being reconfigured. But this analysis has also worked to show that this reconfiguration is not simple, linear or predictable. The analysis does suggest that the university with this programme in this website is positioning itself within one of the newer educational discourses in this ceremonial place. It does locate itself within a relationship of working and learning, of economics and education, by looking to and reporting on alliances with various players. But it also shows that this location is indeed a delicate one and one that continues to be worked on by a number of ceremonials that seem to be almost playfully taken up and down. It might also indicate that this rhetorical playfulness suggests a discursive freedom which, in turn, allows for a number of textual and rhetorical possibilities. While academics may speak of their concerns with a troubling of their disciplinary areas and an inability to hold their subjects still, as can be seen in the above analysis, this instability is a site that opens up rhetorical spaces and provides possibilities for both discursive connections and freedoms.

Chapter 7

Action at a distance
The rhetoric of research management

In our discussion of workplace learning in the last chapter, we made mention of the significance of the changing rhetoric both about and within organizations and, in particular, the rhetoric of managing. The managing of educational institutions has become a significant aspect of the curriculum and discourse of education over recent decades, with much talk of 'new public management' and 'managerialism'. Both of these are held to have emerged from the New Right agenda of the 1980s, inscribed in the slogan that managers have the 'right' to manage. Since then, the rhetoric of management has itself moved to one emphasizing leadership, with charismatic leaders trying to create enchanted and enchanting workplaces.

All of this could be read as part of the struggle between workers and employers that predates the birth of capitalism. And indeed it is. But what is significant for us is that those struggles have themselves begun to be examined rhetorically in the organizational studies and management literatures. The notion that management is simply a rational process, governed by technical rationality, is a recognizable nonsense, even if it plays into the scientific rhetoric that we have discussed as so powerful in modern culture. Thus, greater attention has been paid to the cultural and emotional work of managing, which has immediately pointed to the importance of rhetoric. The rhetoric of managing and leading and the manager as rhetor has therefore been explored in various contexts (for example, Townley 1994; Legge 1995; Westwood and Linstead 2001; Dent 2003). Much of this work, although not all, continues to view rhetoric with suspicion and locates it as masking exercises of power.

In educational discourse, managing has tended to remain a much drier concern, with a great deal of muck-spreading about the encroachments of management on the democratic, professional, collective ethos of educators. The latter offers a framing of a rosy past that might have a certain pathos but for which there appears to be no substantive evidence. In his neo-Luddite analysis, Ball (1990c: 157) implicitly points to the rhetorical role that the discourse of management has played in relation to the reform of education, in his case in 1980s Britain:

> ... management theory views the social world as locked into irrational chaos, as needing to be brought into its redeeming order. It constructs its superiority

via a set of potent discursive oppositions; order is set over and against chaos, rationality against irrationality, sanity against madness, neutrality against political bias, efficiency against inefficiency, and meritocracy against political influence. It is the linguistic antithesis of crisis and as such it has a central political role in the 1980s.

Things have moved on, of course, with the introduction of the rhetoric of educational leadership and its associated discourses and practices.

Managerial language is typically upbeat, even evangelical in character, expressing a 'can do' philosophy of positive action and achievement. Managers like to hear and spread the 'good news' and celebrate achievement. Their discourse speaks of 'challenges' and 'opportunities' rather than 'problems' and 'obstacles'. They define their own role in terms of providing 'vision' and articulating the 'mission' of the institution and projecting its public 'image'.

(Humes 2000: 43)

There is a lot of symbolic work at play in managing, therefore, which Humes (2000: 36) considers to be significant, as the 'management of meaning is an important instrument of professional, institutional and ideological control'. Humes' argument is not one we entirely share, as he seems to point to the play of language beyond the rational and yet recoups meaning as something that can be 'managed' in an apparently rational way as an instrument of control. Those who have adopted a more explicit rhetorical approach to management (for example, Dent 2003) provide a far more complex picture of the contest over meaning-making in workplaces.

There is much that we could write about, therefore, in exploring the rhetoric of managing in education. However, as with previous chapters, we have chosen to focus on a specific example in order to add some logos to our discussion through the provision of detail. In this chapter, we look at the management of research in the contemporary university. We recognize that even amongst Organization for Economic Co-operation and Development (OECD) countries, there are distinct differences in national systems of higher education. Nonetheless, we believe that despite these differences, there are enough similarities and commonalities to warrant the broad brush approach we adopt here. Our focus therefore is on the way in which the management of research is being played out through what we term the 'new research regime'. In the terms of the last chapter, this marks another ceremonial space. We argue this regime is operationalized through technologies that embody 'action at a distance', which we relate to the operations of contemporary forms of governmentality. The chapter also focuses more on the *work* of rhetoric while providing a rhetorical analysis of managing.

We are witnessing the emergence of a managerial rhetoric that is becoming influential in the structures, cultures and values of universities. Our conceptual resources to help us in understanding the work it does in research management will be drawn from the work of Foucault. For Foucault (1979, 1980, 1981), a discourse is a body of knowledge whose major characteristic is its disciplinary power. It fabricates a domain of reality by naming and signifying aspects of experience and constituting experience into thought. There is an interactive process at work whereby reality is fashioned into a domain of thought and thought is fashioned into a domain of reality. This process enables documentation, computation and evaluation of particular aspects of existence, rendering them thinkable, calculable and thus amenable to intervention. Discourse and power therefore go together. In challenging traditional conceptions of power, Foucault argues that power is neither thing-like (reified), nor possessed by one particular group, nor simply emanating from the top-down. Rather, power is a network, it is relational and implicit in any social transaction. Furthermore, power is not solely impositional and therefore negative but productive in making things possible.

What is presented here is a very subtle conception of power. It is a way of acting upon acting subjects by virtue of their being *capable of action*. Power therefore does not stand over and against subjects, as it has no existence outside or above acting subjects. Hence where there are acting subjects there is power. Subjects are empowered. But at the same time subjects are also disempowered through knowledge and discipline, which become two sides of the same coin. Power is enmeshed with surveillance and regulation, either externally/panoptically or by self-regulation though the interiorization of the gaze. Foucault also argues that power and knowledge are not antithetical but always found together. There is a simultaneous production of knowledge that is always bound up with specific regimes of power. As such, discourses have a normalizing and regulatory effect, which is why they can be characterized as disciplinary. Power-knowledge is brought together and relayed through discourses. Discourses bring different categories and objects of knowledge into existence, making possible different ways of knowing the world and of acting within it. For them to be taken up, they need to be persuasive.

Discourse therefore comprises an ensemble of practices that involve both representation and action. It is indispensable to what Foucault calls governmentality: that is, governing which is not confined to the state and its institutions but is spread throughout the social formation. This involves the calculated supervision, administration and maximization of the forces, activities and relations of each and all. In order to govern you need to know people and, through this, you maximize their productive capacity by empowering them. Educational institutions such as universities fulfil a vital role here. They are important sites of normalization and regulation in modern social formations, especially as they seek to maximize the capacities of people. Equally the university is itself a site of normalization and regulation for its own workers, with research management a significant technology by which this is accomplished. What then is the exigence for this technology?

A constant rehearsal of truisms

A truism tends to be understood as a cliché, something that is true but trite. As such, it is normally dismissed as an utterance that does not deserve much attention.

It is perhaps one of the few examples of where truth does not have the resonance it normally has because, with the utterance referring to the obvious, the normal force of truth is attenuated. However, to dismiss the truism so readily, to position something as trite, is to neglect the significant rhetorical role it can play in giving discourses their performative power. This role involves the fabrication of 'facts' through the constant rehearsal of truisms, a rhetorical practice we shall have more to say about in relation to policy in Chapters 8 and 9.

Fairclough (2000c: 1) examines the discursive process by which change is constructed as something inevitable, 'as an external matter of fact which must be accepted and cannot be reversed or redirected, as a process without responsible agents'. He points out that representations of change are pervasive, found in every area of social life, education included, and indeed in our own fashioning of a 'new' regime of research management. What is significant is the repetition of change as a fact. He argues that these representations and their constant reiteration, whilst they may now have become truisms, nonetheless do important work. One aspect of this work is that of naturalizing the world. A second is that of mystifying it in the service of elite formations. Thirdly, it attempts to rhetorically 'sell' the techno-rational socio-economic order of neo-liberalism by making what would otherwise be alien, familiar and palatable.

What is happening here is the formation of knowledge and belief through a reiteration of the same. This constant uptake enhances the persuasiveness of assertions of change, as the more this is asserted, the more categorical and authoritative the truisms become. The naturalizing effect means that the world that is asserted to be in a process of constant change is fabricated as disembodied and disembedded, outside of history and location. No questions are asked about how this change has come about and who benefits from it.

> The 'is' that is so constituted works to ground the 'ought', what has to be done in the face of change that cannot be reversed, inflected, or questioned. Both national governments and international agencies ... increasingly construe their task as *managing* change, rather than implementing policies which shape the direction of change. Substantive differences in political ideologies are fading, and instead political parties differ over how to manage mutually taken-for-granted change. Politics and government become technicist ...
>
> (Fairclough 2000c: 13, emphasis added)

We see here that Fairclough, like Ball and Humes, positions management as a rational and technicist power play rather than a set of rhetorical practices. He provides a kind of ideology critique where neo-liberal discourse is cast as an ideology that functions to mystify and conceal the power of an elite. We need to be cautious about this and question how this critique itself functions rhetorically. One way of looking at this is to recognize its function as an oppositional discourse, a form of resistance to the impact of neo-liberalism. We will say more about this later.

However, there are a couple of points to highlight in terms of their relevance to our theme of research management. First, the constant rehearsal of truisms is an important component of projecting an 'ought to be' from the rhetorical fashioning of an 'is'. It is not a question of whether change exists but rather the articulation of change as something that can neither be reversed nor questioned. Rhetorically, all that can be done is to best *manage* change. People's knowledge of change and their belief in its inevitability becomes something so obvious that it assumes the status of the unquestioned. The articulation of change as something both inevitable and in need of management is now a feature of research in universities. Here the constant rehearsal of truisms articulates change as involving survival. Universities need to change in order to survive in a changing world. They must be managed in order for survival in a world marked by competition between countries and between universities. This is now something that is no longer questioned by many.

Second, the argument that ideology and ideologically based debate fades, with governance assuming a technicist form of calculative rationality, is particularly relevant to research management in universities. In many universities, the legitimation for managing research rests on the claimed expertise of a new class of managers. This is an expertise framed in calculative rationality and the collection and manipulation of data, where the latter comes to symbolically represent the performance of research. In Fairclough's terms, the effect of this is to relocate what would have been in the realm of the political to the realm of numerical and online systems expertise. In our terms, this is an unsustainable either–or, as the political does not so much disappear but is reconfigured through the differing organization of research. In a sense, the rhetoric of management as a technical process devoid of politics precisely attempts to perform the work of taking politics out of organizational life. In other words, the critical perspective only adds to the rehearsal of truisms that it positions itself as opposing. These are the sorts of ironies that we can point to through rhetorical analysis.

Another constant rehearsal of truisms that is impacting upon how research is conceived and managed is that universities are experiencing problems in coping with apparently new types of knowledge and new modes of knowledge production (Gibbons *et al.* 1994 – hereinafter referred to as the New Production of Knowledge [NPOK]). We have already made reference to this in the previous chapter. Mode One knowledge production represents disciplinary knowledge and is positioned as traditional and old. By contrast, Mode Two knowledge production is described as new. Rhetorically, this newness points to the modern, the progressive; it is future-oriented. For many, this has now assumed the status of a truism and a truism that is constantly rehearsed. This projects Mode Two knowledge as both new and as an alternative to the disciplinary knowledge produced in universities. It attempts to produce what it positions itself as describing, when it can be argued that there is nothing new about Mode Two socially distributed knowledge at all. What this suggests then is that Mode Two knowledge has hitherto not been *named* as such, nor attributed the significance now accorded to it. Constant rehearsal is a rhetorical strategy through which to attempt to valorize a particular kind of knowledge. The NPOK points to more than one mode and this suggests that there is now a diversity of ways in which knowledge can be produced and a consequent fluidity and boundary permeability in the landscape of knowledge production. But at the same time the NPOK is not just about the valorization of diversity. There is a very strong and clearly discernible sub-text that Mode Two is *best*. Moreover, the constant reiteration of the Mode Two message constructs a situation where there appears to be no alternative but to recognize and embrace this 'new' mode of knowledge production. The uptake of this position resonates with the managerial thrust in universities, for the task of management now becomes that of ensuring that Mode One knowledge takes on those characteristics which make it commodifiable and sellable: that is, it becomes more like Mode Two.

We have examined how change and Mode Two knowledge are fabricated as facts by a constant reiteration of the same. They signify the exigence to which better/greater managing is a response. These facts project or ground values. We argue from this that the new research regime is a discourse working through action at a distance. The values act or attempt to shape practices at a distance through the facts that assume an authority by constant reiteration. So there is no direct imposition of values. It is facts that have to be and are being acted on. To manage is to be steered by the facts. Who can argue with the facts?

Opening the black box

> We ought not to bemoan a paradise that never existed – or at least did not exist for those of us on the margins. We ought not to assume that the unfettered discovery of knowledge existed in a romanticized version of the past ...
>
> (Tierney 2001: 9)

In actor-network theory, a black box is that which no longer needs to be considered, that can, as it were, be taken for granted. It works metaphorically in a particular manner. A black box provides functionality and there is no need to ask how that functionality happens. So it is something that is so stable that it can be treated as a fact. Black boxes are immensely useful because if something is a black box we don't have to deal with endless complexity and the uncertainty which that brings in its train. The implication of this is that while there are situations where a black box will be opened, there is always a cost involved in such an opening. We will deploy this metaphor of the black box to characterize the contemporary university. What we are witnessing can be understood as the opening of the black box that is the university, as the persuasiveness of discourses such as those we have just been discussing are taken up and translated into the managing of organizations. Universities are being positioned as having to relate ever more to the 'real world' defined as the world of enterprise, business and the economy, rather than engage in those other-worldly practices of pure research and curiosity-based inquiry. Universities are under pressure to become more entrepreneurial and to locate themselves in the marketplace of knowledge production and dissemination, to become sellers and even buyers of knowledge. Knowledge for application, technology transfer, the commercialization of intellectual property and research training enter the discourse over and above the disciplinary apprenticeship and professional socialization of the traditional university.

Recently, the vice-chancellor of an Australian university articulated this different real world very clearly: '[this university] is a knowledge organization in the knowledge services sector'. This is a powerful articulation which many educators would and do find unknown and alien. It was also a significant redefinition of what a university is and what it is about. Furthermore, a clear warning followed the statement: 'the nature of the knowledge services sector is changing, requiring existing players to adapt to survive'. Here is the rhetoric of survival and adaptation we have noted earlier, what we will discuss later in this text as being part of a powerful social Darwinian metaphorical complex.

One important and very noticeable element of this rhetoric of survival is the emphasis on the real world. Whatever the nature of this might be (is there for example an unreal world?), it is clear that the world within which the university understood itself to be located was a far different framing to the world it now finds itself in. This is a situation which both lends itself to the rise of the academic manager, but at the same time needs to engage in rhetorical practices that can be both responsive to the organizational context and to manage, lead or enchant those that work within the university.

The rhetoric of the real world is deployed to challenge the perceived *externality* of the traditional university. By this we mean that, whilst always relating to its world, the university nonetheless perceived itself as also always external to it. To put it another way, traditionally the university has acted as if it were internal to itself. Its distinguishing features, such as its collegial way of working and the commitment to disciplinary truth, were both a manifestation and a cause of this externality or interiority. Externality meant that the university did not see itself as unrelated to the currently fabricated real world but the relationship was perceived as essentially one of its own choosing. Or, to put it another way, the university thought of itself as being *of* the real world but not *in* it. What we are witnessing is a breakdown or dismantling of that perceived externality. The university is discoursed into being as an institution that can no longer be allowed to remain internal to itself. It has to become accountable, accounting for itself through many different types of account (Currie and Newson 1998). Once the university is redefined as a knowledge organization, a packager and seller of knowledge in the knowledge services sector, its perception of its externality cannot be easily maintained. It becomes both in *and* of this real world and necessarily so. The metaphor of opening the black box aptly captures this change. The rhetoric of change, survival and the new types of knowledge production are part of the strategies through which this opening is effected, in part through the uptake of particular discourses of management.

While there are many aspects to this opening, here we are largely looking at research management and, in particular, at the discourse that shapes the new research regime. What has happened to research in the university is perhaps the most significant mark of the nature and consequences of opening the black box. We start by looking at the discourse that fabricates new understandings and actions (practices) about the research degree process. The first thing to note is the very use of the term 'research training' in this context. In Australia, at least, if you are a research student, you don't just do a research degree, you engage in a programme of research training which results in the successful and timely completion of a research degree. The latter is positioned as now no longer simply an induction into an academic way of life and a socialization into traditional research paradigms. Whilst the training locution makes many academics uncomfortable and indeed is actively resisted by some, the implication is clear. First, there is more to a research degree than just doing research. Second, a research degree is a process that has to be and can be *managed*. This implies that a research degree is not just about becoming a specialist in a narrow aspect of disciplinary knowledge. Now it is about acquiring the skills and capabilities valued by the knowledge economy. Furthermore, if doing a research degree is about training, then this implies that there is a *curriculum* that can also be explicitly planned and managed (McWilliam and Singh 2002). If training has to be managed, then the research degree process is deprivatized, relocated from the private to the public domain and hence made accountable and measurable. In the process, the educational relationships between people, their identities and what is produced, and the context of their work, are reconfigured. Irrational chaos is redeemed through the practices of managing. It all makes perfect sense.

The rhetoric within which these developments are taking place is one shaped by the arguments of government that universities must give up some of their traditional autonomy (their externality) and become more accessible and accountable to society. They can no longer remain aloof from the national economic agenda. They have to do things which society, or perhaps more accurately government and business, needs. Moreover, what they do must be measurable through some kind of accountability that makes sense in the context of a knowledge economy. Universities must be seen to be adding value and the most obvious way of accounting for this is through the operation of a research performance regime. Society and the economy are therefore rhetorically mobilized as actors to reshape university practices and their wider relationships.

Accountability for research training is being addressed through quality assurance and improvement processes that work to enhance and tighten accountability in the name of quality. Such quality measures do not only affect the central university level but also trickle down into faculties and departments or schools. Closer scrutiny of supervisory practices as well as of student progress has resulted from these measures. These are some of the technologies of managing that result from those actions at a distance through which change is rhetorically articulated as an exigence for differing ways of doing things.

The increasing push for high levels of accountability has arisen from the need to demonstrate performance in response to the constraints of limited timelines and the emphasis on timely completion. The rhetoric explicitly brings to the fore the accountability of supervisors and the transparency of the supervisory process. Both supervisors and research students need managing. The latter are positioned as valuable yet risky resources. Whereas once students could be allowed to ponder their research questions within fairly loose timeframes, this is no longer the case. Funded research degree places are now precious commodities, severely rationed and limited to carefully designated research concentrations. Thus students are obliged to demonstrate satisfactory progress in ways more overt and explicit than ever before. Mechanisms, such as regular progress reporting, scrutiny by review panels, as well as presentations of proposals and work in progress, and 'at risk' procedures, all embed students in a disciplinary regime and constantly remind them of the need to proceed in timely ways.

Earlier we mentioned that black boxes were potent because they metaphorized a world without complexity. Thus they function as a means of reducing uncertainty and, by implication, risk. We have argued that the research degree process, and particularly supervision with its private characteristics, has traditionally functioned as a black box. The opening of this black box is in the service of reconfiguring and enhancing accountability through a managed performance regime where the cost of opening is to bring a notion of risk to the fore. In a sense, there is no point in having management if there is no risk. With the deprivatization of the research degree process comes an accompanying risk and the consequent need to manage it. It is hardly surprising therefore that the rhetoric of risk has been articulated as a key aspect in emerging research performance regimes. Risk management through a variety of instrumentalities, perhaps the most of which are to do with quality assurance and improvement, becomes an indispensable feature of a performance culture. This is also the case for the wider rhetoric of managing within education and organizations more generally.

This management of risk therefore mirrors the oft-repeated assertion by government that risk cannot be left to self-management by universities. Universities are therefore in a position where they cannot be seen to allow risk to work itself through in a spontaneous way, and so the management of risk cannot be left to trial and error. If universities are to manage, they must subject themselves to self-scrutiny and this in turn requires self-knowledge. Self-scrutiny, it is argued, can only work effectively through the deployment of common performance measures. Hence the need for quality reviews. Here then we have a rationale that shapes the formation of a discursive domain, a realm of thought and action about how to manage research. With this comes the mobilizing of appropriate technologies in the form of efficient systems of data collection and dissemination to build that knowledge.

The processes we have been discussing are further examples of management through action at a distance. It is the performance of researchers, both staff and students, that is cast as requiring management over and above, and in some cases instead of, the traditional forms of organizing provided by location in academic cultures. However, performance cannot be managed directly and explicitly but through acting on researchers at a distance, indirectly and by implication, with an array of instrumentalities such as performance indicators, quality reviews and risk management. All of these instrumentalities are deployed through a rhetoric of accountability and transparency.

Bypassing the academic heartland?

> The core of our thesis is that the parallel expansion in the number of potential knowledge producers on the supply side and the expansion of the requirement of specialized knowledge on the demand side are creating the conditions for the emergence of a new mode of knowledge production.
>
> (Gibbons *et al.* 1994: 13)

It is generally agreed that the state now expects universities to do more, but with reduced resources. It has therefore partly, but significantly not entirely, withdrawn in favour of control by the market. At the same time, greater responsibility is placed upon universities to support and progress national economic competitiveness. This trend inevitably has had consequences for the way universities perceive their mission. We have touched upon this in the earlier discussion of the relationship between the university and the real world. Here is an example of this emphasis from a mission statement of an Australian university:

> The values that will characterize University X as a service organization, and will be embraced by both staff and students of the university are: client focus, quality processes, practicality and relevance, global imagination, cultural diversity, fairness to all, innovation and enterprise, environmental care, learning and personal growth, ethical behaviour and responsibility, and technological/professional orientation.

And from the strategic objectives: 'To provide outcome-related research and consultancy services that address real world issues'.

This is an example of the rhetoric of managing to which Humes referred above, mediating the performance culture through a vision that positions the organization as both desirable and desiring. It is a vision that we could replicate from elsewhere. Here research is increasingly expected to enhance the performativity of universities in ensuring national economic competitiveness. External funding has become an indicator of the success. It is a mark of how success is no longer something defined purely by a knowledge-producing academic community. Research becomes more geared towards pay-offs and the furtherance of systemic efficiency, valued in terms of how much funding it attracts and how happy the clients are with its outcomes. What used to be the means of doing research – that is, funding – has become the end itself and most significantly the measure and sign of its value.

Looking at the way research is being rhetorically reframed allows us to highlight that, precisely because it is the subject of such practices, it now has a clear semiotic dimension immanent in its discursive character. Given this semiosis, we can see that securing external research funding is significant for its sign value as well as its substance. It clearly signifies that the university is no longer confined within its own walls but is becoming more flexible, reaching out to the real world and adding value to it. It becomes a signifier of excellence where this is defined as success in an environment fashioned through competition and where competition provides the mechanism for allocating both public and private resources.

Pressures for accountability are accompanied by demands for transparency, where the latter is articulated as the means of achieving the former. Processes such as research assessment exercises in various forms are important here. They function as a technology responding to transparency, or deprivatization as we have expressed it earlier, where just simply doing research is no longer enough. The kind of accountability demanded of university-based research insists on a semiotic process of *showing and telling*. Research has to be demonstrated in terms of the relevance of its outcomes and its impact. In other words, a performativity regime also implies and indeed requires a *performance* (in both senses of this term) regime for its realization. We shall write more on this in relation to the writing of research in Chapter 10.

Research assessment exercises are now a matter of producing signs to be consumed by certain target audiences increasingly located outside the academic community. This process of sign production serves as a public and transparent demonstration of accountability. These public signs are now taking over the hitherto dominant role of disciplining communities. Some of this is impression management, an increasingly important activity for universities. But there is more to it than that, since it is also a means of fashioning that ambiguous contemporary figure, the 'active researcher'. As Ball (2000: 2–3) puts it:

> ... it is the uncertainty and instability of being judged in different ways, by different means, through different agents; the bringing-off of performances – the flow of changing demands, expectations and indicators that make us continually accountable and constantly recorded ... Are we doing enough? Are we doing the right thing? How will we measure up?

We wrote earlier of the breakdown of the traditional externality of the university. Another metaphorical way of expressing this is to highlight how the discourse of research management is bypassing the academic heartland. What we have highlighted so far are rearticulations of knowledge, who produces it and how, where and how it is stored and disseminated. These have all become critical to the way the university frames itself and is framed by wider discursive networks. What these framings project is that universities are no longer interior to themselves but part of a wider and globalized knowledge market. Producing knowledge is no longer an activity reserved for a select group of academics. This environment is often referred to as one where knowledge is *decentred* and where there has occurred a dedifferentiation or breakdown of fixed and bounded rules about what constitutes knowledge and knowledge production. With the greater permeability and fluidity of hitherto tightly defined disciplinary communities, accountability is no longer left solely to the gatekeepers and epistemological policing of these communities. What is happening in the university in terms of research being managed in the service of performativity is that it can no longer be left purely to the researcher. This is a clear indication of how the academic heartland is being bypassed (Usher 2002). All of this has consequences for the articulation of the university as an autonomous knowledge-producing institution. One outcome of this is that research work has intensified through shorter contracts, job insecurity for research workers, and greater control over the content and direction of research by state and quasi-state bodies and commercial organizations. Is it any wonder that, at least for some, this situation has also produced a persuasive rhetoric of management?

Our discussion points once again to the place of action at a distance in the new research regime. There is another form of deprivatization at work in the management of researchers. Deprivatization is brought about by a rhetoric of accountability and transparency, measured by metrics of performance. At one level, because they are rhetorically fabricated as universal and impersonal, the metrics provide the means for acting at a distance. No researcher is acted upon or managed directly, but indirectly through the metrics. However, there is another less obvious level where the metrics do their work. Research assessment exercises, as semiotic processes, function through signifiers of excellence and relevance. These hook into the desire to be recognized as an active researcher. Researchers are managed at a distance through the stimulating and energizing of this desire.

Managing the researcher

We have talked about changes in the way knowledge and the sources of knowledge have affected the university and researchers located within it. What is happening inside the university, in particular the trend towards managerial practices and a performance economy of research, interacts with these changes. While the university is being framed or re-framed by practices centred on changing configurations of knowledge and new fabrications of knowledge about knowledge, this is not the whole story. As we noted earlier, the university is itself forging knowledge in a particular way, simultaneously a reinforcement of and a resistance to managerial rhetoric. It is to this we now turn.

In a recent study of the governance of Australian universities, Marginson and Considine (2000) discuss the extent to which management structures and a management ethos have become embedded in Australian universities. The position is summarized in the following way:

- universities are now characterized by strong executive control with managerial structures that support this;

- the new class of managers gain their power through mediating and brokering the relationship between the university and the external world;
- traditional governing bodies such as Academic Boards have been rendered marginal or obsolete;
- research in universities is organized through a performance economy;
- academic disciplines are weakened;
- there is an emphasis on marketing and short-term revenue raising;
- universities are dominated by institutional perspectives where the university's corporate interest in revenue and prestige maximization becomes an end in itself.

The trend towards the management of research as if research were a *system* has its roots in pressures external to the university. There is a growing stringency in public funding, reorganization of higher education as a market-oriented competitive system, and new methods of input/output measurement employed by governments when calculating and allocating research support. The external pressures are construed as given and immutable. It is significant that universities as institutions have largely shown little resistance to these rhetorical practices but rather have embraced the truisms of 'there is no alternative' and 'we must change to survive', in the process redefining themselves increasingly as corporate entities. With this has come a strong incentive to treat research in economic terms as a performance economy.

The role of university managers and their positioning as *managers* has become crucial. It is they who now have the role of mediating and interpreting these external pressures. It is they who translate the requirements now placed on universities. They do so by rechannelling the externals into a structured system of internal pressures, incentives and measures. As a consequence, the managerial trend has fabricated research as both a knowledge-producing system and an economic system. In effect, an internal knowledge economy mirrors the external knowledge economy and a research performance economy. According to Marginson and Considine (2000), these overlap and interact, with research reinvented as a system of money, measures, targets and comparisons within a competitive economy and an enterprise culture. The management of research is thus fashioned by double and interactive moves. Research is first fabricated as an economic system with inputs and outputs, research management then colonizes the identity of researchers themselves as they become active researchers. The effects are there for all to see.

Research management therefore is not simply about formulating procedures and measures. That is only part of the story. More significant are the changes that are brought about in the way that researchers understand research and how they fashion themselves as researchers. The rhetoric of research management affects culture and subjectivity. On the one hand, many academics welcome and applaud the very emphasis now placed on research by governments and universities. As Ball (2000) points out, with this emphasis academics can fashion themselves as 'triumphant selves' with a subjectivity that encompasses feelings of pride and achievement. Ball argues that there is something very seductive about being ascribed excellence, being relevant, about performing well and having that *recognized*. The epideictic or ceremonial role of assessments of quality in allocating praise cannot be overlooked. What this implies is that the research performance economy is more than calculation. It is also about building a culture and forging identity, where these appear not to be forged precisely on the basis of calculation. Another way of putting this is that the research regime stimulates and is stimulated by desire, one powered by signifiers of excellence and relevance. This requires a rhetoric of management and by managers, which, as we indicated at the start of this chapter, goes beyond technical rationality to embrace the cultural and emotional, the visionary, even if this might be met by resistance, scepticism or even irony.

The rhetorical practices of the research performance economy are not ones that all academics would regard as appropriate. Many feel uncomfortable with the language of excellence, performance and relevance precisely because these are the outcomes of managerial rather than disciplinary practices. It is because research is now *managed* and often managed by those outside disciplinary domains that there is this critical difference. In the bypassing of the academic heartland, the managed economy means that research is now no longer worth pursuing *in itself* as truth-telling or for what it might teach us. This is not sufficiently persuasive to justify the allocation of public funds. Research has to be managed as a means to another end, viz the competitive position of the university as measured in terms both of cash and prestige, which act as signifiers of excellence and relevance. Research as an economic performance system is not easily grafted on to traditional academic discourse, culture and identity. Rhetorical struggles take place in and around this on a regular basis.

The academic heartland is not bypassed so easily of course. The management of research must to some extent live with the older research regime whose work practices are located in an older academic paradigm. This other research economy is in many ways in conflict with the newer managed research economy. This conflict is often manifested as resistance to the rhetoric of research management and the fulcrum of the resistance is the articulation that too much management is likely to lead to too little research. Marginson and Considine (2000) express this as the dilemma of research management or, as they put it more metaphorically, how to make the butterflies fly in formation. From the viewpoint of the research manager, controlling research is eminently desirable. It is self-evident that research will benefit from a continual flow of performance information and greater accountability. If it were channelled more efficiently into fulfilling institutional goals, there would be more and more useful research and everyone, researchers and institutions alike, would be better off. Research managers have internalized the rhetoric of concentration and excellence. How persuasive this is to academic researchers is another matter of course.

There is another discourse, equally strongly internalized and not just by academics, that research can only come from creative people. The dilemma, it is said, is that creative people do not flourish when they are marshalled to fly in formation (Marginson 1999a). They want to do their own thing, to break formation, to do things that *they* consider important and worth doing, not what others say will bring in most money and prestige. This breaking of formation, this doing one's own thing, is what the older research regime is all about, even though it did not always do it very well. The articulation of research as 'unmanageable creativity' highlights a systemic issue that goes to the heart of the resistance to the managed research economy. In the face of external drivers, the older research economy is rhetorically fabricated as having little chance of continued existence without the newer managed research economy. Without research management, the older economy, it is argued, would eventually be destroyed. At the same time, the resistance frames the newer research economy as in need of the older research economy to deliver the goods: in effect, without this older economy there would be no research to manage. An impasse perhaps. Hyperbole, almost certainly.

'Resistance is futile'

The current research regime fabricates a performance economy *and* simultaneously colonizes the identity of the researcher. The research regime would not work without this double move. However, this is not a straightforward expression of repression through ideological masking. The matter is more complex. At the very least, as indicated by Ball (2000) above, it is necessary to bring to the fore the complicitous way in which academics have helped to bring about and service the new research regime. Many find it problematic but equally academics have allowed themselves to be captured/captivated by its rhetorical power and the desires that it serves. In this context, it is important to note that the research regime we are highlighting is part of a wider regime that seeks to frame the university as a business to be run on businesslike lines. Already, for example, many academics are expected to be flexible workers. They are expected to be excellent researchers and thrusting entrepreneurs. The rhetoric of the enterprising self, to be found elsewhere in many economies (du Gay 1996), is therefore also one deployed in relation to the education workforce.

There are those who see this as a threat to academic freedom and the independence that the knowledge producer needs. As we have seen, this in itself becomes a rhetoric of resistance to the encroachments of the managerial university. At the same time, there are those who see things quite differently, amongst them those now inscribed as active researchers and those enthusiastically embracing Mode Two knowledge. In some cases these may be one and the same. These see the new regime as a kind of freeing-up. For many, it is an opportunity to forge new and productive subjectivities framed by the rhetoric of relevance and excellence.

We referred earlier to Foucault's notion of governmentality and we now need to develop this further. This points to the co-implication of rhetoric and the exercise of power. Governmentality, as we noted, is about disciplining into a *freely accepted* form of life that works by shaping subjectivity through the 'educating' or 'training' of individuals who would otherwise remain 'undisciplined' and therefore economically unproductive. It is important to emphasize the place of education, because disciplining through force or coercion is not approved of in much contemporary culture. Individuals become active subjects by developing their capacities. The development of capacities becomes a technology of success, the means of empowerment and of regulation. Governmentality involves non-coercive pastoral power that works through infiltrating regulation into the very interior of the experience of subjects (Rose 1989). Individuals educate themselves into accepting, valuing and working to achieve the congruence of personal and organizational objectives, a process where subjective experiences are simultaneously shaped and yet paradoxically remain uniquely one's own (Ransom 1997). This non-coercive but powerful regime needs active subjects who are self-developing, self-motivating and self-regulating. It requires the management of subjectivity.

What is framed in the rhetoric of managing is researchers with an enterprising relationship to the real world, but perhaps more importantly an enterprising relationship to *self*, exhibiting qualities of autonomy, self-management and personal responsibility. Managing is not coping or just getting by. Through the managerial rhetoric of excellence, technologies of the research regime (power) and technologies of the self (subjectivity) become aligned with technologies of success (motivation and enterprise). The rhetoric of excellence attempts to link and align the organizationally desirable (more productivity, flexible working, increased efficiency, maximization of outputs) with the personally desirable (greater self-fulfilment through performing excellently and being recognized as such). Researchers are fashioned both as active researchers and as self-regulating subjects. The subjectivity stimulated is one that regards the maximization of capacities and dispositions appropriate to maximizing research productivity and output.

What all this would indicate is that the management of research cannot be simplistically interpreted as the coercive imposition of management power from above. Nor that the rhetoric of managers is simply ideological mystification. The research regime can only work if it works at a distance. It can only work if it persuades rather than coerces. The changes required by the regime cannot occur unless they are self-imposed and unless researchers are disposed to be self-managing and self-regulating. Internal imposition works through the distancing of external imposition. For some at least.

The necessary shaping of subjectivity is not as radical or as difficult to achieve as might be thought at first sight. The enshrining of competition for research funds and prestige is after all a feature that the new research regime shares with the older research regime. The discourse of selectivity, concentration and performance resonates with the older discourse of academic excellence. Many academics have spent their life being excellent and being rewarded for that. They are no strangers to performing; careers are shaped by winning out against the competition. Furthermore, they are used to being examined and to examining others. In a sense, the new research regime is nothing other than a different yet familiar form of examination. It would not therefore be unreasonable to argue that researchers' subjectivity was susceptible, or receptive, to the development of the capacities, dispositions and behaviour demanded by the new research regime. It is in this sense that academics have been complicitous.

Another feature worth noting in this context is that the new research regime is shaped by a rhetoric with an apparently humanistic dimension. The language is one of structures that are lateral, working through informal networks and the interpersonal relations developed within these. Boundaries or 'silos' are to be dismantled enabling shared vocabulary and working together across boundaries and multidisciplinary research to match the inter-professionality and team working that is demanded more widely. The emphasis is clear. It is all about the informal, about networks, about multidisciplinary teams, about crossing boundaries, about conversations rather than managing, and about cultures of change. Yet at the same time as this humanistic and apparently participative rhetoric takes hold, as Marginson and Considine (2000) point out, the executive powers of vice-chancellors are on the increase. In Australia at least there is also the growth of a plethora of pro vice-chancellors with executive responsibilities. The diversity of rhetorical games that are now required to be played need to be managed and, thus, require more managers.

We would emphasize that we are not arguing that a gigantic deception is being perpetrated on academic staff, that they are in effect being 'conned' by humanistic discourse into going along with a repressive regime. Neither are we necessarily questioning the sincerity of the managers. For us, this is not the issue. Throughout this chapter we have highlighted the various complex external and internal exigencies with which universities must cope. In this situation, universities have no choice but to manage in some form. Furthermore, even though they are increasingly being fashioned as such, at the end of the day universities are not businesses. Their response to these exigencies and the need to manage cannot be to adopt a command discourse. The only way that universities can manage given the exigencies they face is through rhetoric that emphasizes the humanistic, because it is this which is needed for the formation of active subjects and therefore active researchers. A managerial discourse which in apparent contradiction contains a significant humanistic dimension is the way in which managing at a distance can be realized. Governmentality works through the action at a distance of pastoral power.

Having said all this, however, we would equally not wish to be construed as advocating a bowing to the inevitable as the only course. Nothing is inevitable. If governmentality is effective then there is a sense in which resistance truly is futile. It could be argued that self-regulation is so effective that colonization of identity becomes total. However, we do not accept this argument fully but rather, again following Foucault, argue that there is no power without resistance, in the many forms that can take. Without resistance, power is not only not needed; it would have nothing to gain purchase on to be exercised. Insofar as the new research regime is an exercise of power, albeit subtle, pastoral and at a distance, it is inevitably met with resistance. Indeed, it could be argued that it came into being precisely because the resistance in the form of the older research regime, and more broadly the academic culture of the autonomous researcher and research 'managed' by disciplines, was already present.

Resistance to the new research regime takes many rhetorical forms. It is partly motivated by the possibilities that cherished roles will be lost and a fear of not being able to 'keep up with the game', of being squeezed out and marginalized. It is also motivated by a suspicion of the new forms of self-regulating autonomy, a suspicion that is articulated as a loss of academic freedom. We find oppositional discourses that attack the very premises of the research management discourse, that actually it is inefficient because of the increased paperwork required by accountability, and the increasing control exercised by the bureaucracy of the university. Earlier, we noted a resistance that articulated the central place of creativity in research and how creativity is not amenable to the form of management demanded by the new regime. Nor have disciplines entirely lost their potency. The need to take account of disciplinary differences is articulated as an opposition to the universalizing thrust of performance indicators as the means of measuring and rewarding excellence. Even the humanistic language we noted can be turned around and deployed in the service of resistance.

These are just some manifestations amongst many of the oppositional rhetoric that shapes the many forms resistance takes. The conclusion must be therefore that resistance is never futile. Indeed it is clear that resistance is inevitable. Rhetoric generates further rhetoric, discourse stimulates more discourse. There are always more texts to write. For every move, there are countermoves. What emerges from this is that the management of research is a site of contestation in the university where any consensus between contesting discourses involves hard-fought struggle and is likely to be only temporary. In this situation, it is very difficult to articulate the scene of research and the struggle for control as anything but messy and complex. Managing does not overcome messiness and complexity, but merely adds to it.

It could be argued, therefore, that the task of managing research, universities and educational institutions more generally is neverending. Some of the reasons for this are not hard to find. The new regime lives in an environment which values competition between institutions, where universities are configured within a performance economy and where the government funding pot is static. Any advancement in research standing by one university is therefore relative. It takes place at the expense of other universities. This is the logos in the rhetoric of managing change and uncertainty.

However, it could be argued that there are other reasons, perhaps ones that are not so obvious. The new research regime embodies, and is powered by, a dream of perfect knowledge and perfect control. This dream is a fantasy given that the scene of research is messy, complex and conflictual. The calculative rationality of the research regime is overlaid by a desire to know and, through knowing to control, to be able to intervene and through that intervention to keep ahead of the game. Yet as we have seen, keeping ahead of the game is itself a fantasy because the rules of the game are always changing and the nature of the game is such that there can be no absolute winners. This is the power of the rhetoric of change and uncertainty. Equally, the same is the case for the resisters. Here the dream is of a romantic past, a fantasy of the 'unfettered discovery of knowledge', as Tierney put it above. As he goes on to point out, this was a paradise that never existed, certainly not for those whom it marginalized. But the desire to remain unfettered and unaccountable within the cosiness of the familiar is very much present.

Managing rhetoric

In this chapter we set out to explore the rhetorical in the practices of managing through a particular case. We have argued that there is a growing potency in rhetoric of research management, and demonstrated how it has fashioned the university into a site of normalization with the deployment of calculative technologies that function to both empower and regulate academics and students. This development is a microcosm of a larger trend where government at all levels is based on knowledge of people and the need to maximize their productive capacity through that knowledge. The rhetoric of research management triggers an interactive process whereby reality is made into a domain of thought and refashioned as the real world. In this world, the research process must be managed so that the income and prestige of the university is maximized. Equally, thought is made into a domain of reality, a real world of research performance and research training amenable to intervention and shaping by appropriate technologies.

Managing research is an exercise of power but this power is neither impositional nor negative. It works through action at a distance, making things possible, creating networks of active, productive researchers. With networks, social transactions are relational, operating within a framework of humanistic language but at the same time competitive. Is this surveillance? In one sense, it is. Power through regulation is enmeshed with surveillance either panoptically or through self-regulation and action at a distance, being seen without seeing. It is enmeshed in both forms. But we must be careful, as surveillance is not a neutral term. On the contrary, it has clear pejorative overtones. We would not wish to be understood as saying that the new research regime and the rhetoric of managing per se is bad. It is creating new kinds of knowledge, researchers, new forms of autonomy and, as we have seen, there are empowering as well as disempowering elements for all researchers, whether staff or students.

We have brought to the fore a new discursive regime that is fast gaining currency in the research domain of universities. By casting it as a discourse we highlight its rhetoricity and hence fashioning power. Yet we ourselves, through our own rhetoricity, have fabricated this regime in a particular way. We have therefore managed our own rhetoric in the process of writing about the rhetoric of managing.

Chapter 8

Sultans of spin?

> We *are* in a *new* age – the age of information and of global competition. Familiar certainties and old ways of doing things *are* disappearing. The types of jobs *we* do have changed as have the industries in which *we* work and the skills they need. At the same time, *new* opportunities *are* opening up and *we* see the potential of new technologies to change *our* lives for the better. *We have no choice* but to prepare for this new age in which the key to success *will be* the continuous education and development of the human mind and imagination.
> (Department for Education and Employment [DfEE] 1998, emphasis added)

To assert a 'new age' within policy discourse, as does this extract from the United Kingdom (UK) consultative Green Paper *The Learning Age*, is to attempt to configure a description of the world that is persuasive to us. It is an attempt to mobilize an audience, translating the concerns of different individuals and groups into a single narrative of change and adaptation. We may accept the assertion as a literal description of the state of the world, as if the new age exists and is unproblematic. We may also argue that the notion is merely 'spin' or, perhaps more accurately, hyperbole, designed to deceive, and thus search for the meanings behind this deception. But to respond in such ways is to fail to recognize that rhetoric is involved in all descriptions of reality and always has been, including those of policy. It is also to miss the opportunity to examine the work that rhetoric does in fabricating and mobilizing the new age. What rhetorical strategies are involved in representing it? For what audiences? With what effect? If we can go some way to answering such questions then we may begin to understand how policy works as persuasion. We also become more discerning as to the way in which the possibilities of our world are fabricated. We may also be able to reconfigure our responses to policy.

Earlier in this text we argued that part of the rationale for a rhetorical exploration of educational discourses arises from the contemporary concern over 'spin', and the more general undecidability associated with the proliferation of media and messages. Nowhere is this more pronounced than in the world of policy. Thus, as Fairclough (2000b: 3) suggests,

> ... language has ... always been a relevant consideration in political analysis. But language has become significantly more important over the past few decades because of social changes which have transformed politics and government. An important part of these changes is a new relationship between politics, government and mass media – a new synthesis which means that many significant political events are now in fact media events ...

Indeed, the mediation of those events points to the rhetorical strategies engaged in, not only by politicians but also by the media, as they attempt to engage in political struggle and mobilize their own audiences in the name of reporting (MacMillan 2002). Listen to the radio news and the struggles that take place between reporters and politicians over whether or not the chosen topic – for example, schools funding, problems with exams results, student debt – does or does not represent a 'crisis'. Crisis narratives provide an imperative for policy action and therefore invest situations with political importance, almost regardless of the relative weight of evidence and analysis by all concerned. They engender a certain policy hysteria (Stronach and MacLure 1997).

Distrust of policy making and policy makers has become more common as politics has become positioned as more concerned with the spin of media presentation than with substance. Of course, this is itself a powerful rhetorical achievement, as to position a political party or interest group as engaged in spin is to attempt to undermine and delegitimize its position – to position audiences as needing to distrust what is written/said. In some ways this might appear to be fair. To suggest that an increase in funding is sufficient to achieve the policy goals set when, in real terms, it signifies a decrease in funding, is rightly challenged. However, to position a particular perspective as 'politically correct' is another matter. As Fairclough (2003) points out, in the UK, sections of the media and the political Right have been very successful in positioning the stance that gives more attention to the questions of language – for example, referring to adult females as women rather than girls – as politically correct (PC) and part of the policies of the 'loony Left'. Here 'the isolation of "PC" from the more general process of cultural and discursive intervention has proved to be a remarkably effective way of disorienting sections of the left' (Fairclough 2003: 21). In earlier work, Fairclough (2000b) analyses the language of the 1997 New Labour government in the UK, arguing that to suggest that New and Old Labour reflect different ideological positions is to manipulate language to control public perception. Are Third Way politics, attractive to social democratic parties in the 1990s and beyond, substantively different from traditional Left and Right policies, or 'mere words, empty rhetoric' (Fairclough 2000b: ix)?

Of course, Fairclough is falling into that trap that haunts the discussion of rhetoric, attempting to make a literal description of its emptiness, which only points to the rhetorical work being done. In our view, to put forward the view of policy as spin, concerned only with presentation, in some ways misses the point, as acts of persuasion are inherent in policy and political processes, just as they are within all communications. To suggest that a policy discourse is 'simply' spin or 'empty' rhetoric implies that there is a more truthful or honest political discourse. To suggest that language has become more important, that 'New Labour is involved in a "reinvention of government" which in itself entails a greater salience for language' (Fairclough 2000b: 5) is to leave space for the reinforcement of a reading of spin. A heightened awareness of policy discourse is in part wrought through media and other representations of it as spin. Views of policy as spin or governance as discourse management take us back to earlier critiques of rhetoric as appealing to the emotions and lacking evidence or substance, politics as manipulation, rhetoric as propaganda. Politicians who are said to spin are positioned as those who are interested in presentation alone. Perhaps in a more sinister way, it is suggested that they are prepared to mask the truth, which it is up to others to uncover. The latter is an argument much favoured by many in the media, thereby ignoring their own rhetorical work while positioning themselves as having a certain ethos in their reporting of politics. While having some sympathy with this view – it is rhetorically powerful – we wish to take a slightly different tack, as we feel the type of ideology critique that underpins such an approach overlooks important issues about what is going on and what our responses might be. Similarly, we would suggest that some of the discursive analysis of policy drawing on understandings of rhetoric (Fairclough 2000b) or the work of Foucault (e.g. Ball 1990a, 1990b and 1998), although valuable, pays too little attention to the work of rhetoric in its own formulations. What we wish to do in this chapter, therefore, is explore the rhetorical work in education policy discourse, in order that we can understand the rhetorical practices of politics and locate spin as doing particular rhetorical work of its own.

Here we will explore a particular example of a policy notion that has become popular in recent years in many nations and among certain international organizations, such as the European Union (EU) and the Organization for Economic Co-operation and Development (OECD). This is the notion of lifelong learning, which is supported by the new age discourse – the new age *is* the learning age – and is often accused, by analysts at least, of being high blown in terms of what it is meant to achieve, masking more sinister economic interests. Policy discourses position lifelong learning as supporting economic competitiveness and social inclusion, yet there is arguable substance to these claims, its logos resting more on the logic and coherence of the claims than the empirical evidence perhaps. Policy statements on what is being achieved in terms of widening access to education and training among adults are not matched by statistics and there remain significant disparities in participation. The espoused contributions to economic competitiveness, health and social inclusion of lifelong learning are subject to question. Reality is contrasted with policy rhetoric and both are found wanting. The classic division between rhetoric and reality is thus reworked in the discussion of lifelong learning, with a resulting cynicism towards the latter as reality fails to match rhetoric. In the discussion of lifelong learning policy, therefore, there is little engagement with the rhetorical work at play on all sides, in which the rhetoric of spin itself acts as a corrosive undermining of the importance of political processes themselves.

Our view is that the notion of spin is part of a particular rhetorical strategy to counter previously persuasive acts of policy. However, it is a strategy of opposition that is in danger of undermining policy processes altogether, as cynicism can result in a debilitated polity, as possibly evidenced by falling participation in elections in many countries. Our argument is that such an approach fails to deliver a productive politics through which to engage in and counter policy processes. By contrast, a rhetorical analysis helps to bring forth such possibilities. The legitimacy of rhetorical acts in policy processes therefore needs to be recognized and (en)countered, as

> ... to be truly persuasive one has to *imagine* the other view, and be able to 'play at' addressing it. Such an act of playful imagination continues to be necessary even in the act of addressing someone with another view.
> (Leith and Meyerson 1989: 100, emphasis in original)

The problem for some may be that this would appear to involve participating in the processes of spin, becoming spindoctors ourselves. Such imaginings are part of what we are involved in with this text and which we feel is lacking in much analysis of educational policy.

Lifelong learning and rhetoric

Few could deny the contemporary significance of lifelong learning as a way of framing policy in relation to post-school education and training, whether in the UK, other nations or in regional and international organizations. In many countries, one can hardly open a newspaper or watch television without some mention of lifelong learning. This is often from unexpected sources and in unlikely contexts. As lifelong learning has developed as a way of framing policy for certain parts of education and training, there has been a diversification of:

- the practices that are considered to be contributing to lifelong learning – these include workplace and community-based learning, as well as more formal provision;
- the practitioners who contribute to lifelong learning – not simply adult educators, but human resource managers, and staff in institutions traditionally more concerned with younger age groups;
- the stakeholders who contribute to debates about lifelong learning – the role of employer organizations and trade unions is particularly significant here.

Lifelong learning here seems to be a far more embracing notion than might be said to be the case in more traditional sector-based understandings of education and training. This in itself can be explored as part of rhetoric. Rhetorical analysis examines the ways in which audiences are positioned or created in the performance. To whom is the text or discourse addressed and how is the audience positioned? This is important, for as we mentioned earlier, creating an implied identity between author and audience is one strategy of persuasion (Leach 2000). Thus, for instance, the audience for policy texts on lifelong learning may be large and diverse. Yet the very bringing together of such an audience through a discourse of lifelong learning aims to create and cement affinities that might not be possible through other types of discourse. Thus, for instance, a policy on higher education would have a lesser audience than that addressed through policy discourses of lifelong learning. As such, lifelong learning appears rhetorically to mobilize a very diverse audience. This is not to say that all are equally mobilized or mobilized in the same ways, of course. Audiences are active and disruptive.

The concept of mobilization we have been drawing upon in this text is taken somewhat liberally from actor-network theory (Callon 1986; Latour 1987), a set of ideas that we briefly introduced in Chapter 5 and that has, to this point implicitly, provided some of the vocabulary for this text. The latter has been influential in the sociology of science and increasingly in the social sciences more generally in recent years, in particular among sociologists pursuing a 'sociology beyond societies' (Urry 2000). Actor-network theory (ANT) is part of the shift from individualized, psychological approaches to the understanding of knowledge-building to more social and cultural interpretations. Knowledge-building is taken to be a joint exercise within a network that is spread across space and time and includes inanimate – for example, books, journals, pens and computers – as well as animate objects. The symmetry between inanimate and animate objects in ANT arises because 'human powers increasingly derive from the complex *interconnections* of humans with material objects ... This means that the human and physical worlds are elaborately intertwined and cannot be analysed separate from each other' (Urry 2000: 14, emphasis in original). Policy and subjectivity are themselves distributed through the range of networks within which one is interconnected. These networks 'expand, contract and shift configuration over time, and even the most stable and predictable of them are constantly being reappropriated and redefined by the nature of the flows that animate them ...' (Nespor 1994: 12).

Educational policy practices, therefore, can be seen as actor-networks in which participants and participation are ordered in time and space. This entails not only people, but also inanimate objects, such as policy documents, computers, printers, microphones and television cameras. Audiences are mobilized as actors in the process. For example, as Popkewitz (1996) argues of school-based reforms, changes in governing entail the repositioning of actors and problem-solving in the educational arena, in particular increasing the role of parents and downplaying that of professional teachers. Similar processes have been at play in the mobilization of groups and individuals in the production and delivery of lifelong learning policies, and in the development of a wide audience willing to participate within such a discursive space. Thus, as Ball (1998: 124) suggests, 'policies are both systems of values and symbolic systems ... policies are articulated both to achieve material effects and to manufacture support for those effects'. In this situation, an effective policy might well appear to be one that is affective, appealing to many educators, employers and others who belong to the polity, which is itself an intertextual and interdiscursive space. As MacLure (2003: 95) argues,

> ... the ties, therefore, that bind people into a polity are, partly at least, inter-textual ones: ways of reading (and viewing) built on past encounters that deliver familiar ways of reading, and being in, the world. If you don't share an immersion in those texts, you mark yourself out as not belonging.

Here the play of pathos and ethos may be more significant than the logos of the text. Part of the mobilization entailed is through the rhetorical work of those involved in policy, and in who is included and excluded as the audience for particular policies. Lifelong learning policy rhetorically attempts to constitute new and wider audiences, as who can oppose the notion of lifelong learning?

Policy descriptions are significant within those networks where knowledge of lifelong learning is built. They are active in working up the facticity of lifelong learning as a solution to particular problems of the world. These descriptions can be examined for the rhetorical strategies that make lifelong learning persuasive. Even though descriptions vary, the rhetorical strategies that are drawn upon in their fashioning may be quite regular and amenable to analysis in terms of the work that they attempt to do. The importance here is to find some form of analysis that can get to the detail of the rhetorical work done within policy discourses and texts, as in the case with the new age of lifelong learning.

> Potentially, there are a huge number of ways in which the production of descriptions is involved with actions. Descriptions are closely bound up with the idiosyncratic particulars of settings ... The point, then, is that although the details of what is talked about may be endlessly varied, the sorts of procedures for constructing and managing description may be much more regular, and therefore tractable in analysis.
>
> (Potter 1996: 111–12)

For those, like us, who are interested in analysing these regularities, it is the details of the procedures and the strategies on which we wish to focus. Here we take the UK Green and White Papers on lifelong learning (DfEE 1998 and 1999), although for a more persuasive argument about regularity we would have needed to have worked more broadly. The Green Paper is a consultative document, while the White Paper proposes legislation to Parliament. We have found that our focus needed to be narrow in the first instance to capture enough of the detail.

We work in part with the notions of offensive and defensive rhetoric outlined by Potter (1996). Rhetoric can be taken to work offensively to reify and defensively to ironize positions.

Reifying means to turn something abstract into a material thing ... These are accounts which are producing something as an object, be it an event, a thought or a set of circumstances. In contrast, we will refer to discourse which is undermining versions as *ironizing*.

(Potter 1996: 107, emphasis in original)

Reifying is a strategy to put something beyond question, to naturalize or ontologically gerrymander it. Ironizing attempts to undermine an alternative position, by, for instance, positioning it as spin. These are useful notions as they emphasize the struggle that goes on within policy discourses, the struggle to produce descriptions that can be taken as literal, and the way in which they work defensively to counter alternative possibilities. Policy 'facts' are represented as facts to do specific work, and representing such facts is itself action. Discourses of lifelong learning represent and in so doing are action orientated.

While we consider studies that point to a lack of substance in lifelong learning policy as important, we feel that they devalue and misunderstand the role and purpose of rhetoric. Implicit in many such studies are forms of ideology critique, which construe certain representations in texts as mystifications of the material world by those who exercise power. Here the notion of rhetoric is collapsed into ideology, and a transparent view of reality, clear of rhetorical traces, is posited as possible. By contrast, our argument is that the study of lifelong learning precisely as rhetoric can illuminate our understanding in slightly different ways – ways which point to the very real and powerful practices that are in play, and the significance of the work we are doing. The question is not so much about whether reality matches rhetoric or not, but which rhetorical performance is more persuasive and why. Here presentation and representation are taken to be substantial actions in their own right.

A rhetoric of lifelong learning

'*We are* in a *new* age – the age of information and global competition ... *we have no choice* but to prepare for this *new* age' (DfEE 1998: 9, emphasis added). The context for the emergence of the policy papers on lifelong learning in the UK (DfEE 1998 and 1999) was the election of the New Labour government in May 1997 following a landslide victory that brought an end to 18 years of Conservative rule. The new government was committed to a project of modernization in all aspects of economic, social and political life. 'Newness' was to the fore, including in the name of the party taking power. The government was to be unencumbered by the Labour Party's historical roots in the labour movement and previous commitments to nationalization and the welfare state in their established forms. Third Way thinking, between state and market, was to the fore. 'Thinking the unthinkable' and 'joined-up government' became important rhetorical acts, reflecting the need to modernize the state as well as other institutions, to ensure departmental disputes did not get in the way of the delivery of policy goals. The agenda was embodied in the Prime Minister, Tony Blair, himself representing a new generation of politicians, unencumbered by previous experience of government.

This was also the period of the run up to the end of the century, during which there were numerous attempts to characterize not only the last century but also the last millennium, and to look forward to the next. Attempts to characterize changes in society and economy have been many and varied. The knowledge society, the information age, post-industrial society, the learning society, globalization and postmodernity, among others, have all vied with each other, each attempting to create a wave upon which to surf into the new century and participate in the then Californian dream of Silicon Valley. In many discourses, such characterizations have become personifications, as we ourselves have done in the previous sentence. The UK government, attempting to locate itself in the radical dimension of change associated with the growth of the Internet and new technologies, adopted the notion of the information age and knowledge society and linked this to the millennium in terms of an urgent need to prepare for the next century. Central to that preparation was education and training and lifelong learning. The information age and knowledge society are thereby reified as the conditions and exigence that make lifelong learning necessary and possible.

A whole raft of education policy and initiatives have therefore emerged in the years of the Labour government, including those to engender 'a renaissance for a new Britain', the subtitle of *The Learning Age* (DfEE 1998). Newness therefore became a key signifier of the modernizing aspirations of the Labour government, matching the newness of Labour as a political party itself. In a sense, the discourse of *The Learning Age* seeks to promote the very thing that is said to be lacking in British society, a culture of lifelong learning. The new age of lifelong learning therefore seems to be conducive to a type of new age discourse, wherein the harnessing of emotions, attitudes and values is emphasized over the requirement for rigorous argument, evidence and debate. A culturalist set of assertions on the desirability and necessity for lifelong learning is posited both as the way forward and in a way which is consistent with this aim, a position inscribed in the notion of a *renaissance* for a *new* Britain. Renewal rather than reform provides a critical impetus for lifelong learning. This echoes the Renaissance of arts and letters and growth of humanism in parts of Europe between the fourteenth and sixteenth century. The notions of renaissance can be said to perform in a number of ways within the text. The location of the Renaissance in continental Europe points to and codes the European credentials of the policy at a time when policy towards the European Union was fraught by division in the UK, when government wanted to be 'good Europeans', but not to be seen to be 'too good'. The Renaissance was also a rebirth of arts and letters, a challenge through culture to the absolutism of monarchy and the orthodoxies of mediaeval church. It therefore points to the importance of culture to lifelong learning, itself indicated in the desire to promote a culture of lifelong learning. Such resonances draw upon a deliberative genre to engender and mobilize an audience who may wish to participate in the processes of renewal. It sets the tone for the policy rhetoric.

The exigence in the policy texts of lifelong learning is clearly identified in the consultative Green Paper – 'learning *is* the key to prosperity … investment in human capital *will* be the foundation of success in the knowledge-based global economy of the twenty-first century' (DfEE 1998: 7, emphasis added). 'Familiar certainties and old ways of doing things *are* disappearing' (DfEE 1998: 9, emphasis added). Thus, 'to continue to compete, we *must* equip ourselves to cope with the enormous economic and social change we face, to make sense of the rapid transformation of the world, and to encourage imagination and innovation' (DfEE 1998: 10, emphasis added). The imperative is established, the need to continue to compete. The implied threat and urgency here is that failure to 'equip ourselves' will result in a lack of competitiveness that in turn will undermine 'our' capacity to cope with and make sense of change. This is the type of crisis narrative so important to policy discourses that we mentioned earlier. The exigence is beyond the realms of interpretation and choice. It is a factual description and the only certainty is the need to change. The ethos and logos of the text is built up through its use of the definite article and the imperative that arises from an acceptance of the exigence as persuasive.

In Potter's terms (1996: 108, emphasis in original), *The Learning Age* offers a description oriented to action:

> On the one hand, a description will be oriented to action. That is, it will be used to accomplish an action, and it can be analysed to see how it is constructed so as to accomplish that action. On the other, a description will build its own status as a factual version. For the most part, the concern is to produce descriptions which will be treated as *mere* descriptions, reports which *tell it how it is*.

The exigence of the policy is reifying as it asserts the fact of competition as the logos for the imperative to act. If we take the description literally, an act is performed by the text, and at the same time a requirement for our own action as readers is also implicit. This reification is achieved through the forms of representation within a hierarchy of modalization (Latour and Wolgar 1979). For instance, 'we *must* equip' is used rather than 'the authors of this text think we must' or 'I feel we should'. Descriptions can be located at various levels on a hierarchy depending upon whether they are treated as unproblematic or provisional in some way. Generally the less provisional and more separated out from the speaker, the more solid the description. The elision of the speaker and the lack of provisionality in the assertion of 'must', work to try and make the description secure and to persuade the readership of the correctness of both the description and the action identified.

As we previously discussed in Chapter 4, reification is also achieved through narrative organization and nominalization. The point at which a description starts is important to its rhetorical strategy in this as in all settings. Narrative organization depends upon the ordering of events and who takes part. It is in part through the narrative structuring of the text that particular meanings are made possible. In *The Learning Age*, by beginning with the new age of information, global competition and economic and social change as the description of the world, the narrative is structured to act in various ways. By asserting particular forms of competition and change as the starting point within a narrative structure, a whole prior debate about the reality of this representation of the world can be circumscribed. Some, including ourselves, would want to contest this view, and suggest that it is as much an outcome of policy as the context for policy. Beginning the narrative with certain props already on the stage avoids having to more obviously bring them on later and this attempts to take our attention away from them as props. It is an ironizing strategy as it undermines the potential for alternative descriptions. At the same time, there is another rhetorical strategy in use here. The props are brought on as real objects rather than as things that are being done by actors. Fairclough (2000b: 27) points to the significance of this kind of nominalization, where words are used as nouns instead of verbs.

> Instead of representing economic processes as people applying means to materials to produce things, the actual processes and people and things involved are backgrounded, and we have instead 'the economy' as an entity. The phrase 'the new global economy' presupposes that there is a new global economy – that is, it takes it for granted, as something we all know.

Global competition, the age of information and change are commonly represented as nominalizations within policy discourses. What this does is to set up a range of objects that appear to exist external to our action. At the same time it allows the writer to avoid the attribution of the activity to any particular population or group.

This description involves a strategy of gerrymandering a division between that which is taken as real and that which is socially fabricated within the description. An ontological problem is obvious when we consider the consequences of the action that is implicit within the imperative of 'the continuous education and development of the human mind and imagination' (DfEE 1998: Introduction, Section 1). The activities that are proposed as the response to the age of information and global competition produce that which they are positioned as assuming. The actions by individuals and institutions fashion the very future developments that have been described as already occurring, rather than simply being a response to them. Of course, we know that this kind of accusation of ontological gerrymandering is valid, as it is identified as a quite general problem of descriptions elsewhere. However, particular gerrymanderings work in part because they are so all-pervasive and are positioned and accepted within policy and other discourses as unproblematic. They are felicitous. The description is not surprising for us as readers. It is familiar. It resonates with descriptions of change and globalization that are found (and accepted) elsewhere, and not only within policy discourses. They are uptakes. Indeed, to put this another way, it would perhaps be quite strange if policy descriptions of the world differed greatly from each other. We expect continuity because plausible accounts are commonly understood to be produced by putting facts, which correspond with reality, within a coherent narrative structure.

We have looked at various reifying strategies that are used to work up the facticity of lifelong learning as a way into the rhetorical analysis of policy discourses. We have argued that policy texts commonly draw upon these kinds of activities. Our analysis does not, however, need to stop here. Reification is effected by presenting authoritative individuals and groups as in agreement with the description, or positioning them as supporting a description in general terms. Gilbert and Mulkay (1984) argued that empirical discourses draw upon specific linguistic and rhetorical features, which form a more or less systematic accounting system. These cluster around themes of grammatical impersonality, data primacy and rules of procedure. Potter (1996) explores the possibility that this empiricist repertoire, or elements of it, are drawn upon outside scientific situations, including in policy discourses. What we want to do here is to explore the notion that policy discourse may display elements of a linguistic and rhetorical repertoire that are to some extent common within particular policy contexts. Thus, the combination of particular nominalizations and the structuring and gerrymandering of the narrative of lifelong learning found within *The Learning Age* may be common to a broader policy repertoire. In a way perhaps similar to the primacy of data within empiricist discourse, particular nominalizations may become primary with regard to policy discourse.

We will develop this notion later on. For the moment we want to go on to explore the forms of corroboration or warranting that are used within this policy document. Empiricist discourse uses citations and references as a warranting strategy, but other forms of discourse – for example, a journalist's descriptions of events – do so less formally: for example, in the form of 'unnamed government officials'. Within a policy consultation paper such as *The Learning Age* (DfEE 1998), corroboration activities occur both in the form of consultation adopted and through various strategies deployed within the text itself. The document thus works both externally and internally to distance its own writers as agents and confirm that others are in agreement with it. However, as we will show, there is also work that it does in support of the following legislative White Paper (DfEE 1999). This illustrates a form of rhetorical work effected through formal policy documents in providing support for each other and policy discourses more generally.

Let us first scrutinize the work of *The Learning Age* as a policy consultation document and its role in relation to the subsequent White Paper. In both guises it has a specific rhetorical action. Consultation papers are requested by government ministers in order that policy proposals may be forthcoming at a later date. Policy proposals need to be greeted with minimized opposition when they are announced and consultation processes operate in advance to help achieve this. Green Papers build up 'footing' for the White Paper and, because the latter is an outcome of a consultation process, help to undermine the potential subsequent reading that the government might have a 'stake' in what is decided – usually not very success-fully. Readers commonly interpret government decisions in terms of stake and interest, and a prior paper and consultation process is a strategy to help avoid this. This is a strategy of stake management, which is, again, common within all forms of communication, because:

> ... people *treat one another in this way*. They treat reports and descriptions *as if* they come from groups and individuals with interests, desires, ambitions and stake in some versions of what the world is like. Interests are a participant's concern, and that is how they can enter analysis. Management of stake is one of the central features in the production of factual discourse.
>
> (Potter 1996: 110–11, emphasis in original)

The consultation process helps to displace this kind of treatment. However, the consultation text itself draws upon further rhetorical strategies to help manage issues of interest or stake. The situation for a minister is tricky. In setting up a consultation process, the signal to the public is one of ensuing decision-making and action. This may be unsettling for those who might be affected. At the same time, it may afford dangerous potential for discourses to get out of control. A consultation process could potentially produce suggestions that sit quite outside what is politically acceptable or rhetorically felicitous. The danger is that there may be formulations of discourse that give rise to alternative possibilities. A consultation process is not just a situation for previous discourse to be reiterated, but has potential to be one for the formation of a new verbal act or primary text.

Given the rhetorical importance of the possible affinity between writer/speaker and audience, it is important to note the implied identity between authors and audience in the use of 'we' within both the lifelong learning policy texts. In work on European Union policy discourses on unemployment, Straehle *et al.* (1999: 90, emphasis in original) have noted similar rhetorical strategies:

> By giving the impression that the problem of unemployment affects not only those individuals who are unemployed, but *us*, the *European citizens*, and *Europe* as well, the speakers demonstrate that *we* – politicians, bureaucrats and ('ordinary') citizens – are all in the same boat ... citizens consequently look like active participants in EU politics and, conversely, politicians and bureaucrats turn out to be, first and foremost, ordinary citizens.

They also point to the way in which the use of we 'helps to shift responsibility away from the individual; the individual politician "disappears" in the collective and no longer bears direct responsibility' (Straehle *et al.* 1999: 90). Parallels can be drawn with the policy texts on lifelong learning. Readers do not know who the authors are, apart from the Preface of the White Paper by the then Secretary of State for Education and Employment, David Blunkett. Even here we might question whether he wrote the text or merely added his name to a text written by someone else. The use of 'we' in both cases positions the government as not imposing policy, as it is as subject to the competitive imperative as everyone else. However, one can also disidentify with the 'we' and position the crisis narrative in this text as saying something about the current state of government and the need for policy makers to equip themselves to cope and make sense of change in a context where the state is no longer positioned as capable of governing in quite the same ways (Field 2000). The exigence elides these possibilities and the unequal positions that we may hold in relation to the requirement to 'continue to compete' and that some may not wish to compete.

Reification of the imperative to learn is supported within *The Learning Age* through the presentation of evidence of national weaknesses in performance with regard to learning within a section called, 'The scale of the challenge'. However, rather than the argument being that global competition provides a logos for learning, the implication here is that because of weakness in learning, or more specifically attainment as measured by the proxy variable of qualification, we need to improve so as to globally compete. Evidence is provided through a forensic analysis of the strengths and weaknesses when compared to other nations:

> The country's current learning 'scoreboard' shows strengths, but also some serious weaknesses. A great strength is our universities which educate to degree and postgraduate level and set world-class standards. The UK is second only to the USA in the number of major scientific prizes awarded in the last five years. The proportion of graduates in the working population has almost doubled over a decade. Our research excellence is valued by many companies which choose to base their research capacity in the UK. A further strength is the existing commitment among many people to gaining qualifications. Fourteen million people have National Vocational Qualification (NVQ) level 2 (equivalent to five or more higher grade GCSEs) ... Our weakness lies in our performance in basic and intermediate skills. Almost 30 per cent of young people fail to reach NVQ level 2 by the age of 19. Seven million adults have no formal qualifications at all; 21 million adults have not reached level 3 (equivalent to two A levels), and more than one in five of all adults have poor literacy and numeracy skills ... we lag behind France, Germany, the USA and Singapore in the proportion of our workforce qualified to level 3. In the case of graduates, even though we have a high number, we need to encourage more of our highly qualified people to update their skills through continuing professional development.
>
> (DfEE 1998: paragraphs 21 and 22)

These national scores ostensibly offer empirical evidence to support the logos for change. They are national measurements that pit the UK against other nations in a competition over specific forms of learning achievement. In so doing, the text fabricates and orders both competition and particular geographical and political divisions. It turns our attention towards particular domains of activity, through which we may recode these divisions. It is not a global inscription, as it ignores significant parts of the world, but positions 'us' in relation to those nations that we might view as 'our' competitors. There is an implicit spatial strategy in play in such policy discourses:

> ... this representational practice is so familiar it seems natural (i.e., not a practice), but this representation of bounded areas partakes of a venerable rhetorical gesture; the map is a spatial trope which, far from simply representing (natural) boundaries, is an aggressive practice, delivering up the discursive territory within which legitimate speak about bounded areas can occur.
>
> (Shapiro, quoted in Potter 1996: 218)

By describing the world in such a way that evidence of the UK's lack in learning is clear, the activities of we, the reader, become required in amelioration of these deficits. We become mobilized in this international competition. National and international competitiveness are

> ... recoded, at least in part, in terms of the psychological, dispositional and aspirational capacities of those that make up the labour force ... Personal employment and macro-economic health is to be ensured by encouraging individuals to 'capitalize' themselves, to invest in the management, presentation, promotion and enhancement of their own economic capital as a capacity of their selves and as a lifelong project.
>
> (Rose 1999: 162)

Thus, lifelong learning is positioned to harness the desires and values of those working in the terrain; it attempts to seduce. In addition to the need to adapt for economic reasons, *The Learning Age* also points to the wider role of lifelong learning. It helps 'make *ours* a civilized society, develops the spiritual side of *our* lives and promotes active citizenship ... That *is* why *we* value learning for its own sake as well as for the equality of opportunity it brings' (DfEE 1998: 7, emphasis added). It also, as we have seen, contributes to the development of 'the human mind and imagination'. This is both inspirational and aspirational, appealing to the values and emotions of many practitioners within the arena. There is the attempt to develop a sense of affinity between author and audience through the text, part of which rests on an appeal to the emotions of the readership through a certain pathos. How many educators working in the post-school sector, or a more general audience, would not support lifelong learning when it is positioned as having so many beneficial and inspiring outcomes?

Following consultation, although later than expected, the legislative White Paper (DfEE 1999) was published the following year. It begins with the Preface by the then Secretary of State for Education and Employment, David Blunkett.

The opening sentence refers back to the earlier paper: 'In the Green Paper *The Learning Age we* set out our vision of how lifelong learning *could* enable everyone to fulfil their potential and cope with the challenge of rapid economic and social change' (DfEE 1999: 3, emphasis added). Here the policy text repeats the nominalizations that were the narrative start of the consultation text. In so doing it gerrymanders the same division between that which exists – that is, rapid economic and social change – and learning throughout life as our response to that reality. However, it differs as it builds up its own footing upon *The Learning Age* and consultation that has gone directly before. The description, through repetition, is rhetorically presented as quite literally the case, with no sense of the agency that engenders particular forms of change and the implied possibility of alternatives. We do not know what happened in the consultation process, apart from what we are told of the process. However, we can be sure that aspects of the description within *The Learning Age* that promoted particular opposition are likely to have been modified within this subsequent one. This points to a rhetorical function of consultation, where strategies that are less than persuasive can be identified and modified. In terms of this function, it would be possible to consider the differences between the two texts and what these may signify, but that is not our intention here.

The Preface once again seeks to align the audience's sentiments with the text through an appeal to the wider role lifelong learning can play.

> Lifelong learning *can* enable people to play a full part in developing *their* talent, the potential of their family, and the capacity of the community in which *they* live and work. It *can* and *must* nurture a love for learning. This *will* ensure the means by which *our* economy *can* make a successful transition from the industries and services of the past, to the knowledge and information economy of the future. It also contributes to sustaining a civilized and cohesive society, in which people develop as active citizens and in which generational disadvantage *can* be overcome.
>
> (DfEE 1999: 3, emphasis added)

Lifelong learning is deployed to rhetorically translate and appeal to a range of different audiences, some of whom may feel themselves to have been misled – a failure of logos – or let down – a failure of pathos – once they move from the Preface to the rest of the policy document with its emphasis on human capital development. However, this precisely points to the importance of the rhetoric. Important here once again is the use of the conditional and definite articles. However, there is more conditionality in the Preface to the White Paper than in *The Learning Age*. The only definite here is that lifelong learning 'will ensure' the economic transition to the future, as though other factors are less significant. Rhetorically the claims are lesser, even as the White Paper positions itself as a bold response to the audience for the consultation text.

> ... the vision of *The Learning Age* has been welcomed. But many of those who commented recommended a bold programme of change in national and local arrangements. They confirmed our view that current arrangements provided an insufficient focus on quality, failed to give men and women the support they need, and were too provider driven. Above all, there was an acknowledgement of the inconsistency and contradictions in present funding and delivery mechanisms. There was, therefore, widespread support for fundamental change ...
>
> (DfEE 1999: 3)

The two policy texts use the exigence of the changes existing out there to build up a context to which we must respond. There is the attempt to build a consensus that such a response is necessary. It seeks to position this as the logos for lifelong learning. Thus, the first chapter of the White Paper, entitled 'A vision for the new millennium', begins with '*The challenge*', the use of these terms already positioning the reader as needing to engage fully and imaginatively with that which they face. Yet this challenge is primarily economic.

> The challenge *we* face to equip individuals, employers and the country to meet the demands of the 21st century *is* immense and immediate. In the information and knowledge based economy, investment in human capital – in the intellect and creativity of people – *is* replacing past patterns of investment in plant, machinery and physical labour.
>
> (DfEE 1999: 12, emphasis added)

In this situation:

> Standing still *is* not an option. The world has changed and the current systems and structures *are* real obstacles to success. *Our* aims can only be achieved through new arrangements at national and local level which build on the strengths, and eliminate the weaknesses, of the present arrangements.
>
> (DfEE 1999: 15, emphasis added)

This represents a deliberative genre of persuasion, future-orientated and often speculative. Having been presented powerfully in this way at the beginning of this document, lifelong learning is then the premise upon which the document as a whole can unfold naturally. However, as with the 'we' in *The Learning Age*, there is a similar ambiguity in the 'we' and 'our' in the White Paper. It seeks to build up affinity between the authors and audience, to position the vision as shared. This is enhanced by reference to the range of responses to the consultation the government had received, thereby building its authority to speak not only as a government policy document, but also as a document belonging to those groups who have participated in the policy-making process. However, it also suggests a certain authoritarianism in its style, presenting to others the government's view of what the vision should be. There is a certain dissonance between the use of 'our' for the vision and the positioning of 'everyone' as 'their'. Who are the subjects of this vision and who are subject to it? Similarly, who is the 'we' that faces the 'immense and immediate challenge'? One senses a certain unease and insecurity underneath the authoritarian edge to the policy rhetoric. There would appear, therefore, to be rhetorical tensions between ethos and audience in the use of 'we' and 'our' in these texts.

Lifelong learning is positioned as a reasoned response to the processes of change. Yet this in itself is an exigence, because of the weaknesses of provision identified in the UK through a forensic genre of rhetoric. Here, as we have suggested, the use of comparison is crucial, drawing attention to the lack of productivity and qualifications in relation to key economic competitors, attempting to align individual and national self-interest and legitimize the need for particular changes. Thus, certain weaknesses in provision are outlined to which the policies laid out are a necessary response. The weaknesses are quite different from those presented within *The Learning Age*:

- low rates of learning and staying on rates after 16;
- a cycle of deprivation and disadvantage – people without skills and qualifications tend not to be able to access opportunities and become excluded;
- particular groups face specific difficulties – people with disabilities and adults with basic skills problems;
- skills shortages and recruitment difficulties;
- limited guidance support – particularly significant given the increasing range and complexity of provision;
- lack of flexibility in provision.

These provide the more specific logos for legislative proposals, although the causes of these weaknesses are not examined. It may be significant that the description of comparative measures of learning, which set the UK against other nations within the Green Paper, do not figure here. They are now taken as read. It is also possible that they provided focus for alternative descriptions within the consultation process and thus weakened that which was presented. We will not address these specific weaknesses here, or whether they are weaknesses at all. To do so would involve more than can be contained in a single chapter and our intention here is merely to illustrate the fruitfulness of a rhetorical approach to the analysis of lifelong learning policy in particular and education policy in general.

For us, the very rhetoric through which lifelong learning is fabricated points to the importance of rhetorical analysis to an understanding of the processes and practices in play. There is almost the sense of the revivalist meeting in some parts of the two policy papers we have examined – salvation through lifelong learning – an appeal to values and emotions. And, as we have pointed out, a certain set of imperatives – 'can', 'will', 'must'. Field (2000: 250) refers to this as part of the government's 'active attempts to mobilize civil society – including education and training providers'. This mirrors the rhetorical attempts to mobilize and motivate workers in the discourses of the learning organization and knowledge management. To question lifelong learning would appear to involve questioning that to which it can contribute at the economic, social and personal levels. Yet, we, like others (for example, Coffield 2002; Keep and Rainbird 2002), would question the logos of those claims, as the evidence for some of them looks at best sketchy. However, this appeal is to reason more than values – the rhetoric of the academy rather than that of politics – whereas pathos more than logos may be more important for policy, despite or maybe because of the calls for more evidence-informed policy. Thus, it may only be in understanding the invention of policy and the other aspects of rhetoric that we may be able to more fully engage in the rhetorical struggles in and around lifelong learning.

Policy as persuasion?

'Political differences have always been constituted as differences in language, political struggles have always been partly struggles over the dominant language, and both the theory and practice of political rhetoric go back to ancient times' (Fairclough 2000b: 3). However, while it is common to say that the policy rhetoric in general and that of lifelong learning in particular is grandiose, the reality is far more complex and messy. Such arguments tend to assume that the goals of policy are achievable, something to be striven for and delivered. Here there is often an implicit suggestion that if only the government got it right and put in more re-sources, a learning society would be both possible and achievable. Lifelong learning could play a role in achieving all those goals of personal fulfilment, social inclusion and economic competitiveness that are to be found in policy rhetoric.

We have not adopted that approach here. Instead we have sought to argue that there is a need to explore the work the rhetoric does more seriously. Where policies present particular descriptions of the world as literal, analysts, such as ourselves, are strongly positioned to do work to support, critique or undermine the facticity of these descriptions. We have only a limited number of approaches that operate persuasively for this, and all have their particular productivities and constraints. What they have in common is, however, the question of truth. What a rhetorical analysis makes possible is a different kind of approach. It refuses to focus on whether or not descriptions of the world are or are not factual or possible. By contrast, it examines how rhetorical strategies are deployed in order to make descriptions felicitous, and the work that these do in the translating of interests and mobilization of audiences. This idea is of course not new, despite the academic pull to claim newness to our position. We have known for a long time that different narratives of the world operate powerfully at particular times and that the analytic resources that we deploy, both to contribute to and to engage with these, are finite and limited. What a rhetorical analysis appears to offer is the possibility of a fine grain analysis of some aspects of what is going on. Lifelong learning is a policy discourse that is mobilized in part as part of governing at a distance (Edwards

2002). This is performed in part through the stabilization of a particular narrative of the world, which we can either find acceptable or against which we may argue, engaging in reifying and ironizing of our own. In either case, we all end up working up its facticity through our constant repetition and commentary. Thus, even as we contribute to the analysis of lifelong learning policy, commenting upon it, we help to fabricate its facticity and ontological position. In this sense, we are as much involved in the spin of policy as those politicians and policy makers who are positioned as the darker forces of the art. And let us not ignore the media in these practices too. To argue that lifelong learning policy is spin is to undermine the status of the policy makers involved in promoting it and to reinforce the truth/falsehood binary that keeps us focused on our search for better truths. It masks our own work as sultans of spin. While this may be productive in some ways, it takes attention from its/our rhetorical work and the productivity of forms of analysis that identify how particular truths become worked up and act, and the possibilities for alternatives.

Spindoctoring is usually dismissed as an attempt to manipulate opinion and put its work in the best light. This assumes that politics is a reasonable business, working on the basis of logos. It underestimates the power of what is at play, as for us, spindoctoring is one of the rhetorical practices in which governments legitimately engage in the attempt to persuade and influence. While the increasing mediation of politics might have resulted in this becoming a more significant aspect of policy processes, dismissing it is to undervalue the power of rhetoric in policy practices, in particular the workings of pathos. Rhetorically, we would suggest that lifelong learning is – and note our own use of the collective and the definitive – an attempt to harness us to a 'movement' that might appeal to some of us affectively and in relation to our value systems, but for which the evidence or logos is less than clear. In terms of our argument in Chapter 6, lifelong learning names a ceremonial place. Its logos emerges from the description of the new age as one of information and global competition, but it is a description that is reinforced through the reification of lifelong learning. We are positioned by this rhetoric and position ourselves in relation to it. The rhetoric is therefore very real and very powerful and should not be dismissed as merely spindoctoring, although we recognize this as precisely a powerful rhetorical strategy through which to throw doubt on the substance of policy and the practices of politics.

This chapter has been intended as a contribution to debates that suggest that there can be productive engagements with rhetoric among those concerned with educational policy. It points to some of the ways of engaging in policy analysis drawing upon the traditions associated with rhetorical analysis. We have suggested that there is fruitfulness in examining the acts of persuasion and influence in policy texts. Such analysis can of course be extended far wider than we have done here. How persuasive our own acts of persuasion are remains to be seen. There is a certain logos in our invention, but whether it has the pathos or ethos to persuade we will leave to you to decide and to engage with offensively-defensively. Whether we have been sufficiently forensic to persuade remains to be seen. Our own rhetoric, however, has allowed us to focus on particular aspects of the work of policy. By refusing to enter into debate over the truth or otherwise of lifelong learning, we have been able to consider how this truth is fabricated and what it does rhetorically. We now move on to explore more fully the issue to which we have alluded already, the theme of globalization in contemporary educational policy discourse.

Chapter 9

The migrating and forging of policy

Descriptions of the problems of the world and solutions to them are features of all policy texts. They are the work of policy and the governments that produce them. To make policy is also to rhetorically position the government as 'in the know' about such problems and as able to identify how we should best act. This is a position of authority and reason. Looking across policy texts from around the world, it appears that descriptions within policy discourse are relatively stable; they emerge again and again in quite similar formulations. Policy discourses are increasingly globalized through the influence of international groups and agencies. For example, in the 1980s the micro-economic version of human capital theory put forward through the Organization for Economic Co-operation and Development (OECD) is seen to have informed many OECD countries around that time (Taylor *et al.* 1997). There is an increasing congruence of policy narratives on educational issues within a network of international organizations. While this could be taken as evidence of the reality of such descriptions, we can also explore this phenomenon rhetorically. It may indicate a rhetorical inter-dependence of policy discourses. For example, unless governments' descriptions of the world are relatively similar, then we would be less able to believe in them. A multiplicity of different descriptions across the policy texts of nations may thus be rhetorically ineffective. Common within current policy texts is the narrative of the increasing pace, complexity and undecidability of global change and the danger that we may not be able to successfully compete within global economic markets if we are not able to respond effectively. This is a narrative formulation that may be rhetorically necessary and highly effective. It may be that there are only a limited number of such formulations that would work within a nation at any one time and that these may be more effective if shared by others. Globalization frames an object external to nations that is a threat to them; it positions nations together in a common effort to succeed. Competition positions nations in a relation of threat with regard to each other. Both of these are rhetorically effective in constituting exigence.

They then legitimately focus policy attention on the details of globalization and responses to them, and the relative national success in terms of competition. These are aspects of the world that it is more or less possible to measure and to which we can direct action more readily. It may then be that this rhetorical similarity and positioning across governments is highly advantageous in terms of their ability to persuade us of their authority and knowledge. It also permits particular forms of contestation through metonymy. Yeatman (1994) indicates the productivity of metonymy in the politicization of metaphors that are mobilized as part of governing. This possibility leads us to consider what metonymical relations these permit, how these are pursued, and with what effect. Perhaps also one might explore the possibilities of alternative narratives of exigence. What might it be possible to conceive apart from narratives that are dependant upon globalization, competition, danger, fear and uncertainty?

We have explored the significance of a rhetorical analysis for the study of educational policy in the last chapter. In this chapter, we explore in greater depth two aspects of policy discourse, therefore. These are the notions of globalization – note the nominalization, a noun rather than a verb – and flexibility. Globalization, in particular economic globalization, is part of the way in which change is characterized in order to generate the need for action. Globalization can itself be taken as literal, over which there is much debate (for example, Hirst and Thompson 1996), or as one of the stories that mediates problem setting in the policy domain. Some time ago, Schon (1979: 255) pointed to the significance of such stories:

> When we examine the problem-setting stories told by the analysts and practitioners of social policy, it becomes apparent that the framing of problems often depends upon metaphors underlying the stories which generate problem setting and set the directions of problem solving. One of the most pervasive stories about social services, for example, diagnoses the problem as 'fragmentation' and prescribes 'coordination' as the remedy. But services seen as fragmented might be seen, alternatively, as autonomous … Under the spell of metaphor, it appears obvious that fragmentation is bad and coordination, good.

Schon obviously feels a discomfort over the spell of metaphor, even while pointing to its significance, an ambivalence we ourselves recognize in our own work. What is significant for us here are the ways in which stories of change in educational policy are framed by globalization, to which certain directions of change are a response, in particular the requirement to produce greater flexibility in the labour market, in organizations and in individuals. Here 'using metaphor to manage meaning is an expression of power through which reality is defined for others' (Straehle et al. 1999: 68).

Here we need to pause briefly to point to the multiple meanings that can be invested in the notion of *framing*. All policy and research discourses make assumptions and these help to frame a particular piece of communication. Framing puts some things in the picture while excluding others. But to frame someone is to set them up in some way, to make them appear to do something for which they were not responsible. This form of framing is to do something that appears underhand. This ambiguity of meaning is something to which we have already pointed in our prior use of the notion of *fabricating*. Two of us (Edwards *et al.* 1999) have previously also discussed the cross-national migrations of policy ideas as *forgings*, never complete, and the copies of policies in different contexts, never entirely the same. Each of these ideas points to the actions that make things happen in policy, the judgements and decisions that are enacted and the ways in which we cannot take for granted the meanings that are represented through such policy discourses.

In addition to globalization, flexibility is a key metaphor in governing contemporary change process. Trends towards greater flexibility are to be found in reforms of education and training around the globe (R. Edwards 1997). They are part of a wider profile of changes to workplaces and labour relations within which greater flexibility is pursued. They are developed in part through the public policies of national governments and international organizations. They are to be seen in economic policies that have resulted in the deregulation of financial and labour markets, thereby contributing to the globalizing processes to which they are positioned as a response in much policy discourse (Scott 1997). They are also to be seen in policies that seek to tie education and training more closely to the fabricated needs of an economy subject to global competition. The rhetoric of flexibility is forged in policy and in the migration of ideas of flexibility into different contexts. Reflexively, therefore, in this chapter we are deploying the metaphors of migration and forging through which to explore policy movements, to frame and fabricate our own stories of policy.

What we seek to do in this chapter is twofold. First, we wish to explore the exigence of globalization, which has profound effects in both justifying greater flexibility through policy and in promoting the forging of similar policies around the globe. The rhetoric of globalization is significant in both providing a rationale for educational reform or renewal, but also in promoting the spread of similar educational policies around the globe. We identify flexibility as part of a global and globalizing policy rhetoric. Here flexibility is largely positioned as a necessary response by individuals and organizations to globalizing processes, in particular the competitive demands of economic globalization. Globalization provides the rationale for policies that seek to promote and develop flexibility in different contexts around the world. In this sense, globalization is the most *moving* – if not always the most appealing – of metaphors, promoting the migration of policies, which themselves are meant to be a response to globalization. Globalization might be said to be a storyline that attempts to portray a certain imagery, to mobilize an extended form of interconnectedness as a norm for economic, political and cultural life. In turn, as it migrates, flexibility becomes a global theme of policy discourse. This we will attempt to illustrate in the second section of this chapter. Although given less attention than notions such as lifelong learning and a learning society, we would suggest that flexibility, with its valuing of change and adaptability, is a more important metaphorical resource in current policies, linked as it often is to other policy themes, such as marketization, choice and access.

In addition, we wish to offer some further thoughts on the role that metaphors have in the representation of reality and the readings to which they are subject. We illustrate this through a reading of flexibility within a social Darwinian metaphorical complex. This is in part to illustrate the ways in which memory engenders a shared understanding between authors/speakers and audience. However, we also wish to say something more concrete regarding the possibilities for rhetorical strategies that not only encounter policy, but might also counter it as well. Here we illustrate the significance of our use of (en)counter, pointing to a range of possibilities through which to engage with the rhetoric of educational policy.

Given the centrality of the metaphor of migration to our argument, we have attempted to give an account in this chapter which fabricates reflexively the journey we have made in developing our ideas. In other words, as with this text as a whole, we have chosen a particular way to rhetorically stage the discussion. We could have chosen to represent our research in a more ordered and conventional way, starting with the more abstract discussion of metaphor and applying it to particular policy texts. This would signify the pull of method in providing a footing through which to warrant what we do. However, this would have replicated earlier discussion in part and therefore could have become somewhat tedious. Further, our journey has been and continues to be more circuitous – migrations of exploration rather than more methodological movements from one pre-determined place to another.

Metaphors of migration

> Thrown into the vast open sea with no navigation charts and the marker buoys sunk and barely visible, we have only two choices left: we may rejoice in the breath-taking vistas of new discoveries – or we tremble out of fear of drowning. One option not really realistic is to claim sanctuary in a safe harbour; one could bet that what seems to be a tranquil haven today may soon be modernized, and a theme park, amusement promenade or crowded marina will replace the sedate boat sheds.
>
> (Bauman 1998: 85)

Bauman provides an arresting image of the unsettling impact of globalizing processes, which speaks to its rhetorical importance in positioning the world as changed and changing, with the consequent requirement that we need to change and adapt as well and deal with uncertainty. He also alludes to the modernizing agenda of the new that we discussed in the last chapter.

The discussion of globalization and educational policy has been developing steadily in recent years in response to the apparent increased harmonization of national policies around the world. Notions of 'policy convergence' and 'policy borrowing' have been developed to help understand and explain these processes. Both *Comparative Education* (1998) and the *Journal of Education Policy* (1999) have had special editions on globalization. There are a number of aspects to this emerging debate, not least, of course, the role of economic globalization in providing an exigence for educational reform and renewal. However, here we will focus on two interrelated aspects of this debate. First, the examination of the content of policies as they migrate around the globe. Second, the exploration of the processes of migration of contemporary ideas, of how similar policies are forged in different national contexts. In relation to both we want to suggest that globalization, although often positioned as the context from within which educational responses need to be developed, provides a rhetorical rationale for the very moving of policies from one context to another. Globalization as a policy thesis has therefore only become significant insofar as its proponents have been able to make it persuasive. For, apart from anything, globalization is not a new situation (Hirst and Thompson 1996). And, as we shall suggest, it is not a situation at all but a set of practices, despite the attempts to persuade otherwise.

In some ways, the discussion of globalization and educational policy has remained bounded by the assumptions and conventions of comparative education, insofar as there is a focus on the unifying effects and homogeneity of policy development around the globe. This draws significantly from notions of globalization as 'one-worldism', in which ideas of harmony and homogenization play out as both fantasies and fears. Here previously powerful notions of First, Second, Third and even Fourth Worlds are elided, as each is articulated, even if in very different ways, to the global economy, policy and culture. However, more interesting work has started to emerge which attempts to locate such policies within the wider understandings of globalization, wherein trends towards similar policies contain difference and diversity within them (Dale 1999; Marginson 1999b). Here globalization is both an exigence and motor for policy migrations, within which differing responses may be inscribed. Thus, even as certain policy goals and strategies have an increasingly global reach, their substance will be very different because of the particular locations in which they are forged. Policies are recontextualized and contested according to the membership resources upon which people call in their interpretations of texts and situations (Fairclough 1999; Wodak 2000). Here the one-worldism of globalization also contains diversity and difference and, indeed, globalization itself is subject to such interpretative processes.

The attempt to articulate these processes, therefore, itself results in the emergence of different concepts through which to bring forth for investigation the unfamiliar, metaphors such as *migration* and *forging* among them, of course. Each is attempting to evoke a felicitous understanding of the world. However, much of the analysis of globalization and education policy pursues a realist trajectory, attempting to define and provide evidence for and against one argument or another. Researchers therefore look for evidence of homogeneity or heterogeneity in policy to prove and disprove that there is a globalization of approaches to education.

Policy migrations can be seen in relation to all sectors of education and training, impacting upon institutional structures, curricula and pedagogic practices. As a condition for these impacts and a result of them, the cultures of education and training are being transformed in various ways and with various effects. For instance, Levin (1998) identifies a certain commonality of themes in the construction and substance of education policy. Although Levin is discussing policy in relation to schooling, the themes can be generalized to some extent to many aspects of education and training. First, he suggests the need for change to be cast largely in economic terms, the enhancement of human resources. Second, there is increasing criticism of education and training and their failure to deliver what is required. Third, changes in education and training are being required without a significant increase in resourcing from governments. Fourth, educational reform is promoted through changes in forms of governance. Fifth, education and training organizations are being required to work in more commercial and market-like ways. Sixth, there is an increased emphasis on standards, accountability and testing. These common themes increasingly have a global reach, they migrate.

Ball (1998) identifies the influences that are resulting in certain commonalities. These are: neo-liberal approaches to education; new institutional economics; performativity; public choice theory; and new managerialism. These policy approaches have migrated around the globe, the reasons for which rest in an acceptance of a closer integration of the global economy and certain positions on the effects and effectiveness of that process. The acceptance of this integration is literal, although we would suggest it is produced in part through the metaphorical work that stories of globalization do, which point towards a shared requirement to adopt certain policies in order to be successful in the emerging globalized economy.

The identification of these trends and influences as literal is important. Yet caution is also necessary. First, the spread of these trends is most readily identified in the English-speaking centres of economic power. Not all countries are in a position or seek to pursue the policies outlined. Other models of education and skill formation are in existence. Second, their identification as 'trends' is itself interesting for the work it does in suggesting certain starting points and trajectories as a norm. These may reflect those of certain nations, but cannot be generalized necessarily to include nations where, for instance, initial schooling is not available to all, or those wherein direct control of the curriculum has been tight historically. If one is located outside a trend, one cannot be trendy. Third, the possibilities for curriculum control and influence by bodies external to the providing institution may differ from sector to sector. For instance, universities may be more resistant to working with employers than technical and further education institutions. Thus, as we seek to examine the migration and forging of policy, we need to be cautious of the assumptions and effects inscribed in taking trends and influences as literal descriptions. Here we are pointing to the rhetorical role policy analysts also have within the workings of policy, as they stage their own arguments in certain ways rather than others.

This is not to deny the importance of examining policy migrations, but there are questions of what is identified, by whom and where, for the migrations will look different from within different locations. Nor will the migrations be singular or unidirectional, as the 1990s reviews of higher education in the United Kingdom (National Committee of Inquiry into Higher Education [NCIHE] 1997) and Australia (West 1998) illustrate. Both reports drew upon experience in the other country for their analyses and recommendations, each rhetorically building the authority of their own national policy statements by comparing and contrasting with the other, a strategy that both inscribes a territorial threat and provides a footing for the particular analysis put forward. The substance of the migration process is not universal, unidirectional, nor uniform, but nonetheless begins to mobilize a globalized and globalizing socio-rhetorical network of policy practices.

Ball (1998: 126) summarizes the practices of migration:

> ... national policy making is inevitably a process of bricolage: a matter of borrowing and copying bits and pieces of ideas from elsewhere, drawing upon and amending locally tried and tested approaches, cannibalizing theories, research, trends and fashions and not infrequently flailing around for anything at all that looks as though it might work.

'Bricolage', 'cannibalizing' and 'flailing' are interesting metaphors for policy analysis, all suggestive of untidy policy processes that do not walk in tune with the sweet reason of globalization, although globalizing processes may themselves be both an impetus for and an outcome of the forgings taking place. For Ball (1998: 127), as with Wodak (2000), generic policies are polyvalent, 'they are translated into particular interactive and sustainable practices in complex ways'. Part of that translation is, as we have argued, through the work of rhetoric. In addition, and as with policy within nation states, there can be various strands in tension and conflict with each other. They also change with the emergence of different economic, social and cultural circumstances. The key point, however, is that the location of policy forgings and the processes by which they are taken up as literal descriptions are as important as the migrations themselves.

We have said that much of the impetus for this migration of policy is the exigence of globalization, even as such migrations contribute to globalizing processes. Look at any recent major educational policy statement and you are likely to find some statement of the need to compete more effectively in the global economy. In order to succeed, nations, organizations and individuals will need to compete far more effectively and efficiently and this requires a labour force with greater levels of skills and/or qualification. The imperative and implied threat is there. Adapt to the new or fall by the wayside. And on (y)our own head be it. And so on. Globalization is therefore presented as a context, to which policy is a timely response.

Two things to which we have already alluded concern us. First, there is the nominalization of globalization, where it is presented as a condition or situation about which nothing can be done, rather than as an outcome of actions. It is ontologically gerrymandered and naturalized. As we indicated in the previous chapter, this is a particularly powerful rhetorical strategy, as it turns situations that are the outcomes of action, and therefore could be other than they are, into reified matters of fact or common sense. Rhetorical struggle over what is a taken-for-granted context and what is not is fundamental to politics and policy, including educational policies. What we are pointing to is that globalization, however we want to understand that term, is represented as beyond debate and discussion, despite, and possibly because of, the attempts of anti-globalization protesters to disrupt this idea. It is a context that has to be worked with and that is a fact. However, by contrast, we could shift the argument by seeking to examine global-izing practices. These would have to include those practices of policy as well as the economy and culture. Here we might end up agreeing with Scott (1997), who argues that globalizing practices are the outcome of policies rather than simply a context to which policy is a response – in particular, the neo-liberal economic policies of the major economies, the OECD, the International Monetary Fund and the World Bank. To make this rhetorical move is not necessarily to make a moral judgement on the rightness or wrongness of such policies. Their source is not a sufficient ethical or political basis for either acceptance or rejection, despite many attempts to suggest otherwise. What it does do is to help identify and call to account those who are responsible for such practices; it supports a politicizing of the taken for granted in relation to globalizing practices.

Our second concern is of the timeliness of educational policy responses to globalization. As we have said, an important aspect of exigence in rhetoric is to establish the timeliness of the response. In other words, a timely solution is put forward to address the identified problem or issue. In terms of much policy rhetoric, it would appear that governments and their populations are almost running out of time. Globalization is positioned as a context to which there must be an urgent and immediate response, if it is not to be too late. Once again, we point to the implied threat in policy rhetoric. So there is a sense in which the speeding up of time that has been the cause of much commentary in recent years may be both reflected in and contributed to by the rhetoric of globalization. For those who see globalizing practices as contributing to global warming, and increasing differentials between rich and poor, the timeliness is also equally urgent, as time is running out to address such issues. With all such messages being communicated on a regular basis through the practices of the global and globalizing media, it may be unsurprising that a sense of crisis and crisis narratives abound. Responses to the exigence of globalization are almost overrun as soon as they are articulated. However, in writing this we have to be cautious, as we are in danger of contributing yet further to the rhetoric of crisis, another pointer to the way in which analysis – as with journalism, public meetings and chats over dinner – is not simply on what is occurring, but is also part of what is occurring – it remains a form of action in the world.

There is a danger then, when considering globalizing practices and educational policies, of suggesting there *is* a globalization of policy, i.e. that this is a condition or context, which we have to take for granted. Some of the above analyses could be seen in this light, even if the various authors might have different under-standings of globalization; one can disagree over definition, but agree over positioning it as a context or condition. Addressing this nominalization brings us to the question of the practices of policy migration. Dale (1999) provides a helpful typology of the mechanisms through which the globalization of policy is effected – harmonization, dissemination, standardization, installing interdependence and imposition. He contrasts these with more conventional notions of policy bor-rowing and policy learning that work from a more national policy focus. Dale is therefore pointing to the multiple trajectories in and significance of globalizing policy practices. By contrast, Levin (1998) suggests that there is little systematic learning in the processes of national policy borrowing and that the latter may be largely symbolic. He suggests the notion of 'the policy epidemic' to assist in under-standing such practices:

> New agents of disease tend to spread rapidly as they find the hosts that are least resistant. So it is with policy change in education – new ideas move around quite quickly, but their adoption may depend on the need any given government sees itself having. Although many people may be infected with a given disease, the severity can vary greatly.
>
> (Levin 1998: 139)

This adds to the metaphors used by Ball above in indicating the significance of recontextualization to the understanding of such processes. In addition to globalizing practices, flexibility and lifelong learning might be said to be related diseases, part of the contemporary policy epidemic. Here it is possible to suggest a relationship between the notion of policy epidemic and Foucault's notions of biopower and biopolitics (Nicoll 1997), as such epidemics spread through the body politic. The former can be seen as a contemporary extension of the latter, as it seeks to renew education and training to extend their capacities to produce healthy, productive and flexible people as part of the administration of populations (Dean 1999). These are the enthusiastic workers who engage in an enterprise of the self in support of their own lifelong (l)earning. A medical metaphor might be appropriate as well, as it is suggestive of the need for health warnings, which in respect of the current discussion might be said to present the view that one should become flexible or perish.

The spread of these diseases may be through a variety of direct and indirect means. The direct means can be through the circulation of ideas based on the movement of individuals among and between certain networks. Politicians, policy advisors and members of 'think tanks' migrate around the globe spreading certain messages. The same is true for many academics and employers and managers. Lingard and Rizvi (1998: 262) suggest that such processes point 'towards the emergence of a global policy community, constituted by an overlapping member-ship of globalizing bureaucrats ... senior public servants, policymakers and advisers'. Conferences are sponsored to develop and promote certain themes and policy options. There is also the influence of members of international organizations such as the United Nations Educational, Scientific and Cultural Organization (UNESCO), the European Union, the OECD and the World Bank. For instance, Lingard and Rizvi (1998: 271–2) suggest that the role of the OECD in higher education policy has been

> ... as an institutionalizing mechanism for the idea of an integrated global economy underpinned by the ideology of market liberalism ... the OECD has been a significant mechanism for encouraging the global flows of people, information and ideology, and, indirectly, of educational policies.

The indirect means of spreading policy may be through the reports, books, the Internet, etc., produced and circulated by individuals and organizations and through the media, including the text you are reading here. The global diaspora of people and ideas through processes of migration enable policy epidemics and the forging of policies around the globe. Globalization is therefore used as an impetus for change and as a social imaginary through which to translate interests and mobilize changes.

Flexibility as a migrating metaphor

An examination of a range of policy texts concerned with the reform of post-school education and training from around the globe brings forward a number of common themes. We are suggesting that a central but overlooked theme is the notion of flexibility. We cannot provide a full genealogy of the migration of this notion, although we consider it a useful and important project upon which to engage. We intend to draw upon a small selection of recent policy documents to illustrate the substance of the policy emphasis on flexibility. In a sense, therefore, we are using an examination of flexibility in policy texts as an illustration of practices of globalization within educational policy more generally, rather than examining the relationship between flexibility and globalization as such.

In relation to the latter, there are a number of possibilities. In many texts, flexibility is positioned as a response or outcome of policy. The exigence of globalizing practices *requires* greater flexibility in order that individuals will be able to adapt to a world of constant change. Flexibility may also be considered a *part of* globalizing practices. For instance, Harvey (1989) provides an analysis of late twentieth-century capitalism that suggests a new, flexible regime of capital accumulation has become necessary, part of which has entailed a closer integration of nations into the global economy. A third possibility is to consider the role flexibility plays in *contributing to* globalizing practices. As we shall see, flexibility signifies a certain 'freeing up' of certain patterns of organization and behaviour. As such, it can be said to contribute to the flows of people, goods, services and information that support the denser interconnectedness associated with globalizing practices. This list is obviously not exhaustive, but what we are pointing to is the multifaceted complexity of the relations between the globalizing practices and flexibility and that the rhetorical location of this relationship is significant in terms of what is being argued and its persuasiveness. A similar point can also be made of analyses and critiques of policy, including our own, of course.

There are two aspects to the discussion in this section. First, we examine the deployment of flexibility within the texts of certain international organizations. Second, we even more briefly illustrate their existence within national policy documents. Underlying this is an interest in the various representations of flexibility that have been forged globally. We want to indicate the diverse ways in which flexibility is deployed, but also the underlying logic of adaptability that is being promulgated.

Flexibility is a powerful metaphor in international policy statements. For example:

> The sheer pace of technological change has convinced business communities and nations alike of the need for *flexibility* in the quality of the labour force. Education systems can therefore no longer be expected to train a labour force for stable industrial jobs; they must instead train individuals to be innovative, capable of evolving, adapting to a rapidly changing world and assimilating change.
>
> (UNESCO 1996: 71, emphasis added)

This quote, from a report produced under the direction of the former President of the European Commission, Jacques Delors, positions flexibility as a key goal of education systems, to enable individuals to be adaptive to the changes they confront. Certain aspects of this quotation are of interest. First, it positions change as a transcendental and inevitable process to which individuals adapt rather than one to which they contribute. Here change is positioned rhetorically as a nominalization. As we have already indicated, it is ontologically gerrymandered as an economic fact of life. The directions and forms of change are assumed to be uncontested through reification. Second, there is an elision of business communities and nations as one overall community to which policy must respond. Thus, while the report overall evinces significant concern for the issues of social exclusion, the underpinning assumption remains that individuals and communities must take on the flexibility, read adaptability, that is demanded of them. It is this requirement that becomes a policy driver for, among other things, lifelong learning.

A later UNESCO report (1997) uses the term 'flexibility' to identify and signal the advantages to adult learners of open and distance learning. 'For the student/ open learner open and distance learning means increased access and *flexibility*, as well as the combination of work and education' (UNESCO 1997: 1, emphasis added). Flexibility does not only entail individuals being responsive to change, it also means they have more decisions about what and how they learn as the provision of learning opportunities itself becomes more flexible and subject to choice. To be a flexible individual in the context of change, more flexible forms of learning need to be available, of which open, distance and increasingly distributed learning are often fabricated as paradigmatic. 'Open learning also means a more learner-centred approach, allowing greater *flexibility* and choice of content as well as organization of the learning programme' (UNESCO 1997: 8, emphasis added). Here flexibility signifies more accessible and student-centred, and maybe even consumer-oriented, education and training systems. However, this remains linked to the production of more flexible work organizations.

> The emergence of more *flexible* work organization is clearly linked to the development of technology. One of the new challenges for education is that high level skills are needed not only by an elite, but also by the population in general.
>
> (UNESCO 1997: 8, emphasis added)

Without the exigence of the emerging work organization, the imperative for more flexible forms of learning to support upskilling would fall. The question remains as to the extent to which policy follows that emergence or, through its social imaginary, seeks to produce it.

The importance of flexibility can be seen also in the policy directions of the European Union (EU) in relation to the labour market and in moves towards open and distance learning. For instance, during the decade 1985–95 the European Commission undertook a wide range of policy initiatives, established a number of networks and invested significant funds in projects which had at their core the necessity of increasing the competitiveness of the EU within world economic blocs through education and training. Central to the importance ascribed to open and distance learning has been its 'capacity to reproduce through its teaching and learning strategies the qualities of independence and *flexibility*, which have become the virtuous qualities of the workplace within the EU and elsewhere' (Tait 1996: 235, emphasis added). Here we find an additional aspect to the rhetoric of flexibility, as it is not the economic flexibility, nor the flexibility of education and training systems that are being pointed to. It is the flexibility of individuals, able to move from job to job and task to task.

A more general EU White Paper on lifelong learning additionally associates flexibility with the increased mobility of the labour force (Hake 1999). This points to an increasingly important rhetorical link between flexibility and lifelong learning, wherein to be flexible one needs to be capable of learning throughout one's life, while to be a lifelong learner, one needs to be flexible and have access to flexible learning opportunities (R. Edwards 1997). In the EU document, in addition to the route of expanded availability of paper qualifications

> ... this White Paper advocates that a more open, more *flexible* approach be adopted alongside it. This approach would in particular encourage the mobility of workers – employers, teaches, researchers – and students. It is

today striking to observe how much easier it is for goods, capital and services to move around Europe than it is for people and knowledge.

(European Commission 1995: 7, emphasis added)

Here the flexibility of mobile subjects is the goal to be achieved through more flexible forms of organization. Thus we have a further dimension of flexibility, specifically the need for the working population to follow the availability of work and learning opportunities within the EU. The undesirable inflexibility, by virtue of opposites, would presumably be to assert that one had a legitimate loyalty to a place or region, and that one was rooted there. It would appear that routes rather than roots underpin policy rhetoric. The potential to be flexible in seeking work also means that learning opportunities are available on a flexible basis to these mobile subjects. This is a view also put forward by the OECD who suggest that universities, at least, develop a 'single idealization of appropriate organizational behaviour', whereby 'organizations must have the capacity to make a *flexible* response to uncertain market conditions caused by commodity saturation' (de Wit, quoted in Lingard and Rizvi 1998: 271, emphasis added). International, regional and transnational organizations therefore deploy flexibility as a metaphor of reform and renewal, which in part contributes to the forms of mobility/migration associated with globalizing practices. Staying still is positioned as not an option.

Flexibility emerges also as a powerful metaphor within national policy statements. For instance, when discussing the changes in the nature and organization of work, and the need for learning opportunities to equip substantial sections of the population with the means to manage that change process, the UK Government's National Advisory Group for Continuing Education and Lifelong Learning (NAGCELL 1997: 13) argued for 'a shift away from the crude, entirely market-driven and sometimes threatening rhetoric which has too often informed the debate about change at work, with its implied lack of alternatives of choice for both individuals and companies'. Flexibility is used thereafter in this document primarily as a term denoting the desirable organization of learning opportunities to permit wider participation. In other words, there is an attempt to decouple the rhetoric of economic flexibility from that of the flexibility of educational and training systems. Interestingly, of course, this is based upon positioning the former as a 'threatening rhetoric', with the implication of its illegitimacy as an argument. For the NAGCELL (1997: 35, emphasis added), in order to make a reality of lifelong learning, methods must be adopted encouraging 'a variety of forms of learning characterized by *flexibility*, including distance and open learning, through modules, by using the new communications and information technology, in the home, in the community or at work'. The UK government's subsequent consultation paper on lifelong learning, which we discussed in the previous chapter, echoed the need for greater flexibility, but also positioned the UK as already a market leader in this area. 'We currently lead Europe, and possibly the world, in learning technology and *flexible* learning delivery, and we intend to maintain that lead' (DfEE 1998: 22, emphasis added).

We therefore witness flexibility being deployed in a number of ways in educational policy discourses. In relation to the labour market, flexibility is associated with a certain freedom to act, unhindered by what are often constructed as the bureaucratic constraints of the past. Thus the significance of the rhetoric of managing that we discussed in Chapter 7. Economic competitiveness, survival and jobs are therefore predicated on greater flexibility. Who can disagree, we ask? In relation to the education and training system, flexibility signifies an expansion and extension of educational opportunities tailored more to the interests of learners than institutions and professions. Who can disagree, we ask? In relation to the individual, flexibility enables people to be mobile in terms of tasks, jobs and geography. More creative and fulfilling working lives become possible. Who can disagree, we ask?

Well, of course, each is contested and struggled over and within. The persuasiveness of discourses of flexibility is contested. Before finishing this chapter, we wish to say something about that struggle and the implications of a rhetorical analysis for it.

Rhetorical struggles

Much policy analysis assumes a realist epistemology. It is representing in some senses the real state of things. Even forms of ideology critique have this assumption; it is the uncovering of the real behind the ideological that is the task of analysis. In realist analyses, the descriptions in policy texts are taken literally rather than there being an examination of the rhetorical work they do in fabricating and forging the real. This results in a set of discourses that seek to provide evidence for the various versions of the real. Logos therefore becomes central to the debate. Yet 'factual and fictional stories share many of the same kinds of textual devices for constructing credible descriptions, building plausible or unusual event sequences, attending to causes and consequences, agency and claim, character and circumstance' (D. Edwards 1997: 263). It is the capacity for story telling or, perhaps more persuasively, communication, which is posited as central to human ontology. In telling tales, tales are told, some of which are more telling than others. Thus, for instance, Potter (1996: 107, emphasis in original) refers to a discourse

> ... which is constructing versions of the world as solid and factual as *reifying* discourse. *Reifying* means to turn something abstract into a material thing; and this is the sense I wish to emphasize, although material should be understood very widely.

Fact fabrication can be seen as a process of attempting to reify the world as real and solid through particular forms of discourse, as we discussed in relation to policy documents which authoritatively state the problems to be addressed as facts earlier. Reification is similar to nominalization, although it points to fact fabrication as a whole rather than simply the turning of particular terms into conditions. These rhetorical practices are part of the attempts to persuade and influence. As we have argued throughout this text, such attempts are pervasive. What this suggests is that in (en)countering policy, we ourselves need to engage in reflexively informed offensive/defensive rhetorical work.

But how straightforward is such work? Central to it is the deployment of metaphor. As we have seen, metaphors are used powerfully and systematically within the political arena, as elsewhere. However, in considering, for instance, flexibility in terms of the metaphorical work that it does, it is important also to identify the complex of metaphors that it may draw from or with which it might be said to resonate. Metaphors do not operate on their own, but in conjunction with others to fabricate a common metaphorical description of the world. In the prior assumptions of the writers/speakers/presenters and readers/listeners/viewers, there can be a predisposition towards accepting certain metaphorical descriptions over others based on rhetorical memory. These are the shared assumptions and cultural memories that exist between authors and audience, affinities that are cemented through rhetorical strategies that enhance the view that we are all in the same boat (Straehle *et al.* 1999). In relation to flexibility, therefore, different metaphorical complexes may be in play and flexibility may be elaborated in a range of metaphorical systems, based upon the memories of those involved. Where a memory is shared between authors and audience, there is the possibility of greater acceptance or uptake of the former's texts or utterances by the latter. In other words, the offensive/defensive rhetoric resonates, rings true, has credibility.

One such reading is within a social Darwinian metaphorical complex. We suggest this because, as we have noted, adaptability and survival are at play in the positioning of flexibility within policy texts. These two notions are central to the secular and popular understanding of the world derived from Darwinian evolutionary science. Social Darwinism extends those notions to the social and national as well as species level, the evidence for which may be dubious, but which nonetheless continues to prove persuasive. Within social Darwinism the social system and its parts are likened to a biological organism, responding to changes within its environment or habitat. A narrative of the social is fabricated from a narrative of the natural. Here the environment is the natural context within which organisms live. Through this separation, the environment is uninfluenced by humankind and to a large extent uncontrollable. This view leads to an understanding of a relationship between the environment and the organism where change in the environment leads to physiological and behavioural misfit between the organism and the environment. Organisms who are able to react appropriately – flexibly – by adapting themselves so that they again fit with the environment survive to reproduce, and the species as a whole survives.

This resonates with our discussion of globalization and flexibility. Flexibility becomes a trait which affords the individual organism, the educational institution and the social system as a whole the ability to respond and adapt to unpredictable changes within the environment, in particular the demands of the global economy for competitiveness. This trait is then the one required for survival. Within policy texts, therefore, the narrative logic is that without flexibility, institutions and individuals will not be able to respond to the uncertain future environment, with the threat of social and economic exclusion. The point here is not to ask whether social Darwinism represents reality truthfully, but rather explore how a prior immersion in this metaphorical description, a shared memory, may predispose the audience to take up a requirement for flexibility and the need for action. Alternative formulations are possible, of course, but depend upon different complexes and readings to fabricate alternative meanings and become persuasive.

This memory, this creation of an audience, is not foolproof. Insight into the rhetorical dimension of EU policy formation is provided by Wodak (2000) who analysed the drafting of an employment policy paper for the EU Council of Ministers. Wodak traces the way in which the text emerged from a succession of events comprising an initial draft, a meeting to discuss the draft, and then a new draft. She uses discourse analysis to reveal a complex dialectical interplay of language and social practice. In creating the document, a rich complex of meanings was constructed by drawing on the membership resources of the worlds the members of the committee represented. These latter included 'their knowledge of language, representations of the natural and social worlds they inhabit, values, beliefs, assumptions, and so on' (Fairclough 1999: 24). However, the process of agreeing a draft overrode this complex interaction and 'the transformations from oral to written constitute a monologizing process which leads to materialization' (Wodak 2000: 203). The result was that while the meaning of the policy that was formulated lay in the way the members of the committee recontextualized each others' meanings, this was lost in the later versions of the text that went forward to the Council of Ministers. The complex negotiations of meaning were ironed out in the construction of the policy text. However, these rematerialize as this text is itself subject to interpretation. We can see that in some ways the project of the European Commission is to build a European space, or 'house' (Chiltern and Ilyin 1993), through the construction of a community of shared membership resources. This space is one that has become based around the metaphor of harmonization rather than standardization over the years to reflect differences between member states. While these resources may make possible the mobilizing of audience or networks, whether they do is another matter, of course. Looking at things in this way means that policy needs to be considered as a constant process of fabricating and reordering networks and less a rational decision that determines action (Barry 2002). Whether this is felicitous in the work of policy rather than the understanding of policy practices remains to be seen, as there is something persuasive about governing on the basis of reason. It harks back to the tranquillity of Plato's philosopher-kings, perhaps.

Inevitably, there need to be more health warnings. Prior acceptance of a metaphorical complex in rhetorical memory can lead to what has been termed 'vassalage' (Potter 1996). This metaphor has been used in relation to the work of the researcher in social sciences, but it might equally be drawn upon in relation to the audience who accepts assertions or judgements of policy texts:

> These sorts of tangles that result in vassalage are not restricted to work on scientific facts, although they are vividly apparent with that topic. In any area where factual versions of some group are taken as a start point for analysis the analyst may end up as a vassal.
>
> (Potter 1996: 98–9)

In opening up the space of policy as a rhetorical practice and pointing to memory as a basis for agreement, we hope to counter such vassalage, a term we find emotive in its own right. More convincing is the need for offensive/defensive rhetorical work in the struggle over both the meanings of policy and in building or working with other cultural memories, membership resources and networks. This might well involve the irony and play of peace camps and satirical comedians as much as the confrontations of the school playground or picket line (Rorty 1989).

What we have been suggesting, therefore, in the last two chapters is that policy and policy analysis depend upon a prior immersion in certain rhetorical practices, whether that be thought of in terms of audience and memory, shared metaphorical complexes, shared membership resources, or being part of a socio-rhetorical network. Analysis of the ways in which policy propositions and their critiques are formed and reified through such processes therefore become important, as any common uptake may circumscribe critical (en)counters. Reflexive consideration of these issues may enable forms of critique and action that refuse or counter practices of reification by drawing deliberately upon rhetorical practices, irony and alternative metaphorical systems. For memories, like rhetoric itself, are not homogeneous. It is in this sense that we have used the metaphor of migration to suggest both the mobility of metaphor and the mobilizing of meaning within such an approach to policy. In examining policy in this way, we start to tell a tale of globalizing practices and flexibility as migrating metaphors and metaphors of migration. In the process, we hope to have illustrated that it is because of the play of rhetoric in policy, including policy analysis, that such an approach can be conceived as a form of social action. To engage in struggle is in part a rhetorical practice. Whether the rhetoric of *struggle* is sufficient to mobilize for social and political action is another matter. Others have tried it, both the powerful (Strachle *et al.* 1999) and those challenging the powerful. Other metaphors may have greater pathos and be more appealing.

Chapter 10

Writing research

On the face of it, a chapter about research in a book on rhetoric seems odd and out of place. It is almost a culturally engrained mind-set that research is an area devoid of the rhetorical. To conjoin research and rhetoric seems oxymoronic. Surely, we say, where research is rhetorical it should be dismissed. Our scientific lens means that common sense tells us to see research as the disinterested pursuit of knowledge represented through a literal use of language. Indeed, researchers are criticized precisely when they/we are seen to stray. Thus, 'politicians and their advisers are castigating researchers for dealing in rhetoric rather than classroom realities, or for failing to write in a "plain language" that would translate those realities without distortion' (MacLure 2003: 4). Where we think at all of the *texts* of research (and generally we tend not to), we see these simply as faithful representations of this knowledge. This is the tyranny of transparency (Strathern 2000). We are back to the rhetoric/science distinction we introduced in Chapters 1 and 2. Rhetorical discourse is ornamental and sneaky, whereas research is about truth and the real world.

It will be clear from what has gone before that this is not a position we hold. Indeed, the very apparent disinterestedness of research texts and the narrative realism that sustains them can itself be seen as a certain genre, a particular way of writing, that in the performance is designed to persuade. Indeed, much has been done to examine the particular genres of research texts (for example, Swales 1990; Bhatia 1993; Berkenkotter and Huckin 1995). These analyses tend to focus on forms of research writing and their broader linguistic structures. By contrast, what we wish to do in this chapter is explore some of the ways of writing associated with different approaches to research, and specifically the rhetorical forms they take. To put it another way, our interest is in the *textuality* and *intertextuality* of research. Here research texts are not seen simply as a way to document reality, but, as texts, they are themselves a documentary reality (Atkinson and Coffey 1997). We argue that research is a particular genre of writing, but that within it there are also many different genres. In the process, we will explore the ways in which some of the epistemological debates about the nature of knowledge can also be conceived as rhetorical debates about the nature of representation and implicitly the rhetoricity of discourse. Educational research, like all research, aims to be persuasive in many different ways, both drawing upon and mobilizing the membership resources of the different socio-rhetorical networks that constitute the stakeholders in research practices – researchers, students, practitioners, policy makers, and even those much talked about 'users'.

To begin ...

In research and scholarship in education, both the focus for research and the approaches to it have been the subject of much debate over the years. The methodological aspects of these debates have also been part of the wider social science literature. Initially, much of the focus was on phenomenological rather than positivist epistemologies and the collecting and analysis of qualitative rather than quantitative data. These debates continue. However, in addition, perspectives associated with feminism, postcolonialism, poststructuralism and postmodernism have raised significant issues of language, discourse and text, all of which impact upon the objects of research, data collection, data analysis, and the representation of outcomes (Stronach and MacLure 1997). This has resulted in what is often referred to as a 'crisis of representation', as the discourses through which research is represented have themselves been questioned. They have come to be seen in certain quarters not as transparent carriers of meaning reflecting the truth of the world, but as imbued with many meanings and embodying the exercise and effects of power. In other words, attention has been and is being given to their rhetorical practices and effects, the way in which they do not just represent a researched world but actually fabricate the research process through which the world is known.

These critiques signal a growing scepticism towards the truth claims of positivist/empiricist/realist approaches to research, although there are elisions here, and an emerging interest in research as a set of social and cultural practices. They raise many questions about:

- why certain phenomena are deemed worthy of investigation whilst others are not;
- the link between the accounts collected by researchers and the reality they purport to represent;
- the ways in which researchers work on these accounts, framing their own representations of reality whilst erasing their own authorial presence;
- the voices and cultures of those Others whom the researcher interprets and represents;
- the pervasive influence of unexamined ontological and epistemological assumptions in the intertextual and interdiscursive work of research.

This has opened up different research terrains and put in question certain traditions of doing research. In particular, it has placed under scrutiny those understandings of research as a technology; a set of methods, skills and procedures which, when applied properly to a research problem, will produce valid and reliable results. The very persuasiveness of method has therefore been thrown into question. Moving away from viewing research as a purely technical and rational activity to viewing it as a social practice, embedded in particular cultural, political and historical contexts and embodied in the persons of researchers, is to induce 'a feeling of strangeness' (Scott and Usher 1996: 9). In other words, where research has traditionally been seen as a process of making the unfamiliar familiar, the focus now is on making the familiar – the research process – unfamiliar. Given the social and political expectations of research as a means of producing useful and objective knowledge and the possible consequences for academic researchers of undermining these expectations, such feelings are perhaps understandable. However, such undermining is well established, ongoing (Nelson *et al.* 1987b; Atkinson 1996) and probably irreversible.

These debates have been prevalent in the social sciences and are also to be found in educational research informed by anthropological and sociological traditions (for example, Clifford and Marcus 1986; Hammersley 1994). However, despite this, the debates remain at the margins of the discourses of educational research. Yet it would seem incontrovertible that in presenting an account of a research project, from whichever perspective, paradigm or approach, we are (re)presenting it and there are choices involved in this process (Clarke *et al.* 2002a). No account, even a totally realist account, can encompass everything. Van Maanen (1988) identifies three types of story written by ethnographers – realist, confessional and impressionist. The first views texts as unproblematic representations of reality. The second provides an autobiographical, experiential account of the research. The impressionistic text is one that is more consciously literary in style. While these stories were identified from ethnographic accounts, there are resonances with other accounts of educational research. The commonality is that each is embodied in a rhetorical practice and attempts to be persuasive, albeit involving different forms of writing, with some more successful than others depending on their felicity. And indeed it is possible to produce a polyphonous account of the research process, which draws explicitly upon different genres of writing in the attempt to either be more persuasive to wider audiences or possibly to alienate them completely by demonstrating that one does not know what one is doing (Edwards *et al.* 2002).

Like Van Maanen, Polkinghorne (1997) also provides a three-fold typology of research stories: algorithmic, strategically improvised and reflexive. Each of these are 'sense-making procedures that members of a culture apply in order to find/ create regularity and stability in the phenomenal world' (Stronach and MacLure 1997: 56). Even accepting that different accounts are possible draws attention to qualities of open-endedness, incompleteness and uncertainty in research practices – there are no definitive findings, no final endings. This points towards the difficulties inherent in drawing any analysis to a close, even though closure, many would say, is precisely the point of research – to find answers, to conclude, to draw a line under it all (Lawson 2001). The multiple possibilities for (re)presenting research in education points to the difficulty of research producing secure and final findings, despite the rhetorical appeal of the evidence-informed policy and practice movement that seems to provide a clear rationale for research that deserves, because of the deployment of evidence, to be funded. We are engaged in ongoing conversations, without end.

For Polkinghorne (1997), the algorithmic tale presents the research process as a logical and sequential series of moves where the generation of research questions leads to methodological design and implementation. Here research is represented as systematic, planned, cumulative and progressive. The emphasis on method and methodology in this account functions to position a certain kind of intellectual labour as research and this then supports claims to truth subsequently made. 'Research articles are thus more persuasive because the articles present an image of determinancy in science and obscure the influences of historical and situational circumstances and possibilities of alternate approaches and judgements' (Prelli 1989: 103). Determinacy is fabricated through the structuring of these research texts rather than found in nature. Predominantly, there are four sections to a research article: an introduction, methodology, results and discussion (or IMRD). This is sometimes enhanced by a summary (IMRDS). In this way, the possibility for rhetorical flourishes and the play of language is apparently reduced, inducing a sense of security in the portrayals within the texts. As Derrida (1980: 125) suggests, 'the method for reducing the frivolous is method itself'. MacLure (2003: 126), following Derrida, argues that method acts as a *pharmakon*, both poison and remedy: 'the "pharmaceutical" or chemical aspirations of method – to disinfect, filter, strain, purify, penetrate, cure, dissolve – will always raise the spectre of the "bad" opposites: the risk that method might infect, adulterate, poison, contaminate, obscure, corrode'. It provides rhetorical footing for warranting results.

This is a familiar and well-established format for presenting research, yet what are rarely brought to the fore are the representational practices deployed in producing this tidy account. For example, Latour and Wolgar (1979) demonstrate how scientific articles attempt to persuade by apparently not engaging in rhetorical practices; science is devoid of rhetoric, as we discussed in earlier chapters. One consequence is an erasure of other insider stories that could have been told. The author is ostensibly absent from the story and yet at the same time strangely present. This absence–presence, it is argued, is a vital factor building and projecting the authority of the text and thereby its persuasiveness. Indeed depersonification is very often a feature of such texts, with, for example, locutions such as 'the article', 'the paper' or 'the chapter' standing in for 'the researcher' (Low 1999), or the pointed eschewal of the first person pronoun – for example, 'studies show' (Lemke 1995). Thus it is the disembodied article that makes the claim and not the researcher who wrote it.

In the early development of modern science there was the need to deploy a rhetorical language that would be convincing in ways in which competing rhetorical practices at the time were not, and to do this through a discourse that precisely appeared not to be rhetoric. The nature of science's rhetoric, as signalled in major publication guides, has shifted over time (Bazerman 1983). According to Swales (1990: 113), this represents a shift in the view of the scientist's relationship with nature from one that 'the nature of things would be easily revealed by direct or manipulated observation to a view that nature was complex, obscure and difficult to get at'. Thus, even within this genre of research writing, there are shifting rhetorical strategies at play over time and space. Two things remain constant, however. First, reading is meaning-taking – the reader is positioned as such – rather than meaning-making. The facts are rhetorically presented to position readers as either accepting or rejecting them. Ostensibly, there is a reliance on the logos and ethos of the argument. There seems to be no deployment of pathos, as the researcher is the emotionally neutral, disinterested scientist, shorn of subjectivity. Nor is there recognition of kairos or contextualization, other than in relation to the existing literature on the subject. Here also is the second constant, the submersion or denial of the rhetoricity of science.

However, Polkinghorne (1997: 12) suggests that 'instead of a performance choreographed according to logically ordered algorithmic methodical steps, the research process consists of often tacit strategic improvisations in the service of a guiding purpose'. Similarly Prelli (1989) argues that false starts and things not working are usually excluded from research texts and Schryer (1994: 119) argues that 'research is essentially an effort of "bricolage"; yet IMRDS turns it into a work of "engineering"'. The second narrative mode therefore seeks to highlight these strategic improvisations, bringing to the fore the inherent untidiness of research practices and making a claim to truth and authenticity by representing itself as closer to the lived experience of the researchers and researched. Here we might once again examine the metaphors of research for what they signify and perform, the experiential meanings they convey. For instance, data is 'granular', fine-grained for the focus of the research, coarse-grained for its context. Breadth and depth metaphors are deployed. Qualitative researchers are encouraged to produce 'thick' descriptions, where we assume 'thick' signifies 'rich' rather than 'stupid'. They are required to produce in-depth and holistic explanations. The characters in the plot are depicted as, for instance 'lads', 'noble savages', varyingly positioned as hero/ines and villains. Here it is as much the pathos that can be evoked through such metaphors and the bringing to the fore of kairos that are as important as the logos and ethos of the argument.

Whilst Polkinghorne's two narratives adopt different rhetorical strategies for fabricating claims to authority, what they both share is a view of language as capable of transparently reflecting reality, of telling the truth. One challenge then might be to achieve a textual strategy that will produce a more accurate and realistic representation of what really happens in the research process. In many such texts, persuasive strategies might involve the deployment of a combination of realist and confessional genres. As we have argued , 'rhetoric enters into every kind of discourse, even the most scientific. That fact is sufficient to overturn the claims of those who demand a bloodless, neutral ideal for language' (Leff 1987: 31). Such an approach is always already a rhetorical achievement, which will be more persuasive in particular times and spaces than others. If 'confession and description are rhetorical practices rather than windows onto minds, thoughts and sensations' (MacLure 2003: 145), then the confessional text may reflect a view of knowledge that all claims involve interpretation, without authors recognizing that they are also deploying a specific genre of writing and their own rhetorical strategies.

In contrast, the third narrative mode, the reflexive tale, points towards the challenges posed by the linguistic turn we have discussed in earlier chapters. This poststructuralist perspective raises important questions, problematizing narrative realism by pointing to the representational practices and textual strategies of any research text and seeking to explore the work done by these. Its focus is on the question of how these accounts are 'made to appear solid, neutral, independent of the speaker, and to be merely mirroring some aspect of the world' (Potter 1996: 1). The challenge of conducting empirical research from this perspective lies in the tension between a commitment to taking account of the everyday lived experiences of informants, while eschewing the production of realist texts that reduce what they do and say to singular and definitive readings. A crucial weakness of such texts is that 'in order to be revelatory ... realist texts have to conceal: they have to iron out inconsistencies, establish coherence and insinuate a shared point of view between reader and writer' (Stronach and MacLure 1997: 53). In the third tale then, there is an attempt to disturb and interrogate some of the easy assumptions that frequently accompany the conduct and reporting of research. This is in order to produce an analytical rather than descriptive or anecdotal reflexivity, one that engages with the performative nature of research and points explicitly to its own rhetorical practices. Thus, for instance, in his discussion of the relationship between psychology and rhetoric, Carlston (1987: 146) agues that there are three levels of interaction:

> First, the particular words that social scientists use to describe phenomena and theories influence their thinking and that of others. Second, the theorizing of social scientists is metaphorical story telling, and many different metaphors can tell the same scientific story. Third, even empirical sciences involve a good deal of argumentation and persuasion: facts rarely speak for themselves, and consequently scientists are required to speak for them.

There is a textual responsibility to be reflected in the narratives of research, a situational context in which they are located and a socio-rhetorical network within which they act.

World making

We have argued at several points in this text that research or knowledge production needs to be seen as a social practice, with the implication that it takes place within knowledge-producing networks. Our position is that research is a set of practices legitimated by a community. Some practices are judged as appropriate and signify that the knowledge produced is valid or at least persuasive, others however are ruled out of order. With this gate-keeping role, knowledge-producing networks *exclude* as well as include. They set boundaries, with language being the principal way of boundary marking. We noted earlier the prevalence of the systems or algorithmic narrative of how research is to be carried out. This is a good example of the boundary-setting function of language.

> Through the systems metaphor a model of research is articulated as both disembedded – an essentially ahistorical, apolitical and *technical* activity, a transcendental, contextless set of procedures and methods – and disembodied in the sense of being carried out by abstracted, asocial, genderless individuals without a history or culture.
>
> (McKenzie *et al*. 1997: 34, emphasis in original)

The articulation creates a discursive domain that shapes the way research is done and the conceptions of their identity as researchers that researchers have.

Our position is that there is no knowledge without inscription and from this we argue that there is no knowledge production without a text. Furthermore, adopting a deconstructive position that all texts are rhetorical, then research texts, even those whose textuality is explicitly 'hard-edged', are structured through rhetoric. This implies that these scientific texts are no different to a literary text. Indeed, going further, we might want to argue that all research texts are a species of literature. This then poses the question, why then cannot research within an experimental science be structured and presented in the form of a literary text? One interesting thing here is that the answer seems so obvious that on the face of it the question seems hardly worth asking. You just don't do that kind of thing! But why not? Fashioning a literary text after all is also a social practice, albeit much less closely defined and bounded than scientific experimentation. Furthermore, as such, worlds are created through the text. Of course, this is not very contentious. Most people would generally accept that is what literature is, after all. But what would be less acceptable, in fact highly contentious, is that scientific experimentation is also world-creating. However, things might be more complex than is apparent once we start considering some commonalities. Like literature, this kind of research is also a social practice, as there is always a scientific network to which research is addressed. Furthermore, like literature, research writing is undeniably textual. At this time, research that exists only in the mind of the researcher is not accorded the status of research in Western culture, although the symbol of Rodin's 'The Thinker' is a powerful sign of a certain form of detached rationality, of course. Research has to be enacted through inscription, thus becoming a text which can be read and re-read. Having a text is critical, since without texts the network could not gatekeep and could not validate outcomes. Without this power, the network would lose its authority as a knowledge-producing network. Part of that power, however, is in only warranting certain genres of writing as research. We would argue, therefore, that it is useful to understand the texts of research as a signifier. Its function is to enact the research through the inscription afforded by textuality. So what we have here is the research text as a performance, or to put it in language we introduced earlier, a speech act.

Speech acts only work, are only taken up, when they are persuasive or appropriate to their context, if the kairos is right. Looked at in this way, we can see why a scientific experiment cannot be presented through a literary text. It is not a matter of literature being fiction and a scientific experiment demonstrating truth. The literary text and the scientific text are equally texts. One could even say both are fictive given that the derivation of this is from the Latin root *fico*, to make. Given that they are texts, both are world-making, albeit that they make very different worlds in different ways for different socio-rhetorical networks. Both are speech acts, examples of world-making through particular ways of reading and writing the world, the fabricating of which we have been alluding to all along. We can conclude two things from this. First, that research, whether scientific or not, hard or soft, is not simply a matter of representing faithfully a world that already exists, waiting to be known. When we do research and when we present or enact it as a text, we are 'knowledging', actively fabricating a world to be known, and doing so in particular and different ways in relation to different knowledge-producing networks. Second, and following from this, scientific research cannot be presented as a literary text because it would fall outside the boundaries of what is constituted as acceptable by that knowledge-producing network. It would be an infelicitous speech act and would not perform as it was meant to, that is, it would not do the persuasive work intended. The kairos would be wrong, the logos invalid, the pathos would evoke the inappropriate emotions and the ethos of the researcher as a scientific self would not be authoritative. Texts have to be felicitous if they are to be taken up (Hutton-Jarvis 1999).

This argument does however have a powerful counter-argument that essentially amounts to asking – if research is about world-making rather than world-finding, why then do research if there is nothing out there to research? This is putting it very starkly and we would argue that the position outlined above is not arguing that there is no world out there, whatever that might mean. We, like most people, trip over pavements, burn our fingers on hot plates, have bodily (en)counters with others. Furthermore, we are certainly not attempting to argue that the world exists only in our minds and that all research is therefore subjective. We find this position equally difficult to understand. In examining this argument, it is therefore not our intention to delve into ageless and somewhat tedious and irresolvable epistemological and ontological debates over the nature of reality and what constitutes knowledge. By contrast, our work is to point to the speech act dimensions of research and, by extension, the significance of the place of rhetoric by bringing to the fore world-making in and through research.

In this context, we highlight the increasing prevalence of notions of reflexivity in research. Rhetoric is often said to be characterized by its reflexivity, so this is a very relevant issue. If research is about the activity of fabricating, then reflexivity is about research bending back on itself where, as it were, research researches itself. Researchers start to bend over backwards in their desire to be helpful. Of course, as we have implied, research carried out in a positivist/empiricist way would deny any place to reflexivity, indeed would find the very notion incoherent. Here research emphasizes outcomes rather than process and is seen as about finding out what is out there, that is its rhetoric. The counter-rhetoric brings to the fore reflexivity, arguing that it is a resource that needs to be acknowledged and used, as in Polkinghorne's (1997) third tale above. Here the question becomes 'Why do research for which you must deny responsibility for what you (the researcher) have found?' (Steier 1991: 10). Reflexivity becomes articulated as a matter of taking responsibility with the clear implication that any research, because it is world-making, has ethical and political dimensions that need to be recognized and taken into (the) account. This is a postmodern rhetoric for, as one of us has previously written, 'a postmodern approach to ... research highlights the need for researchers to be reflexive and to subject themselves, as "knowledgers", to critical self-scrutiny' (McKenzie *et al.* 1997: 36).

> Reflexivity involves ... recognizing our immersion in the historical and the social, the inscription or 'writing' of self in the practices, language, discourses and interpretive culture which constitutes the practice of research ... accepting reflexivity does not assume a subjectivist position that reality is a purely personal construct. Reflexivity ... foregrounds the implication of the personal within what is 'beyond' the personal.
>
> (Usher and Edwards 1994: 149)

However, what is missing here is any acknowledgement that reflexivity is itself a rhetoric. The increasing prevalence of notions of reflexivity in much of the social science and education research literature has not been accompanied by a problematization of reflexivity itself. Or at least, what problematization there is has tended to come from the defenders of narrative realism. They argue that reflexivity might be an interesting notion, but in the end it is pointless. Reflexivity simply ends up as navel gazing. We are so busy being reflexive, we end up doing no research. We become so obsessed with language and style that we end up with incoherent texts that say nothing. Reflexivity may well be enshrined in the realist text but at the same time such texts, its proponents argue, are very effective in ensuring that it is not a problem. All we need to do then is to keep on doing our research in the realist mode.

We have some sympathy with this. Reflexivity has to be felicitous within the specified research networks. However, keeping reflexivity in its place is different from ignoring it altogether. We should not think of research texts as harmless, located in the ivory tower of the academy and thus without effects. On the contrary, research texts can be powerful discourses. They can reinforce and even create social hierarchies. They will often have exclusionary and disempowering effects in naming and explaining the world in specific ways. They can be part of the intellectual technologies for governing at a distance (Miller and Rose 1993). Thus reflexivity can be a powerful tool for bringing to the fore the politics and ethics of research, both in terms of process and outcomes. We should not ignore or marginalize such a tool.

The proponents of narrative realism either ignore reflexivity and the issues it highlights or argue that is not really a problem. If they address the issues at all, their solution is to call for plain language, texts that are transparent and free of jargon. Here then metaphors of clarity and limpidity are being invoked to do their persuasive work. The proponents of reflexivity in their turn are also deploying metaphors to do their, albeit different, work. Here the metaphors are rubbery, those of voice, embedding, constructing and deconstructing, taking apart, bending back and, of course, fabricating, forging, framing and fashioning. The problem is not so much the metaphors deployed but that the proponents of reflexivity are caught in a potentially impossible situation. They wish to deconstruct the texts of narrative realism, revealing their world-making effects by highlighting the metaphoricity of these texts. They are ready to agree that these texts achieve their effects through their rhetoricity. But what about their own rhetoricity? What of our own rhetoricity? Once this is highlighted then an infinite regress is opened up. We have to be reflexive about reflexivity and then reflexive about that reflexivity and so on ad infinitum. It is more convenient therefore to ignore this and thus not to problematize reflexivity. But this will not do because in effect it is claiming that reflexivity is not world-making but world-finding. It is implicitly saying that the language used to convey content must at some point simply be taken for granted, that when it comes to reflexivity the content does not owe its meaning to the particular language and the particular stylistic devices through which it is inscribed and articulated. It is in effect making reflexivity foundational.

Reflexivity therefore is caught in a bind, an aporia. On the one hand, infinite regress, on the other, massive contradiction. Disturbing though this may be, it is not entirely surprising. We have (en)countered it before at the very beginning of this text when we spoke of writing about rhetoric as an impossible task. Our analysis of the rhetoric of reflexivity is simply a variation of this. Impossible, therefore, but does this necessarily mean that we should abandon reflexivity altogether?

Concluding?

How to conclude a text about the rhetoric of educational discourse when we recognize ourselves that we have engaged in certain rhetorical practices? This is the aporia we started with in (en)countering this challenge. If this text persuades you, we have been felicitous in our own use of rhetoric. If it does not, then we have not. If parts have persuaded you and other parts not, it would be interesting to consider why that is the case, and what has enabled some of it to be persuasive. To consider the felicitousness of texts is to take rhetoric seriously and this has been one of the chief aims of this text.

In the process of ourselves fabricating the rhetorical practices embedded in educational discourses, including those of research, and pointing to the work they do in promoting a sense of rationality, coherence and closure, we therefore also introduce ambivalence and doubt about our own text about texts. Accordingly, we have attempted to be reflexive about our own rhetorical strategies and to be reflexive about reflexivity. The purpose of the exercise is not simply to destabilize the authority of those various forms of knowledge fabricated through the texts of research and discourses of education, nor to produce a meta-narrative that then becomes the definitive version. Recognizing yet again the impossibility of the task, we can only strive to indicate the possibilities for a more tentative and rhetorical reading of knowledge claims.

We cannot stop there, however, for the story of this particular text does not have a single narrator. The four writers of this text are part of an interdisciplinary team stretched across time and space, each with our own histories, embeddedness and embodiments. Each of us has a different story to tell, a framing for this text, a tapestry of tales, each with biases that cannot 'be eliminated by first admitting them and then placing ourselves under methodological control' (Usher 1996: 45). In this text we have identified ourselves individually at places, but each of us could tell separate algorithmic, strategic and reflexive tales and do elsewhere – for example, at conferences and the like when we signify to others that we are 'active researchers'. We engage in a range of rhetorical practices in our research and scholarship. While we have reached a temporary consensus for this text, we are still embedded in those processes and practices. And, as we pointed out in Chapter 8, the use of 'we' does certain rhetorical work. We could unravel ourselves as 'I's' but each of the 'I's' needed a 'we'. In the context of the writing of this text, 'we' signifies a critical mass of writers, invoking both authority and power in relation to you, the reader. 'We' signifies both singular and plural, suggesting a single unit. 'We' signifies an assembling of not always aligned actors, differentiated by space and time, yet brought together to translate shared interests in rhetoric into this text. 'We' both personalizes and depersonalizes our writing. It personalizes by locating us actively in the text. However, it depersonalizes by dispersing attribution and author/ity. Who did write specific parts of this text? The 'we' needs an 'I' in order to translate the various texts into one text. There is only one of us sitting here writing this sentence, here, now. And my fellow authors have asked me to unveil myself, for the 'I' translating the multiple texts of the authors into a single text is me, Richard. But without the work of Kathy, Nicky and Robin, I would not be here. So, even though unveiled, 'I' still need a 'we'. Nor are we alone, as there are others with whom we have engaged – colleagues, research participants, peers – who are silent in this particular text, but who would have their own stories to tell. And 'we' also attempt to include you, our audience.

The effectiveness of the performance, the extent to which it enchants and persuades, is in part dependent upon the rhetorical practices in which we have engaged. This text performs through being a *particular* form of text, deploying a range of textual strategies, ones to which we have alluded as we have proceeded.

In the process, we put in question any claim to authority by pointing away from the factuality of our claims, even as authority returns to haunt us in our claim not to authoritatively claim. In writing this text, we have engaged in the ceremonial practices of research and scholarship. Here 'the publishing conventions that makes books the way they are – with covers, titles, bibliographical and cataloguing information, title pages, pages of contents, acknowledgements, prefaces by series editors, footnotes, indexes, glossaries, etc. – are notational frames for the ceremonies of reading' (Freadman 1994a: 60). They are part of the epideictic bringing together of authors and readers through the text in the ceremony of reading research. So how should we conclude?

Bibliography

Adam, B. (1994) *Time and Social Theory*, Cambridge: Polity Press.

Agin, W. (1999) *An Introduction to the .com Phenomenon*. Online. Available http://profs. lp.findlaw.com/e-commerce/ecommerce1.html (accessed 23 June 2003).

Alvesson, M. (1993) 'The play of metaphors', in J. Hassard and M. Parker (eds) *Postmodernism and Organizations*, London: Sage.

Appadurai, A. (1990) 'Difference in the global cultural economy', in M. Featherstone (ed.) *Global Culture: Nationalism, Globalization and Modernity*, London: Sage.

Aristotle (1954) *The Rhetoric and the Poetics*, New York: Random House.

Armitage, J. (2000) *Beyond Postmodernism? Paul Virillo's Hypermodern Cultural Theory*. Online. Available http://www.ctheory.net/text_file.asp?pick=133 (accessed 24 June 2003).

Arnold, J. (1995) *Who Owns Cyberpsace?* Online. Available http://technoculture.mira. net.au/storm/storm10.htm (accessed 23 June 2003).

Atkinson, P. (1996) *Sociological Readings and Re-readings*, Aldershot: Avebury.

Atkinson, P. and Coffey, A. (1997) 'Analysing documentary realities', in D. Silverman (ed.) *Qualitative Research: Theory, Method and Practice*, London: Sage.

Austin, J. (1962) *How to Do Things with Words*, Cambridge, MA: Harvard University Press.

Ball, S (1990a) *Politics and Policy Making in Education: Explorations in Policy Sociology*, London: Routledge.

Ball, S. (ed.) (1990b) *Foucault and Education: Disciplines and Knowledge*, London: Routledge.

Ball, S. (1990c) 'Management as moral technology: a Luddite analysis', in S. Ball (ed.) *Foucault and Education: Disciplines and Knowledge*, London: Routledge.

Ball, S. (1994) *Education Reform: A Critical and Post-structural Approach*, Buckingham: Open University Press.

Ball, S. (1998) 'Big policies/small world: an introduction to international perspectives in education policy', *Comparative Education*, 34, 2: 119–30.

Ball, S. (2000) 'Performativities and fabrications in the education economy: towards the performative society?', *Australian Educational Researcher*, 27, 2: 1–24.

Barry, A. (2002) 'In the middle of the network', in J. Law and A. Mol (eds) *Complexities: Social Studies of Knowledge Practices*, Durham: Duke University Press.

Barton, D., Hamilton, M. and Ivanic, R. (eds) (2000) *Situated Literacies: Reading and Writing in Context*, London: Routledge.

Baudrillard, J. (1988) *The Ecstasy of Communication*, New York: Semiotext(e).

Bauman, Z. (1991) *Modernity and Ambivalence*, Cambridge: Polity Press.

Bauman, Z. (1998) *Globalization: The Human Consequences*, Cambridge: Polity Press.

Baynham, M. (2000) 'Academic writing in new and emergent discipline areas', in M. Lea and B. Stierer (eds) *Student Writing in Higher Education*, Buckingham: Open University Press.

Bazerman, C. (1983) 'Reporting the experiment: the changing account of scientific doings', *Philosophical Transactions of the Royal Society, 1665–1800*, mimeo.

Bazerman, C. (1987) 'Codifying the social scientific style: the APA Publication Manual as a behaviourist rhetoric', in J. Nelson, A. Megill and D. McCloskey (eds) *The Rhetoric of the Human Sciences: Language and Argument in Scholarship and Public Affairs*, Madison: University of Wisconsin Press.

Bazerman, C. (2002) 'Genre and identity: citizenship in the age of the Internet and the age of global capitalism', in R. Coe, L. Lingard and T. Teslenko (eds) *The Rhetoric and Ideology of Genre: Strategies for Stability and Change*, New York: Hampton Press.

Becher, T. (1989) *Academic Tribes*, Buckingham: Open University Press.

Berkenkotter, C. and Huckin, T. (1995) *Genre Knowledge in Disciplinary Communication: Cognition/Culture/Power*, Hillsdale, NJ: Lawrence Erlbaum.

Bhatia, V. (1993) *Analysing Genre: Language Use in Professional Settings*, London: Longman.

Bicchieri, C. (1988) 'Should a scientist abstain from metaphor?', in A. Klamer, D. McCloskey and R. Solow (eds) *The Consequences of Economic Rhetoric*, Cambridge: Cambridge University Press.

Biggs, J. (1999) *Teaching for Quality Learning at University*, Buckingham: Open University Press.

Bigum, C. and Green, B. (1993) 'Technologizing literacy: or, interrupting the dream of reason', P. Gilbert and A. Luke (eds) *Literacy in Contexts: Australian Perspectives and Issues*, St Leonards: Allen and Unwin.

Bigum, C. and Green, B. (1995) *Managing Machines? Educational Administration and Information Technology*, Geelong: Deakin University Press.

Birdsall, W. (1996) *The Internet and the Ideology of Information Technology*. Online. Available http://www.isoc.org/isoc/whatis/conferences/inet/96/proceedings/e3/e3_2.htm (accessed 24 June 203).

Bizzell, P. (1992) *Academic Discourse and Critical Consciousness*, Pittsburgh: University of Pittsburgh Press.

Black, M. (1979) 'More about metaphor', in A. Ortony (ed.) *Metaphor and Thought*, Cambridge: Cambridge University Press.

Boreham, N., Samurcay, R. and Fischer, M. (eds) (2002) *Work Process Knowledge*, London: Routledge.

Boud, D. and Solomon, N. (eds) (2001) *Work-Based Learning: A New Higher Education?* Buckingham: Open University Press.

Boyd, R. (1979) 'Metaphor and theory change: what is "metaphor" a metaphor for?', in A. Ortony (ed.) *Metaphor and Thought*, Cambridge: Cambridge University Press.

Brookfield, S. (1993) 'Breaking the code: engaging practitioners in critical analysis of adult education literature', *Studies in the Education of Adults*, 25, 1: 64–91.

Bukatman, S. (1996) *Terminal Identities*, Durham: Duke University Press.

Burbules, N. (2000) 'Does the Internet constitute a global educational community?', in N. Burbules and C. Torres (eds) *Globalization and Education: Critical Perspectives*, London: Routledge.

Burbules, N. (2002) 'The Web as a rhetorical place', in I. Snyder (ed.) *Silicon Literacies: Communication, Innovation and Education in the Electronic Age*, London: Routledge.

Callon, M. (1986) 'Some elements of a sociology of translation: domestication of the scallops and the fishermen', in J. Law (ed.) *Power, Action, Belief: A New Sociology of Knowledge*, London: Routledge and Kegan Paul.

Callon, M. and Latour, B. (1981) 'Unscrewing the Big Leviathan: how actors macro-structure reality and how sociologists help them to do so', in A. Cicourel and K. Knorr-Cecina (eds) *Advances in Social Theory*, London: Routledge and Kegan Paul.

Cameron, L. (1999) 'Operationalizing "metaphor" for applied linguistic research', in L. Cameron and G. Low (eds) *Researching and Applying Metaphor*, Cambridge: Cambridge University Press.

Cameron, L. (2002) 'Metaphors in the learning of science: a discourse focus', *British Educational Research Journal*, 28, 5: 673–87.

Cameron, L. (2003) *Metaphor in Educational Discourse*, London: Continuum.

Cameron, L. and Low, G. (eds) (1999) *Researching and Applying Metaphor*, Cambridge: Cambridge University Press.

Candlin, C., Gollin, S., Plum, G., Spinks, S. and Stuart-Smith, V. (1998) *Researching Academic Literacies*, Sydney: Macquarie University.

Carlston, D. (1987) 'Turning psychology on itself: the rhetoric of psychology and the psychology of rhetoric', in J. Nelson, A. Megill and D. McCloskey (eds) *The Rhetoric of the Human Sciences: Language and Argument in Scholarship and Public Affairs*, Madison: University of Wisconsin Press.

Chappell, C., Farrell, L., Scheeres, H. and Solomon, N. (2000) 'The organization of identity', in C. Symes and J. McIntyre (eds) *Working Knowledge: New Vocationalism in Higher Education*, Buckingham: Open University Press.

Chappell, C., Rhodes, C., Solomon, N., Tennant, M. and Yates, L. (2003) *Reconstructing the Lifelong Learner: Pedagogies of Identity and Change*, London: Routledge.

Chesher, C. (1994) *Colonizing Virtual Reality: Construction of the Discourse of Virtual Reality, 1984–1992*. Online. Available at http://eserver.org/cultronix/chesher (accessed 23 June 2003).

Chiltern, P. and Ilyin, M. (1993) 'Metaphor in political discourse: the case of the "common European house"', *Discourse & Society*, 4, 1: 7–31.

Cicognani, A. (1998) 'On the linguistic nature of cyberspace and virtual communities', *Virtual Reality*, 3: 16–24.

Clandinin, D. and Connelly, F. (1996) 'Teachers' professional knowledge landscapes: teachers' stories – stories of teachers – school stories – stories of schools', *Educational Researcher*, 25, 3: 24–30.

Clark, R. and Ivanic, R. (1997) *The Politics of Writing*, London: Routledge.

Clarke, J., Harrison, R., Reeve, F. and Edwards, R. (2002a) '"Why don't you give the money back?" Questions of accounting and accountability in the three accounts of educational research', *International Journal of Qualitative Studies in Education*, 15, 5: 555–68.

Clarke, J., Harrison, R., Reeve, F. and Edwards, R. (2002b) 'Assembling spaces: the question of "place" in further education', *Discourse*, 23, 3: 285–98.

Clifford, J. and Marcus, G. (1986) *Writing Culture: the Poetics and Politics of Ethnography*, Berkeley: University of California Press.

Coe, R. (1994) '"An arousing and fulfillment of desires": the rhetoric of genre in the process era – and beyond', in A. Freedman and P. Medway (eds) *Genre and the New Rhetoric*, London: Taylor & Francis.

Coe, R., Lingard, L. and Teslenko, T. (2002) 'Genre as action, strategy and *difference*: an introduction', in R. Coe, L. Lingard and T. Teslenko (eds) *The Rhetoric and Ideology of Genre: Strategies for Stability and Change*, New York: Hampton Press.

Coffield, F. (2002) 'Breaking the consensus: lifelong learning as social control', in R. Edwards, N. Miller, N. Small and A. Tait (eds) *Supporting Lifelong Learning, Volume 3: Making Policy Work*, London: RoutlegeFalmer.

Collin, A. (2000) 'Epic and novel: the rhetoric of career', in A. Collin and R. Young (eds) *The Future of Career*, Cambridge: Cambridge University Press.

Comparative Education (1998) 34, 2.

Cope, B. and Kalantzis, M. (eds) (2000) *Multiliteracies: Literacy Learning and the Design of Social Futures*, London: Routledge.

Cortazzi, M. and Jin, L. (1999) 'Bridges to learning: metaphors of teaching, learning and language', in L. Cameron and G. Low (eds) *Researching and Applying Metaphor*, Cambridge: Cambridge University Press.

Cunningham, S., Tapsall, S., Ryan, Y., Stedman, L., Bagdon, K. and Flew, T. (1997) *New Media and Borderless Education: A Review of the Convergence between Global Media Networks and Higher Education Provision*, Canberra: DEETYA.

Currie, J. and Newson, J. (eds) (1998) *Universities and Globalization: Critical Perspectives*, London: Sage.

Dale, R. (1999) 'Specifying globalization effects on national policy: a focus on the mechanisms', *Journal of Education Policy*, 14, 1: 1–17.

Darkenwald, G. and Merriam, S. (1982) *Adult Education: Foundations of Practice*, New York: Harper.

Davis, B. and Sumara, D. (2000) 'Curriculum forms: on the assumed shapes of knowing and knowledge', *Journal of Curriculum Studies*, 32, 6: 821–45.

Davis, B. and Sumara, D. (2004) 'The hidden geometry of curriculum', in R. Edwards and R. Usher (eds) *Space, Curriculum and Learning*, Greenwich, CT: Information Age Publishing.

Dean, M. (1999) *Governmentality: Power and Rule in Modern Society*, London: Sage.

DEETYA (1997) *Digital Rhetorics: Literacies and Technologies in Education – Current Practices and Future Directions*, Canberra: DEETYA.

Deleuze, G. and Guattari, F. (1987) *A Thousand Plateaus*, Minneapolis: Minnesota University Press.

Dent, M. (2003) 'Managing doctors and saving a hospital: irony, rhetoric and actor networks', *Organization*, 10, 1: 107–27.

Derrida, J. (1980) *The Archaeology of the Frivolous: Reading Condillac*, Pittsburgh: Duquesne University Press.

Derrida, J. (1988) *Limited Inc.*, Evanston: Northwestern University Press.

DfEE (1998) *The Learning Age: A Renaissance for a New Britain*, London: Stationery Office.

DfEE (1999) *Learning to Succeed: a New Framework for Post-16 Learning*, London: Stationery Office.

Drodge, M. and Kitchen, R. (2000) *Mapping Cyberspace*, London: Routledge.

Du Gay, P. (1996) *Consumption and Identity at Work*, London: Sage.

Edwards, D. (1997) *Discourse and Cognition*, London: Sage.

Edwards, R. (1997) *Changing Places? Flexibility, Lifelong Learning and a Learning Society*, London: Routledge.

Edwards, R. (1998) 'Mapping, locating and translating: a discursive approach to professional development', *Studies in Continuing Education*, 20, 1: 23–38.

Edwards, R. (2001) 'Meeting individual learner needs: power, subject, subjection', in C. Paechter, M. Preedy, D. Scott and J. Soler (eds) *Knowledge, Power and Learning*, London: Paul Chapman.

Edwards, R. (2002) 'Mobilizing lifelong learning: governmentality in educational practices', *Journal of Education Policy*, 17, 3: 353–65.

Edwards, R. (2003) 'Ordering subjects: actor-networks and intellectual technologies in lifelong learning', *Studies in the Education of Adults*, 35, 1: 54–67.

Edwards, R., Armstrong, P. and Miller, N. (2001a) 'Include me out: critical readings of social exclusion, social inclusion and lifelong learning', *International Journal of Lifelong Education*, 20, 5: 417–28.

Edwards, R. and Clarke, J. (2003) 'Flexible learning, spatiality and identity', *Studies in Continuing Education*, 24, 2: 153–65.

Edwards, R., Clarke, J., Harrison, R. and Reeve, F. (2001b) 'Flexibility at work? A study of further education', *Journal of Vocational Education and Training*, 53, 3: 373–90.

Edwards, R., Clarke, J., Harrison, R. and Reeve, F. (2002) 'Is there madness in the method? Representations of research in lifelong learning', *Adult Education Quarterly*, 52, 2: 128–39.

Edwards, R. and Nicoll, K. (2001) 'Researching the rhetoric of lifelong learning', *Journal of Education Policy*, 16, 2: 103–12.

Edwards, R., Nicoll, K. and Tait, A. (1999) 'Migrating metaphors: the globalization of flexibility in policy', *Journal of Education Policy*, 14, 4: 619–30.

Edwards, R. and Usher, R. (2000) *Globalization and Pedagogy: Space, Place and Identity*, London: Routledge.

Edwards, R. and Usher, R. (eds) (2004) *Space, Curriculum and Learning*, Greenwich, CT: IAP.

Elliott, R. (1984) 'Metaphor, imagination and conceptions of education', in W. Taylor (ed.) *Metaphors of Education*, London: Heinemann.

Eraut, M. (2000) 'Non-formal learning, implicit learning and tacit knowledge in professional work', in F. Coffield (ed.) *The Necessity of Informal Learning*, Bristol: Policy Press.

European Commission (1995) *Teaching and Learning: Towards a Learning Society*, Luxembourg: Office for Official Publications of the European Communities.

Fairclough, N. (1999) *Language and Power*, Harlow: Longman Press.

Fairclough, N. (2000a) 'Dialogue in the public sphere', in S. Sarangi and M. Coulthard (eds) *Discourse and Social Life*, Harlow: Longman.

Fairclough, N. (2000b) *New Labour, New Language?*, London: Routledge.

Fairclough, N. (2000c) *Representations of Change in Neo-liberal Discourse*. Online. Available http://www.cddc.vt.edu/host/lnc/lncarchive.html (accessed 9 September 2003).

Fairclough, N. (2003) '"Political correctness": the politics of culture and language', *Discourse & Society*, 14, 1: 17–28.

Farrell, L. (2000) 'Ways of doing, ways of being: language, education and "working" identities', *Language and Education*, 14, 1: 18–36.

Featherstone, M. (1995) *Undoing Culture: Globalization, Postmodernism and Identity*, London: Sage.

Featherstone, M. and Burrows, R. (eds) (1995) *cyberspace, cyberbodies, cyberpunk: Cultures of Technological Embodiment*, London: Sage.

Feenberg, A. (nd) *From Essentialism to Constructivism: Philosophy of Technology at the Crossroads*. Online. Available http://www-rohan.sdsu.edu/faculty/feenberg/talk4.html (accessed 23 June 2003).

Fenwick, T. and Parsons, J. (1996) 'Metaphors of adult educators' identity and practice', *Proceedings of the 37th Annual Adult Education Research Conference*, Tampa: University of South Florida.

Field, J. (2000) 'Governing the ungovernable: why lifelong learning policies promise so much yet deliver so little', *Educational Management and Administration*, 28, 3: 249–61.

Fish, S. (1989) *Doing What Comes Naturally: Change, Rhetoric, and the Practices of Theory in Literary and Legal Studies*, Oxford: Clarendon Press.

Foucault, M. (1979) *Discipline and Punish: The Birth of the Prison*, London: Peregrine.

Foucault, M. (1980) *Power/Knowledge; Selected Interviews and Other Writings 1972–1977*, Brighton: Harvester Press.

Foucault, M. (1981) *History of Sexuality, Volume 1: An Introduction*, Harmondsworth: Penguin.

Foucault, M. (1988) 'Technologies of the self', in L. Martin, H. Gutman and P. Hutton (eds) *Technologies of the Self: A Seminar with Michel Foucault*, Amherst: University of Massachusetts Press.

Fox, S. (2001) 'Studying networked learning: some implications from socially situated learning theory and actor-network theory', in C. Steeples and C. Jones (eds) *Networked Learning: Issues and Perspectives*, London: Springer Verlag.

Francis, B. and Humphreys, J. (2002) 'Professional education as a structural barrier to lifelong learning in the NHS', in F. Reeve, R. Edwards and M. Cartwright (eds) *Supporting Lifelong Learning, Volume 2: Organizing Learning*, London: RoutledgeFalmer.

Fraser, B. (1979) 'The interpretation of novel metaphors', in A. Ortony (ed.) *Metaphor and Thought*, Cambridge: Cambridge University Press.

Freadman, A. (1994a) 'Anyone for tennis?', in A. Freedman and P. Medway (eds) *Genre and the New Rhetoric*, London: Taylor and Francis.

Freadman, A. (1994b) '"Do as I say": the relationship between teaching and learning new genres', in A. Freedman and P. Medway (eds) *Genre and the New Rhetoric*, London: Taylor & Francis.

Freadman, A. (1994c) 'Models of genre for language teaching', *The 1994 Sonia Marks Memorial Lecture*, Sydney: Department of French Studies, University of Sydney.

Freadman, A. (2002) 'Uptake', in R. Coe, L. Lingard and T. Teslenko (eds) *The Rhetoric and Ideology of Genre: Strategies for Stability and Change*, New York: Hampton Press.

Freedman, A. and Medway, P. (1994a) 'Locating genre studies: antecedents and prospects', in A. Freedman and P. Medway (eds) *Genre and the New Rhetoric*, London: Taylor & Francis.

Freedman, A. and Medway, P. (eds) (1994b) *Genre and the New Rhetoric*, London: Taylor & Francis.

Fuller, G. and Lee, A. (1997) 'Textual collusions', *Discourse*, 18, 3: 409–23.

Fuller, G. and Lee, A. (2002) 'Assembling a generic subject', in R. Coe, L. Lingard and T. Teslenko (eds) *The Rhetoric and Ideology of Genre: Strategies for Stability and Change*, New York: Hampton Press.

Gabilondo, J. (1995) 'Postcolonial cyborgs; subjectivity in the age of cybernetic reproduction', in C. Gray (ed.) *The Cyborg Handbook*, London: Routledge.

Garrick, J. (1998) *Unmasking Informal Learning*, London: Routledge.

Gee, J., Hull, G. and Lankshear, C. (1996) *The New Work Order: Behind the Language of the New Capitalism*, Boulder, CO: Westview.

Gergen, K. (1989) 'Warranting voice and the elaboration of the self', in J. Shotter and K. Gergen (eds) *Texts of Identity*, London: Sage.

Gibbons, M., Limoges, C., Nowotny, H., Schwartzman, S., Scott, P. and Trow, M. (1994) *The New Production of Knowledge: The Dynamics of Science and Research in Contemporary Societies*, London: Sage.

Gibbs, R. (1999) 'Researching metaphor', in L. Cameron and G. Low (eds) *Researching and Applying Metaphor*, Cambridge: Cambridge University Press.

Gibson, W. (1984) *Neuromancer*, London: Harper-Collins.

Gibson, W. (1989) 'High tech life: William Gibson and Timothy Leary in conversation', *Mondo 2000*, Fall, 7: 8–11.

Gilbert, G. and Mulkay, M. (1984) *Opening Pandora's Box: A Sociological Analysis of Scientists' Discourse*, Cambridge: Cambridge University Press.

Gill, R. (2000) 'Discourse analysis', in M. Bauer and G. Gaskell (eds) *Qualitative Researching with Text, Image and Sound: A Practical Handbook*, London: Sage.

Giroux, H. (1992) *Border Crossings: Cultural Workers and the Politics of Education*, New York: Routledge.

Green, B. (1993) *Curriculum, Technology and Textual Practice*, Geelong: Deakin University Press.

Grubb, W. (1996) 'The new vocationalism in the United States; returning to John Dewey', *Educational Philosophy and Theory*, 28, 1: 1–23.

Hackett, T. (1994) *From Pedagogy to Netagogy: Observations about Resources and Instruction on the Internet*. Online. Available http://is.gseis.ucla.edu/impact/s94/students/timothy/timothy_final.html (accessed 23 June 2003).

Hake, B. (1999) 'Lifelong learning policies in the European Union: developments and issues', *Compare*, 29, 1: 53–69.

Hall, S. (2000) 'Who needs "identity"?', in P. du Gay, J. Evans and P. Redman (eds) *Identity: A Reader*, London: Sage.

Hammersley, M. (1994) 'Ethnographic writing', *Social Research Update*, 5, Guildford: University of Surrey.

Haraway, D. (1991) *Simians, Cyborgs and Women: The Reinvention of Women*, New York: Routledge.

Harris, G. (nd) *Networker: Where is Cyberspace?* Online. Available http://www.greenleft.org.au/back/2000/418/418p11b.htm (accessed 24 June 2003).

Harrison, R., Reeve, F. and Clarke, J. (2002) 'On the road again: the metaphor of the journey in understandings of learning', paper presented at research conference of the Learning and Skills Development Agency, London.

Harvey, D. (1989) *The Condition of Postmodernity*, Oxford: Basil Blackwell.

Hayward, P. (1993) *Situating Cyberspace: the Popularization of Virtual Reality*. Online. Available http://www.cc.rochester.edu/College/FS/Publications/HaywardCyberspace.html (accessed 23 June 2003).

Henderson, W., Dudley-Evans, T. and Backhouse, R. (eds) (1993) *Economics and Language*, London: Routledge.

Hetherington, K. (1998) *Expressions of Identity: Space, Performance, Politics*, London: Sage.

Hirst, P. and Thompson, G. (1996) *Globalization in Question*, Cambridge: Polity Press.

Holmes, L. (1998) 'One more time, transferable skills don't exist … (and what we should do about it)', paper presented at Higher Education for Capability conference, 'Embedding Key Skills Across the Curriculum', Nene College, Northampton, 27 February. Online. Available http://www.re-skill.org.uk/grads/transkil.htm (accessed 9 March 2003).

Huddlestone P. and Unwin, L. (1997) *Teaching and Learning in Further Education: Diversity and Change*, London: RoutledgeFalmer.

Hudson, L. (1984) 'The role of metaphor in psychological research', in W. Taylor (ed.) *Metaphors of Education*, London: Heinemann.

Hughes, C. (2002) 'Beyond the poststructuralist–modern impasse: the woman returner as "exile" and "nomad"', *Gender and Education*, 14, 4: 411–24.

Humes, W. (2000) 'The discourses of educational management', *Journal of Educational Enquiry*. Online. Available http://www.education.unisa.edu.au/JEE (accessed 23 August 2002).

Hutton-Jarvis, C. (1999) 'Test or testament? A comparison of educational and literary critical approaches to research', *International Journal of Qualitative Studies in Education*, 12, 6: 645–58.

Iacono, S. and Kling, R. (1996) 'Computerization movements and tales of technological utopianism', in R. Kling (ed.) *Computerization and Controversy: Value Conflicts and Social Choices*, San Diego: Academic Press.

ILTHE (2003) *The Accreditation of Programmes and Pathways: Guidelines for Higher Education Institutions and ILTHE Accreditors*. Online. Available http://www.ilt.ac.uk/249.asp#jump09 (accessed 4 September 2003).

Inns, D. (2002) 'Metaphor in the literature of organizational analysis: a preliminary taxonomy and a glimpse at a humanities-based perspective', *Organization*, 9, 2: 305–30.

Jameson, F. (1991) *Postmodernism, or the Cultural Logic of Late Capitalism*, London: Verso Books.

Journal of Education Policy (1999) 14, 1.

Kaplan, C. (1996) *Questions of Travel*, London: Duke University Press.

Kaplan, R. (2000) 'Contrastive rhetoric and discourse analysis: who writes what to whom? When? In what circumstance?', in S. Sarangi and M. Coulthard (eds) *Discourse and Social Life*, Harlow: Pearson Education Limited.

Kapor, M. (1993) 'Where is the digital highway really heading?' *Wired*, July/Aug: 3.

Keep, E. and Rainbird, H. (2002) 'Towards the learning organization?', in F. Reeve, R. Edwards and M. Cartwright (eds) *Supporting Lifelong Learning, Volume 2: Organizing Learning*, London: RoutledgeFalmer.

Kenway, J., Bigum, C. and Fitzclarence, L. (1993) 'Marketing education in the postmodern age', *Journal of Education Policy*, 8, 2: 105–22.

Klamer, A., McCloskey, D. and Solow, R. (eds) (1988) *The Consequences of Economic Rhetoric*, Cambridge: Cambridge University Press.

Kollock, P. (1999) 'The economies of online cooperation: gifts and public goods in cyberspace', in M. Smith and P. Kollock (eds) *Communities in Cyberspace*, London: Routledge.

Kramerae, C. (1995) 'A backstage critique of virtual reality', in S. Jones. (ed.) *Cybersociety*, London: Sage.

Krause, S. (2002) *The Immediacy of Rhetoric: Definitions, Illustrations and Implications*. Online. Available http://www.emunix.emich.edu/~krause/Diss/ (accessed 23 June 2003).

Kress, G. (2000) 'Multimodality', in B. Cope and M. Kalantzis (eds) *Multiliteracies: Literacy Learning and the Design of Social Futures*, London: Routledge.

Kress, G. (2003) *Literacy in the New Media Age*, London: Routledge.

Kress, G., Jewitt, C., Ogborn, J. and Tsatsarelis, C. (2002) *Multimodal Teaching and Learning: the Rhetorics of the Science Classroom*, London: Continuum.

Kuhn, T. (1979) 'Metaphor in science', in A. Ortony (ed.) *Metaphor and Thought*, Cambridge: Cambridge University Press.

Lakoff, G. and Johnson, M. (1980) *Metaphors We Live By*, Chicago: University of Chicago Press.

Lakoff, G. and Johnson, M. (1999) *Philosophy in the Flesh: the Embodied Mind and its Challenge to Western Thought*, New York: Basic Books.

Lankshear, C., Peters, M. and Knobel, M. (1996) 'Critical pedagogy and cyberspace', in H.A. Giroux, C. Lankshear, P. McLaren, M. Peters (eds) *Counternarratives*, London: Routledge.

Lash, S. and Urry, J. (1994) *Economies of Signs and Space*, London: Sage.

Latour, B. (1987) *Science in Action*, Cambridge, MA: Harvard University Press.

Latour, B. and Wolgar, S. (1979) *Laboratory Life: The Construction of Scientific Facts*, Beverley Hills: Sage.

Lave, J. and Wenger, E. (1991) *Situated Learning*, Cambridge: Cambridge University Press.

Law, J. (2000) *Political Philosophy and Disabled Specificities* (Draft). Online. Available http://www.comp.lancs.ac.uk/sociology/soc026jl.html (accessed 6 June 2002).

Law, J. and Hetherington, K. (2001) *Materialities, Spatialities, Globalities*. Online. Available http://www.comp.lancs.ac.uk/sociology/soc029jl.html (accessed 22 November 2002).

Lawson, H. (1985) *Reflexivity: The Postmodern Predicament*, London: Hutchinson.

Lawson, H. (2001) *Closure: A Story of Everything*, London: Routledge.

Lawton, D. (1984) 'Metaphor and the curriculum', in W. Taylor (ed.) *Metaphors of Education*, London: Heinemann.

Lea, M. (1998) 'Academic literacies and learning in higher education: constructing knowledge through texts and experience', *Studies in the Education of Adults*, 30, 2: 156–71.

Lea, M. and Nicoll, K. (2002) (eds) *Distributed Learning*, London: RoutledgeFalmer.

Lea, M. and Stierer, B. (eds) (2000) *Student Writing in Higher Education*, Buckingham: Open University Press.

Lea, M. and Street, B. (2000) 'Student writing and staff feedback in higher education: an academic literacies approach', in M. Lea and B. Stierer (eds) *Student Writing in Higher Education*, Buckingham: Open University Press.

Leach, J. (2000) 'Rhetorical analysis', in M. Bauer and G. Gaskell (eds) *Qualitative Researching with Text, Image and Sound*, London: Sage.

Leff, M. (1987) 'Modern sophistic and the unity of rhetoric', in J. Nelson, A. Megill and D. McCloskey (eds) *The Rhetoric of the Human Sciences: Language and Argument in Scholarship and Public Affairs*, Madison: University of Wisconsin Press.

Legge, K. (1995) *Human Resource Management: Rhetorics and Realities*, Basingstoke: Macmillan.

Leith, D. and Myerson, G. (1989) *The Power of Address: Explorations in Rhetoric*, London: Routledge.

Lemke, J. (1995) *Textual Politics*, London: Taylor & Francis.

Levin, B. (1998) 'An epidemic of education policy: (what) can we learn from each other?', *Comparative Education*, 34, 2: 131–41.

Lillis, T. (2001) *Student Writing: Access, Regulation, Desire*, London: Routledge.

Lincoln, Y. (1997) 'Self, subject, audience, text: living at the edge, writing in the margins', in W. Tierney and Y. Lincoln (eds) *Representation and the Text: Re-framing the Narrative Voice*, New York: SUNY Press.

Lingard, R. and Rizvi, F. (1998) 'Globalization, the OECD, and Australian higher education', in J. Currie and J. Newson (eds) *Universities and Globalization: Critical Perspectives*, Thousand Oaks, CA: Sage.

Low, G. (1999) '"This paper thinks …": investigating the acceptability of the metaphor AN ESSAY IS A PERSON', in L. Cameron and G. Low (eds) *Researching and Applying Metaphor*, Cambridge: Cambridge University Press.

Luke, A. (1995) 'Getting your hands dirty: provisional politics in postmodern conditions' in R. Smith and P. Wexler (eds) *After Post-Modernism*, London: Falmer Press.

Luke, T.W. (1996) 'The Politics of Cyberschooling at the Virtual University', paper presented at the Virtual University International Conference, University of Melbourne: Australia.

Lyotard, J.-F. (1984) *The Postmodern Condition: A Report on Knowledge*, Manchester: Manchester University Press.

MacLure, M. (2003) *Discourse in Educational and Social Research*, London: Sage.

MacMillan, K. (2002) 'Narratives of social disruption: education news in the British tabloid press', *Discourse*, 23, 1: 27–38.

Macrae, S. (1997) 'Flesh made world: sex, text and the virtual body', in D. Porter (ed.) *Internet Culture*, London: Routledge.

McKenzie, G., Powell, J. and Usher, R. (1997) *Understanding Social Research*, London: Falmer Press.

McWilliam, E. (1996) 'Touchy subjects: a risky inquiry into pedagogical pleasure', *British Educational Research Journal*, 22, 3: 305–17.

McWilliam, E. and Jones, A. (1996) 'Eros and pedagogical bodies: the state of (non)affairs', in E. McWilliam and P. Taylor (eds) *Pedagogy, Technology and the Body*, New York: Peter Lang.

McWilliam, E. and Singh, P. (2002) 'Towards a research training curriculum: what, why, how, who?', *Australian Educational Researcher*, 29, 3: 3–18

Maffesoli, M. (1996) *The Time of Tribes*, London: Sage.

Marginson, S. (1999a) 'Research as a managed economy: the costs', in T. Coady (ed.) *Why Universities Matter*, St Leonards: Allen and Unwin.

Marginson, S. (1999b) 'After globalization: emerging politics of education', *Journal of Education Policy*, 14, 1: 19–31.

Marginson, S. and Considine, M. (2000) *The Enterprise University*, Cambridge: Cambridge University Press.

Martinez, M., Sauleda, N. and Huber, G. (2001) 'Metaphors as blueprints of thinking about teaching and learning', *Teaching and Teacher Education*, 17: 965–77.

Mayr, D. (nd) *see. think. The History of the Net*. Online. Available http://members.magnet. at/dmayr/history.htm (accessed 15 July 2003).

Mezirow, J. and Associates (1990) *Fostering Critical Reflection in Adulthood: A Guide to Transformative and Emancipatory Learning*, San Francisco: Jossey Bass.

Millarch, F. (1998) *Net Ideologies: From Cyber-liberalism to Cyber-realism*. Online. Available http://www.millarch.org/francisco/papers/net_ideologies.htm (accessed 23 June 2003).

Miller, C. (1994a) 'Genre as social action', in A. Freedman and P. Medway (eds) *Genre and the New Rhetoric*, London: Taylor and Francis.

Miller, C. (1994b) 'Rhetorical community: the cultural bias of genre', in A. Freedman and P. Medway (eds) *Genre and the New Rhetoric*, London: Taylor and Francis.

Miller, N. (1993) 'Auto/biography and life history', in N. Miller and D. Jones (eds) *Research Reflecting Practice*, Boston: SCUTREA.

Miller, N. (1994) 'Invisible colleges revealed: professional networks and personal inter-connections among adult educators', *Proceedings of the 35th Annual Adult Education Research Conference*, Knoxville: University of Tennessee.

Miller, P. and Rose, N. (1993) 'Governing economic life', in M. Gane and T. Johnson (eds) *Foucault's New Domains*, London: Routledge.

Morgan, W. (1996) 'Personal training: discourses of (self) fashioning', in E. McWilliam and P. Taylor (eds) *Pedagogy, Technology and the Body*, New York: Peter Lang.

NAGCELL (1997) *Learning for the Twenty-first Century: Final Report of the National Advisory Group for Continuing Education and Lifelong Learning*, London: DfEE.

Nash, W. (1989) *Rhetoric: the Wit of Persuasion*, Oxford: Blackwell.

NCIHE (1997) *Higher Education in the Learning Society: Summary Report*, Norwich: HMSO.

Nelson, J., Megill, A. and McCloskey, D. (1987a) 'Rhetoric of inquiry', in J. Nelson, A. Megill and D. McCloskey (eds) *The Rhetoric of the Human Sciences: Language and Argument in Scholarship and Public Affairs*, Madison: University of Wisconsin Press.

Nelson, J., Megill, A. and McCloskey, D. (eds) (1987b) *The Rhetoric of the Human Sciences: Language and Argument in Scholarship and Public Affairs*, Madison: University of Wisconsin Press.

Nespor, J. (1994) *Knowledge in Motion: Space, Time and Curriculum in Undergraduate Physics and Management*, London: Falmer.

Nicoll, K. (1997) '"Flexible learning" – unsettling practices', *Studies in Continuing Education*, 19, 2: 100–21.

Nicoll, K. and Edwards, R. (2000) 'Reading policy texts: lifelong learning as metaphor', *International Journal of Lifelong Education*, 19, 5: 459–69.

Nicoll, K. and Harrison, R. (2003) 'Constructing the good teacher in higher education: the discursive work of standards', *Studies in Continuing Education*, 25, 1: 23–35.

Nunes, M. (1995) *Baudrillard and Cyberspace: Internet, Virtuality, and Postmodernity*. Online. Available http://www.dc.peachnet.edu/~mnunes/jbnet.html (accessed 23 June 2003).

Onyx, J. (2001) 'Implementing work-based learning for the first time', in D. Boud and N. Solomon (eds) *Work-Based Learning: A New Higher Education?* Buckingham: Open University Press.

Ortony, A. (ed.) (1979a) *Metaphor and Thought*, Cambridge: Cambridge University Press.

Ortony, A. (1979b) 'Metaphor: a multidisciplinary problem', in A. Ortony (ed.) *Metaphor and Thought*, Cambridge: Cambridge University Press.

Oxford English Dictionary (1992) Oxford: Oxford University Press.

Paechter, C. (2004, forthcoming) 'Metaphors of space in educational theory and practice', *Pedagogy, Culture, Society*, 12, 3.

Papadopoulos, G. (1996) *Education 1960–1990: The OECD Perspective*, Paris: OECD.

Parker, S. (1997) *Reflective Teaching in the Postmodern World: A Manifesto for Education in Postmodernity*, Buckingham: Open University Press.

Petrie, H. (1979) 'Metaphor and learning', in A. Ortony (ed.) *Metaphor and Thought*, Cambridge: Cambridge University Press.

Polkinghorne, D. (1997) 'Reporting qualitative research as practice', in W. Tierney and Y. Lincoln (eds) *Representation and the Text: Re-framing the Narrative Voice*, New York: SUNY Press.

Popkewitz, T. (1996) 'Rethinking decentralization and state/civil society distinctions: the state as a problematic of governing', *Journal of Education Policy*, 11, 1: 27–51.

Porter, D. (ed.) (1997) *Internet Culture*, London: Routledge.

Poster, M. (1990) *The Mode of Information*, Oxford: Polity Press.

Poster, M. (1995) 'Postmodern virtualities', in M. Featherstone and R. Burrows (eds) *cyberspace, cyberbodies, cyberpunk: Cultures of Technological Embodiment*, London: Sage.

Poster, M. (1997) 'Cyberdemocracy: Internet and the public sphere', in D. Porter (ed.) *Internet Culture*, London: Routledge.

Poster, M. (2001) *What's the Matter with the Internet?* Minneapolis: University of Minnesota Press.

Potter, J. (1996) *Representing Reality: Discourse, Rhetoric and Social Construction*, London: Sage.

Pratt, D. and Nesbit, T. (2000) 'Discourses and cultures of teaching', in A. Wilson and E. Hayes (eds) *Handbook of Adult and Continuing Education*, San Fanscisco: Jossey Bass.

Prelli, L. (1989) *A Rhetoric of Science: Inventing Scientific Discourse*, Columbia, SC: University of South Carolina Press.

Ramsden, P. (1998) 'Managing the effective university', *Higher Education Research and Development*, 17, 3: 347–70.

Ransom, S. (1997) *Foucault's Discipline: The Politics of Subjectivity*, London: Duke University Press.

Ree, J. (1999) *I See a Voice: A Philosophical History*, London: Flamingo.

Rheingold, H. (1993) *The Virtual Community*, Reading, MA: Addison-Wesley.

Rogers, C. (1974) *On Becoming a Person*, London: Constable.

Rogers, C. (1983) *Freedom to Learn for the '80s*, Colombus, OH: Charles Merril.

Rohrer, T. (1997) *Conceptual Blending on the Information Highway: How Metaphorical Inferences Work*. Online. Available http://philosophy.uoregon.edu/metaphor/iclacnf4.htm (accessed 23 June 2003).

Rorty, R. (1989) *Contingency, Irony, and Solidarity*, Cambridge: Cambridge University Press.

Rosaldo, R. (1987) 'Where objectivity lies: the rhetoric of anthropology', in J. Nelson, A. Megill and D. McCloskey (eds) *The Rhetoric of the Human Sciences: Language and Argument in Scholarship and Public Affairs*, Madison: University of Wisconsin Press.

Rose, N. (1989) *Governing the Soul: The Shaping of Private Life*, London: Routledge.

Rose, N. (1999) *Powers of Freedom: Reframing Political Thought*, Cambridge: Polity Press.

Sandywell, B. (1996) *Reflexivity and the Crisis of Western Reason. Logological Investigations, Volume 1*, London: Routledge.

Scaife, A., Colley, H. and Davies, J. (2001) 'Setting up collaborative partnership research in FE', paper presented at the Learning and Skills Research Network Annual Conference 2001, Cambridge, 5–7 December.

Schon, D. (1979) 'Generative metaphor: a perspective on problem-setting in metaphor', in A. Ortony (ed.) *Metaphor and Thought*, Cambridge: Cambridge University Press.

Schon, D. (1983) *The Reflective Practitioner*, London: Temple Smith.

Schryer, C. (1994) 'The lab vs. the clinic: sites of competing genres', in A. Freedman and P. Medway (eds) *Genre and the New Rhetoric*, London: Taylor & Francis.

Scott, A. (1997) 'Introduction – globalization: social process or political rhetoric?', in A. Scott (ed.) *The Limits of Globalization: Cases and Arguments*, London: Routledge.

Scott, D. and Usher, R. (eds) (1996) *Understanding Educational Research*, London: Routledge.

Searle, J. (1969) *Speech Acts: An Essay in the Philosophy of Language*, Cambridge: Cambridge University Press.

Senge, P. (ed.) (1994) *The Fifth Discipline Field Book: Strategies and Tools for Building a Learning Organization*, Toronto: Currency Doubleday.

Sfard, A. (1998) 'On two metaphors for learning and the dangers of choosing just one', *Educational Researcher*, 27, 2: 4–13.

Shapiro, A. (1997) 'Is the Net Democratic? Yes and No'. Online. Available http://www. technorealism.org/overview.html (accessed 23 March 2003).

Simons, H. (1990) 'Introduction: the rhetoric of inquiry as an intellectual movement', in H. Simons (ed.) *The Rhetorical Turn: Invention and Persuasion in the Conduct of Inquiry*, Chicago: University of Chicago Press.

Smith, D. (1999) *Writing the Social: Critique, Theory, and Investigations*, University of Toronto Press, Toronto.

Snyder, I. (ed.) (2002) *Silicon Literacies: Communication, Innovation and Education in the Electronic Age*, London: Routledge.

Steier, F. (1991) 'Introduction: research as reflexivity, self-reflexivity as a social process', in F. Steier (ed.) *Research and Reflexivity*, London: Sage.

Sterling, W. (1994) *Hype, Hope and the Information Superhighway: Limited-access Tollways or Multi-access Freeways*. Online. Available http://www.computerlearning.org/articles/ HypeHope.htm (accessed 23 June 2003).

Sticht, T. (1979) 'Educational uses of metaphor', in A. Ortony (ed.) *Metaphor and Thought*, Cambridge: Cambridge University Press.

Straehle, C., Weiss, G., Wodak, R., Muntigl, P. and Sedlak, M. (1999) 'Struggle as metaphor in European Union discourses on unemployment', *Discourse & Society*, 10, 1: 67–99.

Strathern, M. (2000) 'The tyranny of transparency', *British Educational Research Journal*, 26, 3: 309–21.

Stronach, I. and MacLure, M. (1997) *Educational Research Undone: the Postmodern Embrace*, Buckingham: Open University Press.

Swales, J. (1990) *Genre Analysis: English in Academic and Research Settings*, Cambridge: Cambridge University Press.

Symes, C. and McIntyre, J. (eds) (2000) *Working Knowledge: New Vocationalism in Higher Education*, Buckingham: Open University Press.

Tabbi, J. (1997) 'Reading, writing hypertext: democratic politics in the virtual classroom', in D. Porter (ed.) *Internet Culture*, London: Routledge.

Tait, A. (1996) 'Open and distance learning policy in the European Union 1985–1995', *Higher Education Policy*, 9, 3: 221–38.

Taylor, S., Rizvi, F., Lingard, B. and Henry, M. (1997) *Educational Policy and the Politics of Change*, London: Routledge.

Taylor, W. (ed.) (1984a) *Metaphors of Education*, London: Heinemann.

Taylor, W. (1984b) 'Metaphors of educational discourse', in W. Taylor (ed.) *Metaphors of Education*, London: Heinemann.

Tierney, W.G. (2001) 'Academic freedom and organizational identity', *Australian Universities Review*, 7–14

Townley, B. (1994) *Reframing Human Resource Management: Power, Ethics and the Subject at Work*, London: Sage.

Turkle, S. (nd) *Virtuality and its Discontents: Searching for Community in Cyberspace*. Online. Available http://www.prospect.org/print/V7/24/turkle-s.html (accessed 23 June 2003).

UNESCO (1996) *Learning: The Treasure Within. Report to UNESCO of the International Commission on Education for the Twenty-first Century*, Paris: UNESCO.

UNESCO (1997) *Open and Distance Learning: Prospects and Policy Considerations*, Paris: UNESCO.

Urry, J. (2000) *Sociology Beyond Societies*, London: Routledge.

Usher, R. (1996) 'Textuality and reflexivity in educational research', in D. Scott and R. Usher (eds) *Understanding Educational Research*, London: Routledge.

Usher, R (2002) 'A diversity of doctorates: fitness for the knowledge economy?', *Higher Education Research and Development*, 21, 2: 143–53.

Usher, R. and Edwards, R. (1994). *Postmodernism and Education*, London: Routledge.

Usher, R. and Edwards, R. (1998) 'Confessing all? A "postmodern guide" to the guidance and counselling of adult learners', in R. Edwards, R. Harrison and A. Tait (eds) *Telling Tales: Perspectives on Guidance and Counselling in Learning*, London: Routledge.

Usher, R. and Solomon, N. (1999) 'Experiential learning and the shaping of subjectivity in the workplace', *Studies in the Education of Adults*, 31, 2: 155–63.

Usher, R., Bryant, I. and Johnson, R. (1997) *Adult Education and the Postmodern Challenge*, London: Routledge.

Vadeboncoeur, J. and Torres, M. (2003) 'Constructing and reconstructing teaching roles: a focus on generative metaphors and dichotomies', *Discourse*, 24, 1: 87–103.

Van Maanan, J. (1988) *Tales from the Field*, Chicago: University of Chicago Press.

Vickers, B. (1999) *In Defence of Rhetoric*, Oxford: Clarendon Press.

Virilio, P (2000) *The Information Bomb*, London: Verso.

Wark, M. (1997) *The Virtual Republic*, Sydney: Allen and Unwin.

Wark, M. (nd) *The Information War*. Online. Available http://www.dmc.mq.edu.au/mwark/warchive/21*C/21c-cyberwar.html (accessed 24 June 2003).

Wenger, E. (1998) *Communities of Practice: Learning, Meaning and Identity*, Cambridge: Cambridge University Press.

West, R. (1998) *Learning for Life: Review of Higher Education Financing and Policy*, Canberra: DEETYA.

Westwood, R. and Linstead, S. (eds) (2001) *The Language of Organizations*, London: Sage.

Wodak, R. (2000) 'Recontextualization and the transformation of meanings: a critical discourse analysis of decision making in EU meetings about employment policies', in S. Sarangi and M. Coulthard (eds) *Discourse and Social Life*, Harlow: Pearson Education.

Yeatman, A. (1994) *Postmodern Revisionings of the Political*, New York: Routledge.

Zimmerman, E. (1994) 'On definition and rhetorical genre', in A. Freedman and P. Medway (eds) *Genre and the New Rhetoric*, London: Taylor and Francis

Zuber-Skerritt, O. (1992) *Professional Development in Higher Education. A Theoretical Framework for Action Research*, London: Taylor & Francis.

Zukas, M. and Malcolm, J. (2000) *Pedagogies for Lifelong Learning: Building Bridges or Building Walls?* Online. Available at http://www.open.ac.uk/lifelong-learning (accessed 21 January 2001).

Zukas, M. and Malcolm, J. (2002) 'Pedagogies for lifelong learning: building bridges or building walls', in R. Harrison, F. Reeve, A. Hanson and J. Clarke (eds) *Supporting Lifelong Learning, Volume 1: Perspectives on Learning*, London: Routledge.

Index